ENVIRONMENTAL ADJUDICATION

This book provides a detailed study of the role of adjudication in environmental law. It examines theoretical issues concerning the role of judges and other adjudicators, taking account of different legal cultures and contexts, exploring the multifaceted pressures which rest on the shoulders of adjudicators when navigating the tensions between maintaining neutrality, resolving disputes, and providing guidance and assistance for future courts, policy-makers and decision-makers. In addition, it identifies the main adjudicatory 'avenues' which exist in the context of the environmental law of England and Wales and explores the relationship between adjudication and coherence before concluding with an exploration of what constitutes 'good' environmental adjudication.

Environmental Adjudication

Emma Lees
and
Ole W Pedersen

• HART •
OXFORD • LONDON • NEW YORK • NEW DELHI • SYDNEY

HART PUBLISHING

Bloomsbury Publishing Plc

Kemp House, Chawley Park, Cumnor Hill, Oxford, OX2 9PH, UK

1385 Broadway, New York, NY 10018, USA

HART PUBLISHING, the Hart/Stag logo, BLOOMSBURY and the Diana logo are trademarks of Bloomsbury Publishing Plc

First published in Great Britain 2020

A catalogue record for this book is available from the British Library.

Library of Congress Cataloging-in-Publication data

Names: Lees, Emma, author. | Pedersen, Ole W., author.

Title: Environmental adjudication / Emma Lees and Ole W. Pedersen.

Description: Oxford, UK ; New York, NY : Hart Publishing, Bloomsbury Publishing Plc, 2020. | Includes bibliographical references and index.

Identifiers: LCCN 2020019003 (print) | LCCN 2020019004 (ebook) | ISBN 9781509931460 (hardcover) | ISBN 9781509931484 (ePDF) | ISBN 9781509931477 (EPub)

Subjects: LCSH: Environmental law. | Political questions and judicial power.

Classification: LCC K3585 .L43 2020 (print) | LCC K3585 (ebook) | DDC 344.04/6—dc23

LC record available at https://lccn.loc.gov/2020019003

LC ebook record available at https://lccn.loc.gov/2020019004

ISBN: HB: 978-1-50993-146-0
ePDF: 978-1-50993-148-4
ePub: 978-1-50993-147-7

Typeset by Compuscript Ltd, Shannon

ACKNOWLEDGEMENTS

Thanks go to our anonymous reviewers. We also particularly wish to thank Maria Lee, Donald McGillivray, Tiina Paloniitty, Colin Reid, Chris Rodgers, Sakshi S and Stephen Tromans QC for taking part in the Environmental Adjudication Symposium, held in Cambridge, June 2019, and for their enormously valuable contributions which are much appreciated. Finally, we thank each other, for writing the words we didn't.

TABLE OF CONTENTS

LIST OF ABBREVIATIONS

AONB	Area of Outstanding Natural Beauty
EA	Environment Agency
EIA	Environmental Impact Assessment
EIR	Environmental Information Regulations
FTT	First-Tier Tribunal
IC	Information Commissioner
NE	Natural England
SSSI	Site of Special Scientific Interest

LIST OF FIGURES

TABLE OF CASES

Higher Courts

Tribunal Decisions

Planning Inspectorate

European Union Case Law

TABLE OF STATUTES

Statutes

Statutory Instruments

European Union Legislation

International Conventions

1

Introduction

The idea for this book first emerged in 2016. It began as a study of different 'models' for environmental adjudication, and was originally a critique of calls for specialist environmental tribunals. But it transpired that neither our argument, nor those of writers calling for specialist tribunals, could be so simply characterised, and it became apparent that the question of 'how to do environmental adjudication' was logically dependent upon a proper understanding as to the processes driving and shaping such adjudication in practice. Furthermore, the intractability of the link between these forms and processes, and the so-maligned 'incoherence' of environmental law, hinted at our eventual conclusions.

Our question was simple – how does environmental adjudication work? But once we started to answer it, the complexity of the social phenomenon under our microscope revealed a richness in its operation that we have still only begun to appreciate. Nevertheless, in conducting this research, we have concluded that this variety and incoherence is better expressed as bricolage. Environmental adjudication is a patchwork, made up of individually more or less coherent parts. By looking especially at the avenues through which environmental law is channelled, we can understand the operation of this social institution. This improved understanding will hopefully form a base for future scholarly work engaging with and critiquing environmental adjudication.

A central argument is that environmental adjudication takes place across a range of different avenues and that appreciating the variety and differences between these avenues must be the starting point of any attempt to understand environmental adjudication. Consequently, we dedicate the bulk of the book to examining the effects that the different avenues have on adjudication. Those finding little to agree with in our emphasis on the importance of approaching environmental adjudication through these avenues will therefore likely find little pleasure in the book. Prior to developing and defining our avenues of environmental adjudication, however, we develop our conceptual framework for understanding the operation of environmental adjudication in chapter two, where we identify adjudication as a process focused on decision-making with relative winners and losers, based on the attempt to persuade (through internally coherent arguments and rules) an independent decision-maker whose task it is to provide a solution to the dispute before her through the extrapolation of generalisable rules. In order to further develop our description of adjudication in chapter two, we also identify what we consider to be the well-established challenges associated with environmental adjudication as these pertain to politics, policies and values; the strong connection between law and science; and the constant state of flux of environmental law.

In light of this conceptual and definitional base, we examine in chapter three the processes that shape reasoned argumentation and the forces that underpin them from a theoretical and institutional perspective. Here we develop a multidimensional theory of environmental adjudication. The multidimensional characteristics of environmental adjudication are brought out by focusing on the elements, techniques and avenues that serve to 'fix' the parameters of adjudication.

The main feature we identify as controlling environmental adjudication – the avenues (identified as statutory appeals, judicial review, private law and criminal law) – is singled out in chapter four, where we show how the avenues of adjudication shape the purpose of adjudication and operate as power-brokers, as framers of reasoning and as determinants of remedies. In the absence of a 'grand masterplan' for environmental adjudication, to use Warnock's phrase, a central point which follows from the analysis of the avenues and institutional backgrounds of environmental adjudication is, not surprisingly, that institutional context is determinative.[1] The adjudicatory context ultimately shapes the content of the law. One main point to emerge from chapter four is that the application of environmental disputes to avenues of adjudication that have been developed in other areas and disciplines of law leaves a significant imprint on environmental law. This gives rise to an adjudicative fragmentation across environmental law: a fragmentation that takes place across a range of avenues, each with their own modes of reasoning, constitutional functions and sets of procedures.

Having identified the avenues of adjudication, we dedicate chapters five to seven to consider in closer detail the specific impact of the adjudicatory avenues as channels of power (chapter five), as frames of reasoning (chapter six) and as remedy determining (chapter seven). Specifically, we emphasise that in understanding how environmental adjudication works, one of the most critical issues to determine is the power structures that have been established through the avenues of adjudication. These power structures (often self-determined by adjudicators) control important aspects such as *who* has the power to decide and *what* an adjudicator has power to decide. A central element in this power structure and ability to decide relates to four primary blocks: jurisdiction, fact-finding, access to adjudicatory fora, and the power to interpret and create new rules. Following from this, we explore the connection between the avenues of adjudication and the reasons that can be considered in the different avenues, and how these forms of consideration affect the overall processes of adjudication in relation to environmental matters. The impact of the different avenues of adjudication on the kinds of argument considered legitimate in any avenue is critical in the context of environmental law as it evidently shapes the extent to which concerns about environmental harm

[1] C Warnock, 'Reconceptualising Specialist Environment Courts and Tribunals' (2017) 37 *Legal Studies* 391.

and public interest concerns are taken into account. Of central importance in understanding how the different avenues shape the relevant reasons is the degree of seriousness with which an adjudicator is willing to engage with arguments challenging the original administrative decision (in respect to the scientific evidence which underpins that decision and in respect of the level of scrutiny). Importantly, if not terribly surprisingly, particular arguments are simply illegitimate in one adjudicatory forum but not in another – and the patterns of what can and cannot be considered are not the same across the different avenues, skewing how discussion about the environment is conducted in these divergent contexts. Another factor, which plays an important role in shaping the relevant reasons across the different avenues of adjudication, is the relative proximity between an adjudicator and the administrative decision-maker whose decision the adjudicator is scrutinising. As we explore, the line between adjudicator and administrative state can often be very fine, especially in a context where we demand the rehearing and replaying of subjectively balanced environmental values. Often this proximity, and the high degree of expertise that typically goes with it, has been deliberately built into the adjudicatory system and is in many contexts to be embraced.

The important influence exerted by the different avenues of adjudication arguably is most clearly expressed when it comes to remedies which dominate in each and we explore this in chapter seven. Each of the four avenues of adjudication and their purposes significantly shape what steps an adjudicator might be able to order once a decision has been reached. Again, as in the previous chapters, the constitutional role performed by adjudicators in each of the avenues takes centre stage. Although remedies may come across as an 'afterthought' in an adjudication process, the range of remedies available to adjudicators within the different avenues produce the final part of the 'jigsaw' (to mix metaphors) of the bricolage of environmental adjudication. Two main points that emerge from our examination of remedies are, first, that, for the parties themselves, the remedy is what matters; and second, that far from being the inevitable conclusion of the development of a series of rules, the remedies provided are also shaping the substance of the rules. In this context, and without being drawn to discussions about remedialism in adjudication, environmental adjudicators often show a deftness when it comes to taking account of the practical significance of the matters before the adjudicator.

The picture of environmental adjudication as a bricolage is explored in depth in chapter eight. Here we define a bricolage as something that is made up of separate avenues of adjudication, each with their own constitutional roles and purposes that shape the power structures, reasons and remedies. But it is also a bricolage that often gives rise to a paradox of neutrality and independence, expertise and subjectivity, deference and intervention. The bricolage of adjudication is mainly a feature of happenstance and the fact that the discipline of environmental law, as many other disciplines of law, has developed incrementally over a long period of time. When the law, as is the case of environmental law, is a direct result of rough-and-tumble politics, the structure of the law is inevitably going to be untidy. Viewed as a whole, the bricolage is indeed untidy and lacking in structure and order. But viewed more closely through the lens of separate avenues, a certain level of order is restored. Adjudication becomes locally coherent insofar as adjudication within a particular avenue takes place subject to the constraints, rules and forms found in that avenue. One important consequence to emerge from this is, as others have pointed out, that contingency comes to play an important role in environmental adjudication and consequently in environmental law. Equally important, the force exerted by the different avenues alongside the institutional and professional commitment of each adjudicator to a particular avenue means that there are limits to what we can expect of adjudicators when it comes to breaking free of the constraints of each avenue and facilitating overall coherence. Ultimately, we conclude that whilst this might disappoint commentators who favour a higher degree of disciplinary coherence, the commitment to environmental adjudication within defined avenues nevertheless secures important legal qualities, including consistency, integrity and ultimately the rule of law – legal qualities that ought to be central to any discipline of law.

2

Defining Adjudication: Nature and Challenges

I. Introduction

Environmental adjudication as a multifaceted and layered process is an under-explored social phenomenon. The processes by which both judges and other adjudicators reach their decisions, and how these emerge from and through the administrative state, has not been the subject of sustained analysis across the environmental law landscape. The precise parameters of the adjudicator role, both practical and normative, are not easy to draw. One goal of this book is to identify what it is we ask our environmental adjudicators to do when carrying out such tasks and to examine the dimensions of their responses.

Novel scientific arguments, an ever-changing regulatory landscape, and a multiplicity of values and goals make for a challenging, and at worst, impossible, task for 'a judge'.[1] However, it is also a role that is essential where neither scientific consensus nor democratic 'preference' can find a solution that is both acceptable from an environmental protection perspective, and can neatly find a balance between the conflicting values at play *by themselves*.[2] In this sense, the adjudicatory role is but one part of environmental decision-making. However, as we shall see, we call upon that role to achieve different outcomes at different times in relation to different kinds of decisions, and in respect of different forms of decision-maker.

To understand the multifaceted nature of adjudication, we must first examine of what it consists. Section II considers the importance of building a definition of adjudication – of challenging assumptions and the received wisdom that adjudication has as its goal overall coherence – and then proceeds to distil the key features of adjudication. The following chapter (three) presents our theory as to how such adjudication works.

In making these assessments, it becomes clear that whilst, in broad strokes, the process of adjudication can be understood, at a specific level, the steps an

[1] The definitional parameters of our study are considered in section II.E below. Judge here is used simply to mean one who adjudicates.

[2] Fisher et al refer to this aspect of the adjudication process, citing Jasanoff who argues that the judicial forum is needed where science by itself cannot settle the multifaceted nature of the dispute at hand. E Fisher et al, 'The Legally Disruptive Nature of Climate Change' (2017) 80 *MLR* 173, 198. S Jasanoff, 'The Practices of Objectivity in Regulatory Science' in C Camic et al (eds), *Social Knowledge in the Making* (Chicago, University of Chicago Press, 2011) 309.

adjudicator takes become less clear and more fluid. The consequence of this is that far from being understood as a 'model' of a *type* of decision, to be aspired to, adjudication should be understood as a mode of reasoning, and as a process, which flexes according to the nature of the dispute at hand. In this part, we explain and explore a multidimensional theory of adjudication, a theoretical position that is given further expression in chapter three. We also explore the distinctions that can be drawn between judge and adjudicator; between judicial decision-making and adjudication more broadly; and between courts and other kinds of decision-making institutions to explore where the lens of our study should fall.

Section III explains what we mean by 'environmental'. Here, we accept that it is quite futile to attempt to find a definition which precisely delineates the 'environment'. Indeed, a successful comprehensive definition, even if found, would not be reflective of the reality of environmental law. This discipline, by its intimate connection with the 'real', as opposed to the socially constructed, is not isolatable. As a result, we take a 'central case' approach to defining environmental law, an approach we feel provides a sufficiently robust delineation to allow the phenomena of environmental law to be studied, without claiming to be 'perfect'.

Section IV of this chapter takes these findings and applies them to 'typical' features of environmental litigation, demonstrating that the characteristics of adjudication as a process are not well suited to the kinds of decisions which must be made in environmental law. This creates difficulties. That such adjudication is challenging for the reasons mentioned is well documented.[3] Indeed, there is a large volume of literature presenting potential solutions to such challenges, solutions which range from the creation of specialist courts, to moves away from traditional judicial adjudication into alternative dispute resolution mechanisms.[4]

However, as we conclude in section V, it should be recognised that the existence of these challenges is not a unique phenomenon for those attempting to reach judicial decisions in respect of environmental problems. Lots of law is 'hard' in these senses, but has been rendered more straightforward by two infinitely valuable factors: resources (over time),[5] and experience.[6] In environmental law, there

[3] For example, see Brian Preston's analysis of the characteristics of successful environmental courts, which contains a very useful explanation of the challenges faced. BJ Preston, 'Characteristics of Successful Environmental Courts and Tribunals' (2014) 26 *Journal of Environmental Law* 365.

[4] See U Bjällås, 'Experiences of Sweden's Environmental Courts' (2010) 3 *Journal of Court Innovation* 177; Preston, 'Characteristics of Successful Environmental Courts'; G Pring and C Pring, *Environmental Courts and Tribunals: A Guide for Policy-Makers* (UN Environment Programme, 2016); and NA Robinson, 'Ensuring Access to Justice through Environmental Courts' (2012) 29 *Pace Environmental Law Review* 363.

[5] The lack of funding for environmental judicial 'capacity-building' is an international as well as a national phenomenon, Robinson, 'Ensuring Access to Justice through Environment Courts' 378. A practical consequence of a lack of resources available to the Court is emphasised by the positive experience of New South Wales Land and Environment Court, which is well resourced and able to engage technical expertise of its own initiative, rather than relying on the financial resources of litigants to ensure access to high quality scientific information relevant to the resolution of any particular dispute. See BJ Preston, 'Judicial Specialisation through Environment Courts: A Case Study of the Land and Environmental Court of New South Wales' (2012) 29 *Pace Environmental Law Review* 602, 614.

[6] 'Practice does make perfect', Preston, 'Judicial Specialisation through Environment Courts' 612. Robinson notes the 'time-factor' when emphasising that we are some way off from ensuring the

has been over its short history few periods where these two factors have been in abundance. As we strive to utilise more mature environmental techniques, and our judiciary become more used to handling such questions, so too the judicial branch of government, as with the executive, is faced with mounting costs and time pressures; diminishing funding commensurate with that increase in workload; and a less well-resourced legal aid sector to support legal challenges brought by those in a financially vulnerable position.[7] The advantages that other 'legal areas' have had – a well-resourced and experienced justice system – are perhaps denied to those seeking to ensure high-quality environmental adjudication. Whilst, therefore, we may not be able to solve entirely the problem of environmental adjudication, we can understand the process more fully, and recognise the contextual issues which can render decision-making according to an adjudicative process both easier in practice and more legitimate in theory. It is these latter tasks that are undertaken in the remainder of this book.

II. Theorising about Adjudication

This book seeks to answer the seemingly simple question: how can we better understand environmental adjudication, recognising the context within which decisions are being made, and operating effectively within the practical and normative restrictions bounding the adjudicatory role? In very simple terms, our 'research question' is: how does environmental adjudication work in England and Wales? Answering this allows us to assess what the consequences of this deeper understanding of the process of adjudication might be. What is absolutely critical is a recognition from the outset that exploring the nature of adjudication is not simply a means to ensure that the courts and other forms of decision-maker are well equipped to face up to the more challenging aspects of adjudication in the sorts of cases that arise in an environmental context. More fundamentally, 'better' environmental adjudication is adjudication which achieves goals above and beyond that rather pragmatic goal of being able to 'cope' with complex science, with a fast-changing regulatory landscape, and with a multiplicity of values and goals operating simultaneously, and often in a conflicting fashion, in relation to the

realisation of environmental justice through our courts. Robinson, 'Ensuring Access to Justice through Environment Courts' 373. Experience too can be calculated in the shape of a 'critical mass' of decisions, to provide a sufficient range of issues to build up a consistent approach to adjudication. Preston emphasises the importance of creating such a critical mass: Preston, 'Judicial Specialisation through Environment Courts' 611.

[7] For analysis of the relationship between environmental litigation and legal aid, see F McCartney, 'Public Interest and Legal Aid' (2010) 37 *Scots Law Times* 201 and Editor, 'Legal Aid for Environmental and Planning Litigation?' (2017) 24 *Irish Planning and Environmental Law Journal* 54. For views on legal aid cuts and their impacts more generally, see eg F Hawken, 'Failed Justice: The Impact of the Legal Aid, Sentencing and Punishment of Offenders Act 2012 on the Legal System of England and Wales' (2019) 24 *Coventry Law Journal* 129 and E Uncovska, 'The Impact of Legal Aid Cuts on the Right to a Fair Trial' (2019) 24 *Coventry Law Journal* 136.

same pieces of legislation or case-law. Our exploration is therefore cognisant of the need to be reflexive regarding the realities of environmental adjudication. To put this another way, we do not assume that 'good' means 'made easy'.

To demonstrate this we, first, in section II.A, build an understanding of what adjudication involves. In section II.B we explore polycentricism in adjudication. Section II.C considers the role of reason in adjudication. Section II.D explores the role of adjudication as a source of generalisable rules, and section II.E concludes this part with an analysis of adjudicator identity.

A. Defining Adjudication

To commence our process of defining adjudication, we look to Fuller and other articulations of the nature of adjudication.[8] It will be argued in this section that adjudication is characterised by a decision-making process: (i) which results in a decision being reached more or less in the favour of one of the participants in the dispute; (ii) which relies on a particular mode of reasoning to justify conclusions – ie based on persuasive arguments, reason and proof; (iii) where the goal is to provide a solution not only to the instant dispute, but also to provide reasons that can be generalised so as to produce a pattern of decision-making based on persuasive arguments, reason and proof; and (iv) where the identity of the institutionalised decision-maker can be appropriately conceived of as a 'third' party. As we shall see, whether or not any one institution meets these criteria can, in difficult cases, be a question of degree rather than black or white.

The precise nature of the reasons that can form a decision, and their power in each case, will vary (as we shall explain in chapter six) according to the precise mode of the dispute which results in institutionalised intervention. In this respect, we depart from Fuller in arguing that it is possible for a 'legislative' result from a judicial (or other adjudicatory) forum to be legitimised *as adjudication*, depending upon the context of the rules being applied, but that the legitimacy of such generalised rules is contingent upon this wider context.

There is a great deal of theoretical debate in the literature as to how adjudication should be carried out, and as to the central role adjudication plays in the very idea of the social institution of law. Indeed, for Dworkin, his theory of adjudication constituted his very theory of law itself.[9] For others, the role of the judge (or adjudicator more generally) is special in their articulation of the operation of a legal system. Hart, for example, emphasises the importance of judicial acceptance

[8] L Fuller, 'The Forms and Limits of Adjudication' (1978) 92 *Harvard Law Review* 353.

[9] Ronald Dworkin explores the figure of Hercules, the idealised judge. See R Dworkin, *Law's Empire* (London, Fontana Press, 1986). His theory postulates that law consists of the one right interpretation of the existing rules as applied to the facts before the judge when the judge seeks coherence in that set of rules. See also J Dickinson, 'Interpretation and coherence in legal reasoning) https://plato.stanford.edu/entries/legal-reas-interpret/ (29 May 2001, revised 10 February 2010 – accessed 28 January 2020).

of the relevant rules in order for them to form part of a positivistic understanding of what the law is in a particular state.[10] Understanding what adjudication is, and how it works, is seen as a central component of a fully worked-out theory of the legal system as a whole. Examination of the existing literature regarding the nature of adjudication reveals that many theorists assume a model of adjudication (neutral decision-making on the basis of pre-set standards) in creating such an overall theory.[11] Built into this assumption as to the nature of adjudication is a (potentially) normatively simplistic preference for a neutral judiciary which does not make law, but rather, applies it.[12] This approach to understanding the adjudicative process is built upon ideas such as the separation of powers, rule of law and the need to respect democratic decision-making.

However, such theories are often conflating three questions (consciously or unconsciously), as Moore explains:

> Such a theory should do three things: (1) describe what judges actually do when they decide a case; (2) recommend what they ought to do when they so decide; and (3) make assumptions about what is possible for judges to do in deciding cases, in order to give accurate descriptions and sound recommendations. Thus, any complete theory of adjudication will undertake the threefold task of stating what is the case, what ought to be the case, and what can be the case in judicial decision-making.[13]

Failure to note that these three questions can be separated undermines much that is written about adjudication if one uses this literature in the search for a definition. Such conflation allows for a tacit acceptance that *all* that judges/adjudicators do is, or should be, adjudication, and as such, anything not properly described as adjudication is also illegitimate action on the part of the adjudicator. It is important to distinguish from the outset the question of what adjudication is, from what judges should do.

Such theorising therefore sits at an uncomfortable juncture in the description of a legal system, for not only is it a normative description (adjudication at its peak is *x*, so all real-life judges, to earn the title of judge, should adjudicate in accordance with manner *x*), but also an attempt at a practical description (this is what judges are doing). For some theories, the uncomfortable mismatch between description from theory and description from practice undermines the integrity of both. Dworkin's account of the role of the judge struggles for its lack of realism for how judges actually decide,[14] whilst a formalistic account focusing on the

[10] HLA Hart, *The Concept of Law*, 2nd edn (Oxford, Clarendon Press, 1994).

[11] eg B Cardozo, *The Nature of the Judicial Process* (New Haven, CT, Yale University Press, 1921) and the discussion in J M Zane, 'German Legal Philosophy' (1918) 16 *Michigan Law Review* 287.

[12] Cardozo, *The Nature of the Judicial Process* 113 and HLA Hart, 'Positivism and the Separation of Law and Morals' (1958) 71 *Harvard Law Review* 593.

[13] MS Moore, 'The Semantics of Judging' (1981) 54 *Southern California Law Review* 151, 154.

[14] See K Llewellyn, *The Bramble Bush* (New York, Oceana, 1930); MS Moore, 'A Natural Law Theory of Interpretation' (1985) 58 *Southern California Law Review* 277; and B Leiter and MX Etchemendy, 'Naturalism in Legal Philosophy' https://plato.stanford.edu/entries/lawphil-naturalism (15 July 2002, amended 27 March 2017 – accessed 28 January 2020).

legitimacy of information taken into account in reaching decisions is unrealistic in assuming either that judges never use intuition,[15] or in artificially restricting the scope of the factors they take into account. A theory of adjudication is therefore a challenging enterprise, a fact that has been seized upon by the legal realist school, which focuses on the lack of 'legal' content in judicial decision-making in reality.

However, from this theorising we can learn some important lessons for how we can go about building a rich understanding of what English and Welsh judges do, and should do, when presented with environmental law cases. First, rigorous distinctions must be drawn between what judges in fact do, what we feel they ought to do, and what they can do, as Moore highlights.[16] These three questions are conceptually distinct. Second, much theorising about adjudication does not start with an important discussion – what do they actually understand adjudication to be. Is it the entirety of a judicial process? Is adjudication the decision thus reached? Does adjudication extend beyond the judiciary and encompass certain kinds of decisions made at administrative authority level (one thinks in the environmental context of decisions made about prosecutorial approach by the Environment Agency (EA); by planning appeal inspectors; and by appointed but non-judicial adjudicators)?

This is a serious omission, which undermines the power of any claims made about either what is or what should be the nature of adjudication, when the boundaries of the topic under discussion are not drawn. Finally, and as we shall see in the next chapter, any account of what adjudication is and should be is, ultimately, a contextual one as even the most formalistic account of how law operates must accept, not least because there will always be the contextual question as to whether there is pre-existing law in place or not (in Cardozo's expression, whether the law in question has 'open spaces').[17] This means that it is not possible to articulate in advance a complete list of factors a judge should (or does) take into account when adjudicating because that task will shift according to the nature of the case at hand. Indeed, this acceptance is central to our argument throughout this book. As a consequence of these three factors we can conclude that theorising about adjudication requires a clear distinction to be drawn around the scholarly task being undertaken, an answer to the question as to what adjudication actually is, and a recognition that the answer to both what adjudication is, and what it should be, is a contextual one rather than one which can be precisely articulated without understanding the parameters and situation within which and in relation to which the question is being asked.

[15] See F Jackson *From Metaphysics to Ethics: A Defence of Conceptual Analysis* (Oxford, Clarendon Press, 1998).

[16] Moore, 'The Semantics of Judging' 154.

[17] Cardozo, *The Nature of the Judicial Process* 113.

i. Application of a Pre-existing Standard to Facts

There have been numerous attempts over time to define adjudication – be that in the context of *alternative* dispute mechanisms, or in attempting to capture the essence of the judicial role. For example, Moore argues that, '[a]djudication is concerned with the application of a standard to events that have already happened'.[18] This highly formalistic definition pervades US scholarship on the nature of adjudication. As highlighted above, such is not normatively neutral, for it contains within it an assumption that the creation of standards would be beyond adjudication, and therefore beyond the proper judicial role. Such a definition is, however, limited in practice. Whilst it applies without too much difficulty to 'standard' criminal law cases, it is somewhat more difficult when we consider litigation in the form of a primary reference to the Court of Justice of the European Union (CJEU), for example, where the litigation is *not* about the application of a standard to factual events. Rather, it surrounds arguments as to what the appropriate standard is (a distinction can be drawn here between the clarification of a standard, and the creation of that standard, at least in theory). Even if it can be argued that the CJEU action is merely 'part of' a wider process of adjudication, it is perhaps more realistic to conclude that adjudication is concerned not only with the application of standards to facts, but also (at least) with the clarification of such standards, and the proof of facts, amongst others. It is, in this sense, also about 'norm setting and compliance'.[19] These two forms of adjudication are sometimes referred to as the distinction between dispute resolution and expository justice,[20] but drawing a bright line underestimates the need to provide generalisable rules in many cases in order to resolve a dispute, and the two forms of adjudication are not diametrically opposed if we understand adjudication to be a mode of reasoning by certain forms of decision-maker rather than a type of decision based on certain kinds of rules and reasons.

Fisher et al, in considering the disruptive effect that climate change litigation has on adjudication, define the parameters of the subject matter, but use a

[18] Moore, 'The Semantics of Judging' 154–55. In an environmental context this is very often not what judges are asked to do for they are very often making predictions about the future. Yes, they are applying standards to a decision which may have already taken place, or in reference to a plan already drawn up, but the emphasis of the task is different. This is captured by Ulf Bjällås, a former presiding judge on the Swedish Environmental Court, who argues that:

> I am sometimes asked, 'What is the difference between judging an environmental case and judging a criminal case?' I usually say that the criminal judge looks backward trying to find out what has been proved about what happened, while the environmental judge looks forward asking what will happen in the future as a result of my decision.

U Bjällås, 'Experiences of Sweden's Environment Court' (2010) 3 *Journal of Court Innovation* 177, 184.

[19] Fisher et al, 'The Legally Disruptive Nature of Climate Change' 198.

[20] See GA Spann, 'Expository Justice' (1983) 131 *University of Pennsylvania Law Review* 585.

deliberately 'broad' definition, whilst highlighting that there is no clear definition available. Thus:

> [W]e define 'adjudication' in very broad terms to include triadic forms of dispute resolution, which involve some *application* of legal norms. With that said, understanding adjudication is 'no easy task.' It is at once a deeply jurisprudential pursuit, a socio-political consideration of the proper role of judges, and a practical question about the types of issues that can actually be resolved in a courtroom … as a form of decision-making, it can blend into mediation and even representative government. It is also a collective practice. Adjudication is not the act of a single judge or a single party and its form and processes are embedded within the relevant legal, social and political culture.[21]

This definition is therefore, as the authors acknowledge, an attempt to find a simple set of words to describe the phenomenon they study in their paper, a search which requires them to analyse what adjudication is, as well as what it should be, whilst recognising that the exact forms and nature of adjudication will vary across jurisdictions and contexts. This definition, for the most part, looks to the content of the decision made, as does Moore's.[22] It emphasises that adjudication is the *application* of legal norms, and the judicial aspect of the adjudicative process is highlighted. However, there is also embedded within this a hint that judicial decision-making and adjudication are conterminous, which may not be the case. Furthermore, focus on the 'types of rules' being applied may, to a certain extent, presuppose the issues we discuss below surrounding gaps and the creation of judicial legislation.

ii. Adjudication as Process

An alternative approach to defining adjudication therefore is one that looks not at the content of the decision being made (even appropriately caveated by reference to context), but rather the *process* by which that decision is reached. This approach to definition sees adjudication as a mode of reasoning, rather than a type of decision. Of such approaches, one of the most significant articulations is to be found in Fuller's attempt to explain of what 'true adjudication' consists.[23] His argument – which, as we shall see in the subsequent chapters, chimes very well with our findings upon the different scope of adjudicatory powers when answering a range of questions in the environmental law sphere – is that whilst no adjudication system *in fact* meets the definition he devises, adjudication as a social institution is at all times striving towards his understanding of true adjudication. Of course, there is a distinction between what adjudication is, and what *good* adjudication may be, but it is impossible to examine the parameters of adjudication in relation to the environment without some explanation of what adjudication is, and what we include within our survey.

[21] Fisher et al, 'The Legally Disruptive Nature of Climate Change' 175–6 (emphasis added).
[22] Moore, 'The Semantics of Judging' 292–93.
[23] Fuller, 'The Forms and Limits of Adjudication' 355–56.

Fuller articulates three key characteristics of 'true' adjudication. First, the dispute must be one that regulates the relationship between persons. Second, in resolving this dispute, the adjudicator must resort to reason, proof and argumentation. Third, the body through which the dispute is resolved must be an institutionalised one. To this, subsequently, we add two further characteristics: adjudicatory reasoning must allow for generalisable rules in appropriate cases; and the institutionalised decision-maker is also 'independent' from the dispute.

B. Winners, Losers and Polycentricity

Fuller's definition commences, as he highlights, with the obvious: adjudication is 'a means of settling disputes or controversies'.[24] He then continues: 'More fundamentally, however, adjudication should be viewed as a form of social ordering, as a way in which the relations of men to one another are governed and organized.'[25] That adjudication usually involves winners and losers requires some justification, for indeed we can imagine cases where a judge is required to assess whether an individual's act is permissible or not regardless of whether there is any person who wishes that she would not carry out such an act.

We could respond simply: cases like this do not in practice arise, and indeed, Fuller acknowledges as much (even if he suggests that in the majority of cases there is no 'true' polycentrism so that the dispute becomes irresolvable by adjudication – for more on polycentrism, see section IV.D below).[26] In the real world, litigation, and therefore judicial adjudication, involves winners and losers to a greater or lesser extent. If everyone was likely to achieve everything they wished from a situation, then there would be no litigation in the first place. The position regarding non-judicial adjudicators is admittedly less clear cut, but in general this practical point is true. However, Fuller provides a more robust theoretical defence of the idea that adjudication is first and foremost a mode by which decisions are made as to the relationship between two or more legal persons, parties to the dispute. He explains that the natural form of adjudication is to adjudge as to 'right', or to 'fault'. In order for there to be such a claim, there must be one against whom the rightness is asserted.[27] This does not mean, of course, that there cannot be three, four or even a hundred parties to a dispute, but rather, because of the nature of adjudication, there must be relative winners and losers in the resolution of that dispute, and this balance is calculated according to the 'rightness' of the claimant(s), or the fault of the defendant(s). There is, in this sense, inevitable opposition.

In this approach we find already one reason why environmental disputes may appear to be so unsuited to adjudication in this form. Environmental problems

[24] ibid 357.
[25] ibid 357.
[26] ibid 394–404.
[27] ibid 370.

may most naturally present themselves as being disputes between individuals, or between legal persons, as where one industrial concern causes polluting effects to the land of another,[28] but very often the dispute is not between or about two legal personalities. Rather, it is more often a case of the acts of one legal person causing harm or potential harm to 'the environment', a concept not easily captured in scholarship, literature, science or law, and certainly not easily captured in the legal process. When the environment is on one side of the balance sheet in this sense, the calibration of the 'relationship' by a court becomes nebulous and multifaceted and the identification of adjudicators a question of degree. However, in exploring the phenomenon of adjudication, we accept that a situation will only involve adjudication in its fullest sense if it presents a 'winner' and a 'loser', or, more generally relative 'rightness' between parties.

C. Argumentation, Reason and Proof

Our second aspect of adjudication as a social institution – as a means of social ordering – is that it is achieved through the presentation of rational arguments, proof and reason.[29] It is here that we find the core of adjudication (even a roll-of-the-dice decision involves winners and losers but can hardly be labelled adjudication). Per Fuller:

> This whole analysis will derive from one simple proposition, namely, that the distinguishing characteristic of adjudication lies in the fact that it confers on the affected party a peculiar form of participation in the decision, that of presenting proofs and reasoned arguments for a decision in his favour. Whatever heightens the significance of this participation lifts adjudication toward its optimum expression. Whatever destroys the meaning of that participation destroys the integrity of adjudication itself.[30]

Furthermore, in explaining the importance of this mode of participation, Fuller highlights that whilst this does not entail that adjudication has a monopoly on reasoned argumentation, it is the fact that reasoned argumentation here creates a socially constructed institution which is critical, allowing for 'a form of participating in a decision that is institutionally defined and assured'.[31] In this, we find the concomitant need for a decision-maker who listens to the reasoned arguments and is bound to respond to them in a reasoned way, ie the judge. Taken together, this allows Fuller to conclude:

> Adjudication is, then, a device which gives a formal and institutional expression to the influence of reasoned argument in human affairs. As such it assumes a burden of

[28] What we may think of the traditional form of environmental regulation in the shape of nuisance laws. For discussion of the history of pollution control, see B Pontin, 'Integrated Pollution Control in Victorian Britain: Rethinking Progress within the History of Environmental Law' (2007) 19 *Journal of Environmental Law* 173.

[29] Fuller, 'The Forms and Limits of Adjudication' 363.

[30] ibid 364.

[31] ibid 366.

> rationality not borne by any other form of social ordering. A decision which is the product of reasoned argument must be prepared itself to meet the test of reason. We demand of an adjudicative decision a kind of rationality we do not expect of the results of contract or voting. This higher responsibility toward rationality is at once the strength *and the weakness* of adjudication as a form of social ordering.[32]

Acknowledging again that Fuller is describing true adjudication – an idealised form of the social institution – it is nevertheless notable for environmental adjudication that rationality, proof and reason are often not only difficult to find in relation to environmental problems, but in a more radical sense, impossible, due to the nature of the issues at hand. One cannot simply try harder to prove what the effects of substances will be in two hundred years time. This sort of discussion is not susceptible to proof, and indeed principles such as the precautionary principle may be seen to be a solution in the absence of a rational or reasoned response based on the particular facts of any case. They are a generalised solution to intractable problems.[33] This, we may say from the outset, will cause environmental adjudication in particular to struggle to meet adjudication's 'optimum expression'.[34] We consider this further in section IV below.

The demands for such reasoning have an inevitable consequence for the quality of adjudication. This relates to the need for the adjudicator to provide, and make available to both the parties and the general public, reasons for the decision reached. Without seeing the reasons, we can validly argue that the process by which a decision was reached may or may not be properly regarded as adjudication, for without the provision of reasons, the decision could have been reached on an entirely irrational basis, or purely by chance. As Shapiro argues, the process of adjudication and its very nature requires the provision of candid reasons for a decision:

> In my view, the case for candor in the crafting of judicial opinions … draws special strength from the nature of the judicial process … reasoned response to reasoned argument is an essential aspect of that process. A requirement that judges give reasons for their decisions – grounds of decision that can be debated, attacked, and defended – serves a vital function in constraining the judiciary's exercise of power. In the absence of an obligation of candor, this constraint would be greatly diluted, since judges who regard themselves as free to distort or misstate the reasons for their actions can avoid the sanctions of criticism and condemnation that honest disclosure of their motivation may entail. In a sense, candor is the sine qua non of all other restraints on abuse of judicial power, for the limitations imposed by constitutions, statutes, and precedents count for little if judges feel free to believe one thing about them and to say another.[35]

[32] ibid 366–67 (emphasis in the original).
[33] For extensive analysis of the environmental principles, see E Scotford, *Environmental Principles and the Evolution of Environmental Law* (Oxford, Hart Publishing, 2017).
[34] Fuller, 'The Forms and Limits of Adjudication' 364.
[35] DA Shapiro, 'In Defense of Judicial Candor' (1987) 100 *Harvard Law Review* 731, 737.

As this argument shows, the provision of candid reasons is not only an essential part of the mode of reasoning of adjudication, but also of ensuring that other social institutions are able to keep check on the process of adjudication. Indeed, in emphasising the importance of reason and justification in adjudication, we can conclude that an adjudicative process which is wholly irrational is no adjudicative process at all (at least, it is one not worthy of the name). Taking this into account, we assume certain qualities in that mode of reasoning that justify the label of adjudication. This makes the line between what adjudication is, and what adjudication 'should be', a fine one.

D. Generalisable Rules

The dilemma of a court attempting to resolve an individual dispute, whilst also providing generalisable rules, is neatly articulated by Spann: 'The task of the … judiciary is seriously complicated by the fact that it has to play one role while pretending to play another.'[36] This tension in adjudication is one aspect where the formulation as to the nature of adjudication provided by Fuller appears to be unrealistic, or at least realistic only in the context of the most straightforward of cases. He is not alone, however, and Sunstein too highlights the distinction between adjudication and rule-making.[37] In the context of regulatory law, however, it is clear that the rules enunciated are not intended to constitute merely a resolution of a dispute on the basis of new and existing rules, but rather to provide a standard of behaviour that ought to be followed in future action. We agree here with the many arguments made in emphasising the exposition role performed by judges, in addition to the dispute resolution role, with both appropriately being grouped under the heading of adjudication.[38] However, quite how far one role should dominate the adjudication process, and how one reconciles the two roles, is not simple to answer.

Furthermore, the *basis* upon which a judge makes the new rules will determine whether or not the rules can be appropriately considered to have arisen out of a process of adjudication (rather than policy-making). As Rubin emphasises, this distinction depends on the mode of reasoning employed so that, '[t]he common law grants judges the authority to legislate – to announce new legal rules – on the basis of the reasoned arguments that Fuller identified as their particular preserve.'[39] On the other hand, Kress, in recognising the inevitability of legal indeterminacy – of penumbras and gaps – emphasises that '[e]very case of adjudication requires judicial legislation'[40] but that this does not necessarily render judicial adjudication

[36] Spann, 'Expository Justice' 585.

[37] CR Sunstein, 'The Problem with Rules' (1995) 83 *California Law Review* 953, 1015.

[38] Spann, 'Expository Justice' 592ff.

[39] EL Rubin, 'The New Legal Process: The Synthesis of Discourse, and the Microanalysis of Institutions' (1996) 109 *Harvard Law Review* 1393, 1397.

[40] K Kress, 'Legal Indeterminacy' (1989) 77 *California Law Review* 283, 288.

illegitimate. In this section, whilst we are not concerned with this legitimacy question per se, it does suggest that a rich account of what adjudication entails includes an assessment that law is inevitably 'gappy', and that in making pronouncements as to outcome in such cases, the adjudicator in reaching a reasoned decision is nevertheless 'making' law.

However, this inevitable truth about adjudication has dangers, particularly as a means by which rules are created by a partisan advocate through the medium of the adjudicator, but without engaging with the majoritarian democratic process. Thus, as Diver explains,

> Litigation is a social institution inherently dichotomous in nature – it is at once a process for authoritative adjudication of legal disputes and a vehicle for partisan manipulation of bargaining advantage. The balance struck between these roles traditionally has favored adherence to adjudicative ideals. Modern litigants, however, increasingly have invited litigation to perform tasks demanding fuller exploitation of its political potential. …
>
> The enormity and complexity of such an undertaking have created unprecedented pressures on judges to abandon their historical positions as neutral arbiters and to assume the manipulative role of powerbrokers. The conventions of litigation present the judge with many opportunities to influence allocation of bargaining advantages among the parties before him. Decisions he makes – the specificity of his orders, his choice of procedures for planning remedies, which parties he allows or orders to be joined – unavoidably have an impact on the structure and the agenda, and thus the outcome, of subsequent political games.
>
> Having opportunities to play the role of powerbroker is, however, only a necessary, not a sufficient, condition for its successful use. The judge also must possess the knowledge, the time, and the power demanded by such a role. Structural characteristics of the judicial position place inherent limitations on the judge's capacity to gather political intelligence, to oversee a protracted, complex process of adjustment, and to induce desired shifts in individual behavior.
>
> More important, as the political nature of judicial behavior in institutional reform litigation becomes more apparent, courts can draw less and less on the reserve of authority that the revered position of neutral lawgiver confers. The legitimacy that the adjudicatory model bestows on the judge unavoidably is at odds with his using his power to achieve political ends. Only if a simultaneous and fundamental transformation occurs in the popular view of the judiciary can judges long sustain the efficacy of their new role as powerbrokers.[41]

The adjudicator is able through the process of adjudication to allocate power.[42] That allocation may give power to the judiciary, or to another actor within the process. We examine this power-broker aspect in chapter five. To carry out this task successfully, they need the tools – financial and otherwise – to draw on

[41] CS Diver, 'The Judge as Political Powerbroker: Superintending Structural Change in Public Institutions', (1979) 65 *Virginia Law Review* 43, 106.

[42] E Lees, 'Allocation of Decision-Making Power under the Habitats Directive' (2016) 28 *Journal of Environmental Law* 191.

a variety of factors in weighing up their decision. In so doing, however, they may risk the very purpose of the judicial branch, ie its political neutrality in decision-making (if such is an appropriate label, because we can clearly see that adjudicators *ought* to be, and very often are, committed to the values embedded in the rule of law, and cannot in that sense be truly described as politically neutral). By moving away from this position of ostensible political neutrality, the adjudicator risks moving away from the process of adjudication relying on reason and proof, to a process of politics, relying on persuasion, passion and argumentation not held to the same standard of rationality. We consider how this tension between neutrality, politics and power allocation through decision-making plays out in an environmental context in section IV.A.

E. Institutionalised Decision-Making and Independence

Until this point the terms adjudication, judicial decision-making, judge, court and adjudicator have been used relatively interchangeably. This underplays the importance of the identity and characteristics of the decision-maker in adjudication. As explained above, there are two necessary elements to this identity for one who judges to be properly labelled 'adjudicator': institutionalisation and independence.

By 'institutionalised' here is meant that *framework* within which the ability of the individual in question to decide on the dispute at hand is pre-existing to the dispute, and established by a recognised social institution. As Fuller explains, the point is not so much that the framework is one which *in fact* gives a judge the ability to decide an outcome in a dispute between two parties, but rather one which is *intended* to grant this ability *and* where the judge is expected to meet the test of reason, argumentation and proof in fulfilling this role. Thus:

> What distinguishes them [judges at livestock fairs] from courts, administrative tribunals, and boards of arbitration is that their decisions are not reached within an institutional framework that is intended to assure to the disputants an opportunity for the presentation of proofs and reasoned arguments.[43]

We must ask, therefore, what kinds of frameworks are appropriately institutionalised. At the 'clear' end of the spectrum, of course, lie the courts and tribunal systems where there is little doubt that these systems are created with the purpose of providing decision-making on the basis of reason, rather than either chance, or mere subjective, unchallenged preference. In such fora the parties are encouraged to present arguments in support of their position, and there will be restrictions on the kinds of arguments which the decision-maker can take into account. At the opposite end, a situation where a third-party friend is asked to decide between two neighbours as to who is behaving 'properly', the fact that this decision is not

[43] Fuller, 'The Forms and Limits of Adjudication' 365.

one with an institutional backing prevents the friend being appropriately considered an adjudicator. Should one neighbour simply chose to ignore the decision of the friend, there is no sanction, recourse or institutional guarantee in which the outcome of the decision will be reflected.

There are, of course, many situations that sit between these two clear examples. Some of these are 'blurry' because of the identity of the decision-maker and the parties – for example, does first-instance planning authority decision-making by a local council constitute adjudication? – and we consider this kind of blurring below. Others are blurry because the institution in question is of an unusual kind. For example, let us consider the situation where a contractual agreement established between two parties includes an arbitration clause. A clause may provide that the arbitrator is to be appointed at the will of the parties alongside, perhaps, a contractual penalty for failing to comply with the decision of that arbitrator. Is this an institutionalised framework or not? The adjudicator is not chosen, constructed or guaranteed by the state directly. Rather, a failure to operate within the confines of the contractual arrangement is so guaranteed. A binding legal contract is a social institution, but the arbitration process itself is not. We would therefore exclude the arbitration process from the scope of adjudication (not least because there may be no socially developed norms as to the sorts of considerations which that arbitrator may take into account, and therefore we cannot say for sure that this was *intended* to create a forum based on reason and proof). Some arbitrators could of course be included where, for example, a statutory mechanism established a system of arbitration to encourage alternative dispute resolution mechanisms. Here the institutionalisation of the arbitrator is clear. To provide a list of who does and does not 'count' here is not possible. There will be obvious cases, and others where the answer is far from clear and susceptible of legitimate disagreement. However, this is what we have looked for in our search for 'the adjudicator' and we map this, as we see it, onto English and Welsh environmental law, in subsequent chapters.

To this idea of institutional decision-maker, we add 'independent'. This is a difficult concept to pin down. Again, there are very clear cases. A Supreme Court judge, not tainted by any self-interest that would cause her to recuse herself, in a tort dispute between two private individuals, is independent from the dispute. So too are there cases where there is no independence, as, for example, in cases where a public authority would be authorised to make assessments of its own reasonableness in action. The nature of independence in adjudication is in fact most often discussed in the context of human rights and fair trials,[44] and in this we can find many examples where the answer is not clear-cut. There is therefore little to be gained by engaging in an entirely hypothetical discussion. Rather, in chapter four, we answer this question specifically in relation to the decision-making forms apparent in English and Welsh law.

[44] See *R (Holding & Barnes Plc) v Secretary of State for the Environment, Transport and the Regions* (also known as *Alconbury*) [2001] UKHL 23, [2003] 2 AC 295.

Before moving on, it is worth emphasising here, however, that a single body can be both an adjudicator and a 'disputant' at different times. A good example of this, which we consider further in chapter four, is the EA. The role of this body in respect of criminal enforcements is complicated. At times, the Agency operates, in effect, as a prosecutor, bringing the actions of an individual before the traditional courts, seeking a penalty. At other times, the Agency becomes the direct forum within which decisions about guilt are made, and sanctions imposed. In such cases, the Agency is wearing two hats: on the one hand it is proxy decision-maker for 'the environment' and is therefore in a sense a party to the dispute; on the other hand, it is the decision-maker before whom the environment and the defendant are judged against one another. Certainly, the Agency does not have a vested interest in the outcome. Rather, as a representative of the environment its interests are the maintenance of appropriate legislative and policy standards. And yet, in reaching any decision the Agency would be applying its own policy. The reason why this is problematic, therefore, is less about the Agency as prosecutor, but rather about the environment as a 'party' to disputes, as we discuss further below. The scope of the Agency role as an adjudicator is considered further in chapter four.

We may wrap up this section by answering one final question – why is this independence, or 'third-party' status so important to what we conceive to be adjudication properly so-called? It follows from the fact that adjudication involves winners and losers, that the person who decides who wins, and who loses, should not be one of those people. If it does, then the value of the reasoned arguments that are so critical to adjudication becomes much diminished in the face of demonstrable self-interest. Rather, there is effectively a negotiation without an adjudicator, in which the stronger party is able to assert their will. This strength may emerge from the power which that party has been given to make decisions in their own cause.

How this argument operates where the decision-maker, although not impartial, does not have 'self-interest' as such in the outcome of the dispute is brought to the fore in the EA example above. Further cases that spring to mind of this phenomenon are local planning authorities considering a planning application (although given their elected status, it may be said that there is a degree of self-interest); an environmental protection agency considering a licensing request; or a nature conservation body assessing conservation status of a site. These bodies are not 'third parties' – there are only two people in the discussion, the administrative agency, and the party making the application. If we simplify this situation into a 'winner'/'loser' paradigm, then the situation is as follows: the agency decides whether the applicant wins or loses. There is no one on the other side. This situation appears not, therefore, to be one of adjudication *not* because of the presence of self-interest per se (unlike in an internal appeals process where the decision-maker who is embedded in the institution, the decision of which is being challenged), but because there is no possibility of their being both a relative winner and a relative loser. How this plays out against the recognition that 'the environment' can effectively be the winner/loser in appropriate cases, represented by such a body, is considered further later. Whether or not these cases are appropriately conceived of as adjudication is significant, however, since it suggests, if considering how *should* such decision-makers behave, that they should be motivated by rationality and reason, rather than political persuasion.

In bringing this discussion of our theoretical framework to an end, we are now in a position to demonstrate where the boundary lines of our investigation lie in respect of the identity of the decision-maker who can appropriately be considered an adjudicator. Courts, and judges, in the traditional form are without doubt usually 'adjudicators', but may also be administrative bodies depending upon the function that they are being called upon to undertake in any particular context. The EA, for example, can be an adjudicator – it is an institutional decision-maker – but it may not be if in the case at hand it is either not independent, or there is no winner/loser balance to be had. Similarly, a planning appeals inspector will very often be an adjudicator, but obviously will not be so where their own decision is that which is being challenged so that they become a participant rather than the judge. Even a judge may not always be an adjudicator. The example of judicial review of a decision of a magistrates' court demonstrates this, for in such cases the judge herself becomes the potential winner or loser in the dispute. She was an adjudicator earlier in the process, and now has been the subject of adjudication.

Finally, it is also worth noting here – and we return to this theme in chapter three – that whilst we speak of 'judge' and 'adjudicator', we may often be referring to 'judges' or 'adjudicators' in the case of an appellate court, for example, where there will be more than one individual called upon to produce a single 'decision' (even if expressed in multiple agreeing or even dissenting judgments, the result of the adjudication will be a single outcome). These dynamics of multiperson adjudicators are considered later.

III. Defining the Environment

In addition to defining adjudication, we must also provide some boundaries to what we consider to be 'environmental'. To do so is not easy, as is very well documented. As a 'real-world' idea, the environment is not isolatable. In purely legal terms, since England and Wales do not have an environmental code, we cannot simply use legal coverage or legal definitions to do our work for us. As a result, we take, as noted above, a central case approach to definition.[45] That is, there are some situations which so obviously are 'environmental law' that we do not need a precise and concrete definition of 'environmental' to be sure we ought to address them. Nature conservation provisions, pollution controls and environmental impact assessment regulations would all fall into this category.

[45] The 'central case' definitional approach is also adopted by John Finnis. See J Finnis, *Natural Law and Natural Rights* (Oxford, Oxford University Press, 1980) 17–18, though it is Aristotelian in origin. See also V Rodriguez-Blanco, 'Is Finnis Wrong? Understanding Normative Jurisprudence' (2007) 13 *Legal Theory* 257.

However one would define 'the environment' or 'environmental', these provisions would undoubtedly be covered. Similarly, there are definitely areas of the law which we can exclude on the grounds that they sit so far outside that central case that they are not environmental law. The rules of evidence in relation to fraud trials are one of an uncountable number of examples. And, as with adjudication above, there are situations which sit somewhere on this spectrum and are therefore 'difficult'. Are the principles of contractual interpretation 'environmental law', in the sense that they will determine how a conservation covenant is interpreted and will therefore affect the environment? Are the rules relating to proof of intention in a criminal action environmental law, as they may determine whether an individual is successfully prosecuted in a polluting case? As we shall see later in this book, we argue that attempting to decide whether these are or are not properly considered environmental law is positively damaging to our understanding of how environmental law works. They are relevant to environmental adjudication, and by this token may or may not be relevant to our study depending upon the context within which these issues arise.

Given this, not only do we take a 'central case' approach to definition, but we also take a *categorical* approach to defining environmental law, relying on a more or less instinctual understanding of what should be included, considering cases involving potential, actual or alleged environmental harms, degradations or effects. We do not, therefore, make a claim in this book to comprehensivity. Rather, we study the 'core' of environmental law to examine its features. That this does not also result in total coverage of the subject falling under our gaze does not diminish the arguments we can make in respect of this core. Over the course of this book, we consider environmental information, environmental impact assessment, nuisance, waste offences, habitat protection, amongst others, in cases involving potential, actual or alleged environmental harms, degradations or effects. In terms of adjudicators, we explore the published decisions of the Planning Inspectorate, the First Tier Tribunal (FTT) and the Upper Tribunal, the Information Commissioner (IC), and the higher and lower courts. We also look at the adjudicatory role played by the EA.

IV. Challenging Adjudication

As noted above, many if not all of the challenges we identify here have been explored in the existing literature in relation to environmental law, particularly in the context of a series of well-articulated analyses of the merits of specialist environmental courts and tribunals.[46] It is, however, critical to examine some of these

[46] Preston, 'Judicial Specialization through Environment Courts'; Preston, 'Characteristics of Successful Environmental Courts and Tribunals'; and R Carnwath, 'Environmental Enforcement: The Need for a Specialist Court' [1992] *Journal of Planning Law* 799.

arguments here, in order to develop a full picture of the issues facing judges when they seek to reach a binary winner–loser decision in relation to some of the most complex and multifaceted problems it is possible to imagine. The challenges to be discussed here are: politics, policies and values (section IV.A); science and proof (section IV.B); shifting regulatory standards, a lack of resources and inexperience (section IV.C); and winners and losers in the adversarial process (section IV.D).

A. Politics, Policies and Values

We can sum up many of these challenges in three words: politics, policies and values. Environmental adjudication is a process within which these factors marble together to produce an ever-changing landscape of legitimacy, merit and rationality in decision-making. It can hardly be considered unique that environmental adjudication encompasses tensions between these factors. However, we can explore these in more detail to allow for a more comprehensive understanding as to how they shape the rationality and reason-driven adjudicative process.

By politics in this context is meant two things – first it refers to the political processes that shape environmental policy, which are not themselves aligned around a single homogenous goal, or designed to produce a legal system that 'works well'. Their goals will be more varied than this, and the courts are often left to adjudicate on the meaning and reasonable interpretation of such policies, their interaction with 'hard' legal rules, and individual action, without such policies having been drafted with the perspective of litigation in mind. This makes such policies a constraining rather than a liberating voice, and it is certainly not the voice which one would choose to construct a 'pure' series of environmentally perfected rules. But of course, it is also not a voice which should be ignored in an environmental context notwithstanding the fact that the consequence of this voice is likely to be diminution of protection in relation to some issues; an over-focus on other issues; and a desire to ensure low cost and simplicity perhaps above effectiveness over the long term.

Second, 'politics' is a reference to the fact that law, and environmental law within that, is really about power. This is a point which has been made forcefully by Fisher (and which we explore in more detail in chapter five), who has emphasised that rather than thinking about environmental law as a toolbox which contains better or worse rules, being more or less well designed, we should recognise that law is really about conferring power onto or away from certain groups and individuals, and that as a result environmental law just as much as all other forms of law has a power creation and allocation function.[47] Politics in this sense

[47] See eg E Fisher, 'Unpacking the Toolbox: Or Why the Public/Private Divide Is Important in EC Environmental Law' in Mark Freedland and Jean-Bernard Auby (eds), *The Public Law/Private Law Divide: Une entente assez cordiale?* (Oxford, Hart Publishing, 2006) 215–46.

means power.[48] As noted above and elsewhere, the judicial role here is often about deciding the locus of such power.[49] In addition, it is important to realise that much of the legitimacy of judicial action is derived from this power-conferring ability. As Rubin explains:

> More generally, both the common law and the Constitution contain embedded value choices that authorize judicial action. These sources of law establish the proper role of courts as encompassing a blend of positive and normative functions, thus rescuing judicial action from the moral aridity of positivism.[50]

Public perception too is part of politics and plays an important role here, not just in terms of perception of the environment, but also as part of the assessment as to the merits of judicial decision-making and of the adjudicative role. Indeed, in this respect the neutrality and background of the adjudicators we have identified can be a positive hindrance to the public acceptance of decisions made in an environmental context. Some jurisdictions have tackled this by utilising scientific or technical experts to add an element of scientific credibility to the findings of a court, to noted success.[51] Utilising such external assistance does not fundamentally change the adjudicative process. The expertise of the decision-maker does not affect the degree to which a process can or should properly be called adjudication. However, such expertise renders the process of utilising rational and reasoned argument, based on proof and evidence, more straightforward in practice. This is particularly true when we move away from deciding between the instant parties, to the process of creating generalisable rules. The importance of public perception, and of understanding and working within the parameters of environmental policy, whilst respecting the need for rationality, makes the inclusion of such expertise more desirable. It may assist the achievement of 'good' adjudication, but does not in itself alter the very process under scrutiny.

However, the risks associated with the need to understand and respect the political nature of adjudicatory decision-making, even if based on rationality and reason, is the risk that the courtroom shifts from being an adjudicative forum, to one where the values of such adjudication are abandoned in favour of 'political' decision-making in a less positive sense.[52] One aspect of this can be seen in the debate surrounding litigation around climate change. Fisher et al have explored

[48] Following Freeden, it is possible to define the political as, 'the drive to finalize collective affairs through decisions'. These decisions not only produce outcomes, but also dictate who makes specific decisions and how. In this sense, institutional power allocation, whoever the decision-maker, is an inherently political process. M Freeden *The Political Theory of Political Thinking: The Anatomy of a Practice* (Oxford, Oxford University Press, 2013) 22.

[49] Lees, 'Allocation of Decision-Making Power under the Habitats Directive'.

[50] Rubin, 'The New Legal Process' 1397.

[51] Bjällås, 'Experiences of Sweden's Environment Court' 183. Preston too notes the importance of reputation and of credibility, a credibility built in part through where the court sits within the wider judicial hierarchy, Preston, 'Judicial Specialisation through Environment Courts' 613, 614.

[52] This shift in role is examined in A Chayes, 'The Role of the Judge in Public Law Litigation' (1976) 89 *Harvard Law Review* 1281, particularly 1288–1304.

this, emphasising that much relevant literature has 'treated courtrooms as another forum for politics'[53] so that courts are encouraged within the literature to create new rules, to fill gaps left by democratic institutions, to meet the pressing need for effective regulation of emissions so as to tackle the problem of climate change. Whilst judicial intervention in this way may be entirely *legitimate*,[54] at a certain point where the decision is no longer based on rationality and reason, but perhaps on gut instinct or personal preference, then the decision will no longer be *adjudicative* in its true sense. The question as to whether judges should make law outwith an adjudicative mode of reasoning is a different question from whether such law-making should be defined as adjudication.

The difficulty with allowing decisions based on this range of personal preferences, however, is that the multiplicity of values at play in environmental issues, as well as each individual judge's own assessment as to where the merits of a decision may lie, can in themselves lead to incoherence. One of us has previously emphasised the relationship between a value-rich field, and incoherence in decisions with that field,[55] highlighting that 'questions of balance between costs and benefits, perceptions of risk, and questions of trade-offs between such considerations are inherently heterogeneous'.[56] This makes them impermeable in some cases to the kind of reason which generally characterises adjudication. However, in a value-rich field, such values are not to be dismissed as an inconvenience for effective regulation. Rather, they form an important dynamic in the development of the discipline.[57] It is important, therefore, in analysing judicial adjudication in an environmental law context that we do not attempt to 'design out' political conflict. Rather, we must recognise its inevitability and discern what arises from this political nature.

Finally, in respect of the 'political' nature of environmental regulation, there is a tendency within the judicial review branch of environmental law, as we demonstrate in chapter four, for merits-driven claims to be 'dressed up' as legality reviews. Questions about the merits of a development from an environmental perspective become dressed up as a legality review of an administrative authority's handling of expert evidence; of the reasons given in their decision; or of the technicalities of the process followed. Questions about environmental protection become filtered and distorted through the lens of the legality review, and this in turn can hide the degree to which questions are political. Fisher et al note this, arguing that in respect of climate change litigation:

> An obvious disruptive question from a legal perspective is whether disputes over climate change are socio-political disputes (and thus to be resolved in political forums)

[53] Fisher et al, 'The Legally Disruptive Nature of Climate Change' 174.
[54] See MC Dorf, 'Legal Indeterminacy and Institutional Design' (2003) 78 *New York University Law Review* 875, fn 251.
[55] OW Pedersen, 'Modest Pragmatic Lessons for a Diverse and Incoherent Environmental Law' (2013) 33 *OJLS* 103.
[56] ibid 110.
[57] ibid.

> more than legal disputes. If they are, then responsibility for climate change is non-justiciable, and disputes over it are not for resolution in judicial forums.[58]

For a court, the question becomes equally one of whether they are genuinely answering a legality question, or whether the forum is being 'manipulated' (perhaps without necessarily being accompanied by the negative connotations conjured by the use of such a word) for the purposes of merits review. In such cases, the need to rely on reasoned arguments in respect of the legal standards becomes somewhat mechanical and technical, when the reality of the dispute is somewhat different from its ostensible form.

B. Science and Proof

The opposite of reliance on such subjective value-based judgements would of course be reliance upon scientific, evidence-based, proof. However, such is simply not available to those considering many environmental law problems. Of course, there will be cases where the scientific information is easy and uncontroversial, but more common will be situations where although the science can predict possible outcomes, and risks, it cannot provide a definitive answer, neither predictive (what will happen if a certain action is allowed), nor retrospective in terms of causation of particular harms. The problem that this causes for the process of adjudication is twofold. First, as Fisher et al explain, '[t]he need to make legal decisions in circumstances of scientific uncertainty creates fundamental challenges for law and adjudicative processes, particularly because of the value placed on legal stability in applying legal rules and in resolving disputes'.[59] This focus on the mismatch created when the unpredictable and uncertain forces of nature are captured in seemingly stable rules is considered also by De Sadeleer.[60] He highlights that the goals of the disciplines of science and law are different, and that this means that the priorities of each are somewhat at odds with one another. Second, scientific uncertainty can be so acute that it prevents the judiciary from relying on that information in a rational manner. This second problem is perhaps less prevalent than the first, for there can be a rational and reasoned argument made to follow a particular assessment of scientific information, even where that information is not itself definitive. Furthermore, since there is a difference between uncertainty in the science itself, and uncertainty as to the way 'facts will play out' in real life, it is possible for courts to develop a range of rational responses to different forms of uncertainty, one such being the precautionary principle.

However, McEldowney and McEldowney have suggested that the only possible solution to this tension in the longer term is for the two disciplines to work

[58] Fisher et al, 'The Legally Disruptive Nature of Climate Change' 180.
[59] ibid 179.
[60] N De Sadeleer, *Environmental Principles – From Political Slogans to Legal Rules* (Oxford, Oxford University Press, 2002).

more closely together, so that each is better equipped to understand the other's methodological choices, analytical approach and aims.[61] However, even genuine multidisciplinarity cannot change the fact that rule-of-law values and the rules relating to evidence and responsibility demand a degree of certainty. The legal system hinges on standards of burden of proof and of the reliability, or otherwise, of evidence. The fact that in relation to environmental law we know, or at least suspect, that science cannot provide the answers in this form, cannot be changed by asking the scientist to better understand how law handles risk. Similarly, the fact that the real-world processes involved in environmental degradation are uncertain cannot be made more palatable by the fact of our knowing about that uncertainty, for it will still engender uncertain and unpredictable law, and that will always be anathema to legal values.

It is important, however, when we consider this relationship to recognise that just as the adjudicative process will alter depending on the nature of the questions at hand and the evidence before the court, so too there are different ways in which a court may handle scientific evidence and uncertainty. To conclude that scientific uncertainty is a universal problem in environmental law, and that the adjudicative process inevitably struggles with it, is to underestimate the range of scientific 'evidences' which may emerge, and the approach that a court may take to such. As Ky has explained, there are (at least) four ways in which a court may handle science as part of its adjudicative process, and the effect of uncertainty in the science in the processing of reasoning and proof-based decision-making undertaken by the court will depend on the content of the scientific evidence, and which of these methods are utilised for evaluating that evidence from a legal standpoint.[62] These four ways are: first, qualifications approach, where the focus is on 'the qualification or specialised skill of the scientist who produces or expresses the scientific information or opinion in question';[63] second, the weight of opinion approach, which 'involves a kind of popularity contest in which the majority scientific opinion is used as a formal signifier of scientific reliability';[64] third, the methodology approach which 'focuses on the methodological processes or "scientific method" underpinning the generation of scientific information';[65] and, fourth, the peer-review approach which involves an assessment as to whether the paper concerned has appeared in a peer-reviewed journal. In cases where the scientific evidence is uncertain, but the court utilises a methodology relying on the qualities of the person presenting that information, the effect of the uncertainty on the process

[61] J McEldowney and S McEldowney, 'Science and Environmental law: Collaboration Across the Double Helix' (2011) 13 *Environmental Law Review* 169.
[62] P Ky, 'Qualifications, Weight of Opinion, Peer Review and Methodology: A Framework for Understanding the Evaluation of Science in Merits Review' (2012) 24 *Journal of Environmental Law* 207.
[63] ibid 221.
[64] ibid 223.
[65] ibid 230.

of reasoning is much less than in cases where the court attempts to assess the evidence itself. We consider the place of scientific information in adjudication in chapter six.

Furthermore, as Fisher et al, and Davies[66] more generally argue, when a court reviews scientific evidence it need not be engaging in a scientific process at all. Where a court engages in judicial review, it does so from the perspective not of original decision-maker, but as overseer. The consequence of this is that 'the review of agency science is deeply rooted in law and not in science'.[67] The risk may be that this results in 'analytical opportunism'[68] but it may also be that it provides some insight into how an adjudicative process can handle such uncertainty. Fisher et al argue that oversight on the basis of law does not provide a good mechanism for keeping scientific decision-makers held to account, and such is no doubt right, but that conclusion does not necessarily mean that it would always be the role of the judge to perform such a role when adjudicating on disputes. It is only by understanding the shapes, limitations and processes of adjudication that we can examine when and how different modes of scientific uncertainty can and should be accounted for.[69]

C. Shifting Regulatory Standards, a Lack of Resources and Inexperience

Experience is critical in ensuring success in what is being sought in the adjudication process. When commenting on the success of Sweden's specialist environmental courts, Bjällås emphasises how significant it can be

> to balance different interests against each other: for instance, weighing the harm to individuals against the economic benefits of the enterprise of causing the harm and trying to find the balance point. This is a very important – and difficult – task for a judge in an environmental dispute. The court's decisions often have impacts far beyond those of the parties directly involved.[70]

In English and Welsh environmental law, it is arguable that a lack of experience has resulted in an absence of expertise in the judiciary in performing such a task. The advent of the Planning Division of the High Court may ameliorate this somewhat, in that a large number of environmental disputes, at least in respect of land use, emerge in relation to planning law, and of course the criminal courts are clearly

[66] ACL Davies, *Accountability: A Public Law Analysis of Government by Contract* (Oxford, Oxford University Press, 2001) 73.

[67] E Fisher et al, 'Rethinking Judicial Review of Expert Agencies' (2015) 93 *Texas Law Review* 1681, 1686.

[68] ibid and see E Fisher, *Risk Regulation and Constitutionalism* (Oxford, Hart Publishing, 2007).

[69] See Fisher, 'Rethinking Judicial Review of Expert Agencies' 1687.

[70] Bjällås, 'Experiences of Sweden's Environment Court' 183.

increasingly aware of environmental crime and the problems associated with that (see chapters four and seven). With time, and stable law, however, experience and expertise will inevitably build. Specialisation may speed up the process of developing expertise, but it is not necessary (and significantly, expertise is not the only relevant adjudicator quality). The issue is that the environmental law corpus is constantly in a state of flux, a state of affairs that is very unlikely to be improved by the uncertain and highly complex Brexit process; the apparent instability of government policy resulting from this; and changes of personnel within the relevant departments. Add to this the fact that the law will change rapidly in this area not only due to political dynamics, but also due to the changing face of the environment on the ground, and the shape which environmental problems take on. The consequence of this is that however much experience is built up in respect of certain 'kinds' of environmental law problems – fly-tipping, and major polluting events, for example – other more peripheral actions will remain on the fringes of judicial action, so that each new case represents a situation of novelty for the presiding judge. Climate change perhaps represents the clearest example of this, but species protection and developing understandings of the long-term effects of agricultural practices too will pose novel and difficult decisions for an inexperienced court, specialist or otherwise.

D. Winners and Losers in the Adversarial Process

Finally, we must recognise the polycentric nature of environmental disputes, with many 'interested parties' (including the environment itself) not represented in an adversarial dispute which is conducted, according to Fuller's understanding of adjudication, on a more or less 'winner and loser' basis. Environmental law demands a shift in focus away from the individual parties. Woolf highlighted this shift in focus when considering whether the judiciary was environmentally 'myopic', emphasising that whilst early incarnations of environmental rules in the form of the traditional nuisance action do indeed involve the protection of private rights, environmental protection 'properly understood' is different. 'The primary focus of environmental law is not on the protection of private rights but on the protection of the environment for the public in general.'[71] It must be recognised that adjudication as a social function, whether judicial or otherwise, implies a *choice* – either outcome (a) or outcome (b) is right (and any number of other options), but the existence of the choice in an adjudication process means that there will be winners and losers, to a greater or lesser extent. However, what this means is that in the process of adjudication there will be a focus on the outcome and decision as between the parties to the case, rather than a focus on the outcome

[71] H Woolf, 'Are the Judiciary Environmentally Myopic?' (1992) 4 *Journal of Environmental Law* 1, 4.

for those not party to the case. As we shall see below, the tendency of this winner/loser approach to lead to an adversarial adjudicatory process – even where the process is not supposed to work like that – means that any interest not represented as a party in an adjudication is likely to play second fiddle to those interests expressed.

Taking this argument further, we can say that on this understanding of what the very nature of adjudication is, it is not well equipped to handle polycentric questions. Fletcher, defining polycentricity, and supporting Fuller's argument that polycentric problems are not well suited to judicial adjudication, reasons that:

> Polycentricity is the property of a complex problem with a number of subsidiary problem 'centers,' each of which is related to the others, such that the solution to each depends on the solution to all the others. A classic metaphor for a polycentric problem is a spider web, in which the tension of the various strands is determined by the relationship among all the parts of the web, so that if one pulls on a single strand, the tension of the entire web is redistributed in a new and complex pattern … polycentric problems permeate our society, and … for the most part, they are ill-suited to resolution by governmental decision-making authorities.[72]

We could add to this conclusion that polycentric problems are problematic for the process or mode of reasoning in which adjudication consists precisely because they are polycentric. Fisher et al emphasise the legally disruptive nature of climate change litigation – and the same comments could be applied to a variety of other environmental problems precisely because of the polycentricity of such disputes.[73] They explain why polycentric disputes can be so problematic for established modes of adjudication, as 'the issues presented fit awkwardly into existing and well-honed grooves of legal reasoning'.[74] If, as we suggest here, adjudication is indeed a mode of reasoning, then any dispute which does not easily fall within that approach to reasoning will by its nature challenge the adjudicatory model. Climate change is but one example of where environmental litigation has the effect of creating such a challenge, in part because these 'well-grooved' modes of reasoning are not established to handle polycentric disputes.

In highlighting this problem, however, it is important to emphasise that there is a difference between an adjudicative process being able to competently capture a variety of interests, and the persons interested in the dispute being themselves represented in the judicial forum. To put this another way, there is a difference between adjudication as a process, and access to environmental justice as a goal, and an adjudication process can be entirely satisfactory *as adjudication* even if it does not allow for access to environmental justice to *individuals*. This is not to say at all that we ought not to seek both, but rather that the question as to what

[72] WA Fletcher, 'The Discretionary Constitution Institutional Remedies and Judicial Legitimacy' (1982) 91 *Yale Law Journal* 635, 645.

[73] Fisher et al, 'The Legally Disruptive Nature of Climate Change' 174.

[74] ibid.

constitutes adjudication does not necessarily need to shift in the face of polycentric disputes, merely that the approach that a court may take to its adjudicatory task may shift in the face of the multiplicity of interests in play.

Finally, we can note that when dealing with the 'winner–losers' issue, it can, in certain environmental disputes, thanks in part to the scientific issues identified above, be challenging to identify the relevant parties to the dispute.[75] The consequence of this is that whilst an adjudicator may allocate winners in the dispute before them, this may have a negligible effect on the environmental problem itself, since the wrong parties may have been identified. To give but one example, where a challenge is brought against a local authority policy in respect of land use development, the policy itself can be found to be perfectly acceptable in itself, but based on national policy wherein lies the problem. If the national policy is not challenged, then it may be possible for the real locus of the issue to be obfuscated. More complex may be situations where the causal nature of an environmental problem is obscure, or impossible to discern, so that a polluter may be the 'loser' but the real 'cause' of a pollution problem in a river, for example, may well be the introduction of an entirely harmless substance 'upstream' which interacts in a problematic way with the substance introduced by the polluter, but with the causal effect of this interaction being entirely unknown.

V. Conclusions

This chapter has explored the nature of adjudication, and the challenges environmental adjudication poses for the process that characterises it. The question for the rest of this book is: how have adjudicators reacted where it is the very nature of the question being asked to destroy or challenge those forms of participation and process that characterise adjudication, and thus risk to endanger the integrity of adjudication itself? How should we, as scholars, respond to this challenge? Do we alter our forms of adjudication, do we accept that the problem will manifest itself to a greater or lesser extent in different contexts and find a minimum standard of rationality in decision-making with which we will be satisfied, or do we accept that in the context of (in particular) scientific uncertainty, the very nature of adjudication both in practice, and more fundamentally, shifts, so that the goal of those conducting the exercise must adjust accordingly?

Indeed, we suggest that much of the existing literature concerned with what environmental courts might offer, though laudable in many ways, in fact overestimates what courts can and should be doing in this context by suggesting that environmentally specialist judges can act as catalysts for improved environmental

[75] ibid 178.

protection; for coherence within a hugely diverse range of subject areas; and for bringing simplicity and ease to what are enormously difficult policy and scientific questions. We suggest that it is the very nature of environmental adjudication that the courts *cannot* do this for us, and it is only by recognising this fact that we can actually begin to build a system of environmental adjudication which is successful and 'better' in light of both the goals which we ascribe to those *adjudicating*, and in the face of the challenges before those who seek so to do.

3

Multidimensional Environmental Adjudication

I. Introduction

The previous chapter defined environmental adjudication as a social institution characterised by the resolution of disputes on the basis of reasoned argumentation and proof, in cases involving potential, actual or alleged environmental harms, degradations or effects. Having established these definitional features, we turn now to our understanding of the operation of this institution. Our goal with this project has been to answer the seemingly simple question: how does environmental adjudication work? This chapter examines the processes that shape reasoned, 'legal' argumentation and the forces that underpin them from a theoretical perspective. We develop, through this, a multidimensional theory of environmental adjudication. Unsurprisingly, the dynamics of such adjudication, both in instant cases and in broad structural terms, are complex. However, by thinking about such forces through the dimensions we identify here, we are better able to plot and analyse key features of environmental law jurisprudence and other reported decisions, and to understand reasoning contained therein.

In articulating our theory of multidimensional environmental adjudication, this chapter sets the scene for the practical focus of the chapters which follow. In section II, we explain the merits of building such a theory as a starting point of our analysis. In section III, we explore the dimensions we have identified – elements, techniques and avenues – and consider how these produce the multidimensional social institution which we identify. Section IV demonstrates this theory at work in practice using the decision of the Supreme Court in *Dover v CPRE Kent*[1] as a case study. In section V, the issues of inevitability and non-linearity will be considered, emphasising the importance of adjudicator autonomy in decision-making. Section VI then highlights the importance of adjudicatory hierarchies within the overall conceptual framework, before section VII concludes. From this discussion, it will become apparent that the dimensions of environmental adjudication are symbiotic and mutually reinforcing, and contribute to the shifting dynamics of legal reasoning in this context.

[1] *Dover DC v Campaign to Protect Rural England (Kent)* [2017] UKSC 79, [2018] 1 WLR 108.

II. Theory-Building

If it is accepted that adjudication involves the resolution of disputes by reliance on reason and proof, and by the application of norms, both predetermined and generated within the adjudication process itself, the critical questions become what kinds of reasons and reasoning emerge, and how? But there is a risk in building theories about adjudicator reasoning. In focusing on the process of the generation of reasons and the techniques of reasoning, we may lose sight of outcomes. To put this another way, ought we not to be examining the environmental (or other) effects of the reasoning processes we identify, rather than looking at those processes themselves? This challenge for those concentrating, as we do, on explaining how outcomes are reached, rather than the merits of the outcomes themselves, is neatly captured by Levi, who explains that:

> For the judge or lawyer the relevant effects are upon the web of the law, the administration of law and respect for it. These are large items, and the priest who only keeps his temple in good repair is not to be condemned on that account. Yet with all these qualifications, and even with the difficulties which analogous illustrations suggest, the point though battered seems to me to persist. Is the analogy to be to the man of medicine who describes not what the virus does and how it is to be counteracted but rather emphasizes the difficulties and virtues of his diagnostic art? Is it to be to the scientist who cares less about his discovery and more about how he made it? Again it is to be recognized that perhaps the discovery is more the way and less the result.[2]

His conclusion, however, points the way. The significance of our multidimensional theory is that it may help – in a practical way, as explained in chapters four to seven – to appreciate how such outcomes are reached. If change is sought, it provides a route by which such change can be achieved. Furthermore, the previous chapter emphasised the central importance of reasoned argumentation to the very notion of adjudication. We ought, therefore, to consider the nature and source of such reasons. There must be a threshold at which point a 'reason' relied on by a decision-maker is not sufficient to meet the test of adjudication, or is generated according to an improper route. For example, an adjudicator deciding that person A should win a contractual interpretation dispute because person A has a nice jumper on is not adjudication worth the name as it does not rely on the right kinds of reason, although it is clearly *reasoned*. The reason must be related to the nature of the dispute. Furthermore, the reasoning must be impersonal, although as we shall see this does not necessarily remove the possibility of adjudicator autonomy.

Similarly, the consequence of the institutional nature of adjudication is that the reasons applied must also be authorised by the institutional set-up which gives the adjudicator their power. This makes the task of the adjudicator the application of relevant, impersonal and authorised 'reasons' to the resolution of the dispute.

[2] EH Levi, 'The Nature of Judicial Reasoning' (1965) 32 *University of Chicago Law Review* 395, 396.

This chapter explains our theory as to how such suitable reasons are generated specifically in the context of environmental adjudication, and therefore bridges between our explanation of what adjudication is, with our practical examination of decision-making in England and Wales.

It is important to emphasise, however, that we are not examining the internal cognitive processes of reaching a decision. Rather, our theory relates to the institutional and impersonal (although see below on adjudicator autonomy). The goal of this chapter is to build a theory of reasoning in environmental adjudication. The purpose of building this theory is to deepen our understanding of the dynamics which shape such reasoning. We are thus concerned with identification and analysis of those forces which contribute to the creation of power structures; to the process by which sufficient reasons for outcome are generated; and by the responses to these outcomes. In doing so, we explore the consequences of this is for the system as a whole. To understand the effects of the dimensions of environmental adjudication, however, it is necessary to explore what these dimensions are.

First, we show that environmental adjudication is indeed multidimensional. A central element of our argument in this book is that the 'avenues of adjudication', as we term them are, in a hitherto underexplored way, driving not only outcomes but adjudicator approaches to power, reasoning and remedies, in environmental law in England and Wales. These avenues are one of three dimensions we identify. The other two dimensions we term 'elements' and 'techniques'. We show that the practical and normative 'constraints' the avenues provide are central to the practice of environmental adjudication. To see where these avenues sit within the system as a whole, it is necessary to take a step back so as to appreciate their place and role within this multidimensional whole.

Second, we argue that the multidimensional nature of environmental adjudication is the more or less central factor in allowing the avenues of adjudication to operate as they do as shown in chapters four to seven. In those chapters, we demonstrate that the avenues of adjudication, as identified in judicial review, statutory appeals, private law and criminal law, operate as power-brokers, as framers of reasoning, and as determinants of remedy. Taken together, the avenues shape the purpose of adjudication. To understand how the dimensions equally contextualise and shape the applications of the avenues, it is important here to examine the different dynamics which emerge from the elements of a dispute and from the techniques of legal reasoning.

Finally, and to foreshadow our conclusions in chapter eight, it is part of our argument developed here that the best way to understand and to operate within the both apparent and real incoherence of environmental law is to see it as a bricolage[3] – a patchwork of blocks making up a single whole. Thus, to understand the whole, one needs to understand the construction of the blocks. The avenues

[3] We explain the origins of this term and its place within legal theory in ch 8.

are but one element of block design – albeit an understudied and absolutely critical one – but they are not all. This chapter explains the blocks as a whole.

III. The Multidimensional Practice of Environmental Law

We have developed our theory of multidimensionality by considering what adjudicators must consider when resolving environmental disputes. When faced with the need to reach a determination in respect of an environmental dispute, they must contend with three key elements in each case. First, the factual state of affairs is obviously central. The adjudication process must determine these facts and frame the case accordingly. Second, there will be a range of norms which may potentially apply to the dispute. These norms may be more or less precise; more or less general/specific; and more or less relevant/determinative. Third, and by definition in environmental adjudication, there must be actual environmental effects; the risk of such effects; or the allegation of such effects such that the 'value' or goal of environmental protection will be brought into play.[4] It is also almost certain that there will be other relevant values, but these will vary from situation to situation. Every dispute will involve facts, norms and values. So far, so simple. Adjudicators will generate reasons for their decision from these elements. This much is obvious: the adjudicatory resolution, whatever it is, if it is adjudication worth the name, will come from the combination of these key elements, as interpreted and reasoned with.

The key to understanding environmental adjudication is not in this simple picture, however, but rather lies in exploring the dynamics which form the balance of that combination. How will this combination be found – and what are the reasoning processes which will be followed? First, whatever style of reasoning adjudicators prefer (or are constitutionally mandated to use) – deductive, analogical etc – they will use two 'forms' of reasoning, or 'techniques', to reach their resolution. They will 'explore' within the parameters of the dispute, and from time to time make 'fixings'. 'Fixings' in this sense, represent a temporary or permanent closing-off of routes of discussion to simplify in respect of the resolution of a single issue or question. Given the fact that there is an ever-changing balance within the elements, the fixings allow the adjudicator to keep one part 'still', whilst they explore the others. We use the terms fixings and explorations here, rather than *ratio* and *obiter*, although there are certain elements of overlap, to emphasise the importance of processes of reasoning, rather than merely outcome. To give an example, when a court is required to assess liability for environmental damage, and the parties dispute the extent/existence of such damage, the court may 'fix' the

[4] See ch 2.III.

facts on a conclusion that there is damage, and apply liability rules on that basis but then re-engage with uncertainty when it comes to assessing remedy or sentence.

As a result, these techniques form a critical part of legal reasoning, as a mechanism to manage the interactions of the elements (facts, norms and values) identified above. But these techniques are not purely functional. The use of such techniques, and the ways and points at which they are used, creates dynamics of its own within the overall process. This means that to understand an adjudicatory outcome, and its systemic relation to other such decisions, it is necessary to understand the dimension of reasoning; the interplay between fixings and exploration; and how that affects the balance between the elements of the dispute, and vice versa.

This balancing act, and mutually reinforcing dynamic, cannot, however, in anything approaching an efficient or predictable system, be left to each individual decision-maker, without the help of guidance. Rather there should be a route by which these shifting parameters are made more manageable. A guide is required. Of course, in cases where rules are very precise, determinative, specific and relevant, help may not be needed. But otherwise adjudicators need to know how closely to look at facts; which facts are relevant; how they relate to other decision-makers; what their decision-making reach is; what kinds of reasons will suffice to justify outcomes; what remedies best capture the situation; etc. This guidance comes from the 'avenues' of adjudication as we have termed them.

The avenues direct frame, shape, etc, and, as such, they act as translators between the general principles which we might think of as values, and those very specific norms which are rules. But these avenues are not entirely functionary either. Rather, they too bring value-balancing, modes of reasoning and dynamics of their own which are native to the avenues (as we analyse in chapter four) rather than native to the dispute themselves. They are not a neutral translator, but rather bring their own views to bear on the question at hand. In these avenues we find the third dimension of environmental adjudication.

The consequence of using this 'structural translation', which is not normatively neutral, is that you can sometimes encounter a clash existing between the values and guiding principles of the avenues themselves, and those that appear more relevant on the precise factual dispute in an instant case. This can, on occasion, make the values embedded in the avenue feel inappropriate, or even produce apparent inconsistency, which too generates a dynamic of its own. Shortly, we will examine these dimensions in more detail, but first, let us use an (imperfect) analogy to explain this multidimensionality more fully.

A. Playing with Blocks

We have been assigned a task. Our task is to build a wall from 'generic brand' modular interconnecting blocks. We do not know the required size of the wall, or indeed the complexity of the space we are trying to fill. The end-point of the task is unknown at the outset.

The team is made up of a variety of more or less experienced members and is provided with a full and messy bag of blocks in a variety of styles (mega, large and normal); shapes (square, rectangle, corner, etc); sizes (1 × 1, 2 × 2, etc); and colours/patterns.

When establishing how to go about constructing our section of the wall, we may commence with an analysis of what is likely to be both the most efficient and effective means of construction. The difficulty in producing the most effective solution is that we do not know the end-point. In making our solution, speed and quantity in terms of wall size must also bend to the need to build flexibility into the wall design. This makes the task of designing a good 'work system' more complicated. Nevertheless, a number of decisions will need to be made: what blocks will be used; who will be building which parts; and what guidance are they being given when they start to build?

1. What blocks will be used?

The starting decision will likely be whether to use the large, medium or small blocks. Their incompatibility means that it is foolish to build a wall made of a mixture of these. In making this initial decision, a number of wall-defining characteristics will emerge. Having discarded all those now unusable blocks, we are left with a still very large bag of (for the sake of argument) normal-style blocks.

2. Who will be building which parts?

The next task is to decide who is to be responsible for building what units – for their professional preferences, decision-making competences, wall-building experience, etc, will make a difference to the final outcome. We might, for example, make the more experienced builders responsible either for building in flexibility (and therefore variation), or they could be in charge of overseeing what the other builders were doing, to try to weed out errors.

3. What guidance will they be given in starting to build?

In an effort to achieve maximum results, we must decide how to approach the work. We might conclude that a series of 'six-block units' is a good solution. A six-block unit is simple and fast to produce, but there is a wide degree of variety available (see Figure 3.1).

Figure 3.1 Six-block units

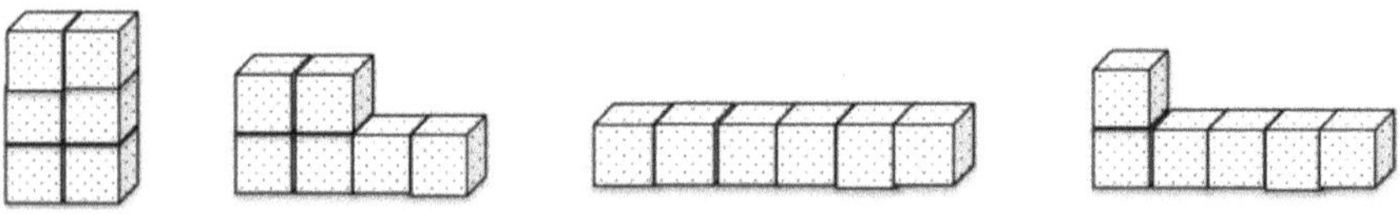

Each of these units can be rotated or modified, giving more variety, and each has different advantages and disadvantages as a style for creating a large yet flexible structure. Since colour is irrelevant to the functionality of the wall, any colour can be used as this will assist in terms of speed and might allow the builders some additional enjoyment in the task. Allowing also for the possibility of human error, the end result will be a range of units, in colour and construction, which can then be more or less slotted together to form the wall.

What are the consequences of these decisions? Whatever the approach taken to creating the wall, the final outcome is very unlikely to be 'perfection'. This is for three reasons. First, the flexibility that was built into the system so as to overcome the problem of not knowing the end-point means that not all the blocks will fit together perfectly. This will certainly look 'messy', and might affect functionality. Second, the range of colour choices means that whatever the functionality of the wall, it will not look harmonious and there will be points that look more 'uniform' and designed than others. Finally, due to the possibility of human error, even with supervision, there will be structural flaws.

i. How Does this Analogy Relate to Environmental Adjudication?

On our multidimensional theory, the blocks analogy allows us to see how the different elements, forms of reasoning and avenues in the adjudication process fit together to produce systems and outcomes of adjudication. Let us return to the decisions above:

1. The *task*, ie the motivation to embark upon the wall-building enterprise in the first place. In terms of adjudication, this reflects the desire of institutional decision-makers to regulate on the issue at hand, and also the challenge of so doing given the indeterminable end-point. In this institutional design, there is a high degree of uncertainty (a) because the institutional design/wall may have been developed/built a long time ago when the need to adjudicate on environmental questions was not apparent (eg in the case of judicial review), and (b) will not have been developed with the specific conflict or with environmental adjudication in general.
2. *Style of blocks*. The style of blocks – the fundamental choice as to which 'system' to utilize – is essentially representative of jurisdiction. It is a meta-decision, which brings into play constitutional norms and principles. This is intimately linked to the 'task' above. Jurisdiction will often be provided by design (eg statutory appeal), meaning litigants have very little choice. Although there might be some scope for challenging an action through multiple routes, eg a *Coventry v Lawrence*[5] - type scenario where the aggrieved neighbour presumably could consider taking a claim against the local planning authority rather than a nuisance case against the operator, such choice will be very limited. The choice is rather a choice of institutional design.
3. *Size and shape of block*. The size and shape of the blocks represent the fundamental *elements* of the dispute. It is not possible to generate different

[5] *Coventry (t/a RDC Promotions) v Lawrence* [2014] UKSC 13, [2014] AC 822.

pre-existing norms (or the absence thereof), facts and relevant values through the process of judicial reasoning. Once certain blocks are used, the range of shapes that can be made is limited.

4. *Builder identity*. The identity of the builder, and their experience, is a function of power-allocating structures in adjudication. These, on our model, emerge from the avenues of adjudication as power-brokers.[6]
5. *Construction*. The pattern in which the blocks are constructed – 3 × 2, 6 × 1, etc – represents the outcome of the adjudicatory process in the form of a remedy, but the process and guidance by which a builder chooses how to construct their blocks represents the reasoning aspect of the avenues of adjudication.
6. *Colours*. Finally, the colours of the blocks represent both individual reasons which apply to the specific case (providing diversity in decision-making) and a degree of builder autonomy.

Each of these steps involves consideration as to the best way to proceed (exploration), and has a conclusion that has determining effects (fixing).

In this analogy, we see the dimensions of adjudication at work, and the interplay that exists between initial decisions and the consequences which such decisions have on the elements of the adjudicatory process, including the range of norms which are relevant to its resolution, and the values in play. More fundamentally, this analogy gives a clear indication as to what the consequence of a system made up of these dimensions might be – somewhat of a messy-looking wall. Whether this mess is more perception than reality, and whether the 'structural integrity' of the wall is thereby affected, is considered in chapter eight. In chapters four to seven we effectively consider the guidance for how to build a wall as it is channelled through the avenues of adjudication.

To recap: there are three dimensions of environmental adjudication identified here: elements, techniques and avenues. Let us consider these now in more detail, keeping in mind the blocks analogy discussed above.

B. Elements

It will be remembered that every environmental dispute susceptible to institutional adjudication will involve three key elements. These were facts, norms and values. We can expand on these categories somewhat. First, in relation to the facts, there are two aspects. On the one hand, there are the factual events that have occurred which have given rise to the dispute in the first place. Second, there is the fact that the parties are both sufficiently motivated and well resourced to litigate/access an adjudicator and one or both are insufficiently compromising to reach a settlement or other amicable conclusion. Similarly, in respect of norms, there will be two

[6] See ch 5.

forms (albeit on a spectrum) which may appear relevant, as explained earlier: clear and close-textured norms, and those less precise rules that, although relevant, may not be entirely determinative or clear on the facts of the case and thus require a higher degree of adjudicator interpretation before they will provide an 'answer'. Finally, in respect of values, again relevant will be at least the value of environmental protection and, since the situation will not exist in a vacuum, this will almost certainly be in conflict with, and supported by, other values rightly given weight in the system.

The adjudicator's task is first and foremost to examine the precise dispute before them, not to provide generalisable or structured rules. This has consequences for the coherence of the rules, as we explore in chapter eight, but it also, obviously, has a critical effect on the outcome of the adjudication process. We see in subsequent chapters that some of the areas where clarity might have been provided by a court cannot be so because the facts of the dispute are not amenable to such a discussion and in these cases guidance as to how to proceed in the face of such uncertainty emerges from the avenues (discussed below). Furthermore, the central importance of the facts to the nature of any generalisable norms which do emerge means that the adjudicator's task of weighing evidence, deciding factual parameters and weeding out the irrelevant plays a critical role in determining outcome.

In addition, there must actually be a dispute in the first place. This requires (at least) three factors to be present: one or both parties must be sufficiently motivated to resolve their dispute in an institutional forum; they must be entitled to bring their dispute before such a forum; and they must have the resources at their disposal to do so. Although in respect of motivation, it is obviously not necessary in such cases for the motivation to emerge from self-interest, the effect that motivation has on outcomes ought not to be overlooked, for this will colour the arguments presented in the case and the 'angle' of claimant attack.

Even with motivation, however, not all claimants, as is well documented, are entitled to bring a claim before an adjudicator, however heated their dispute.[7] As a result, there must also be an entitlement to come before a decision-maker as part of the factual make-up of the case. In cases involving judicial adjudication, this requirement is best understood as a requirement of standing before the court. In other forms of adjudication, as we shall see in subsequent chapters, the authorisation to bring a dispute before a particular forum is most often accorded to the parties through statute. There will, in any situation, always be a limited (even if potentially broad) class of persons who are entitled to appear before an adjudicator to complain of or seek vindication in respect of any action. The parameters of such 'entitlement' rules have enormous implications for the nature of disputes which arise before an adjudicator, especially when twinned with the motivation point above. Finally, and in practice this is hugely significant,

[7] There is a significant amount of scholarship in the environmental law context which considers restrictions on access to justice and standing. See eg F Ahmed and A Perry, 'Standing and Civic Virtue' (2018) 134 *LQR* 239.

the parties must be sufficiently well resourced to engage in what can be an enormously expensive social practice.

When we move on to think about the relevant norms, it is tempting to think in a three-pillar structure. The first pillar is that of constitutional norms and principles which shape decision-making. Generally speaking such 'rules' will be relatively imprecise, acting more as a guide to the overall structures of decision-making instituted by legal institutions, than as a solution to an instant dispute. The power of such norms comes from allegiance to their spirit as much as it does to their specific content. Such allegiance is a driving force behind 'good' environmental adjudication, and on the assumption (more or less controversial) that the majority of adjudicators will be trying to exercise their task in the best way possible within the limit of their resources and capacities. The second pillar would then be the contextual, but still relatively general, rules that surround a dispute – the principles of tort law, or contract law, for example, or the principles of judicial review. These 'rules' are derived from the avenues of adjudication as we term them. The third pillar is the highly specific norm most relevant to the instant case – the definition of a waste offence, the contractual term breached or the procedures mandatory in seeking planning permission, and the like.

Indeed, this three-pillar approach – as long as it is accepted that the division between any relevant norms is one of degree rather than absolutes – is helpful (and we refer to it in subsequent chapters). However, thinking of the avenues as being *only* a means of providing more a contextualised set of *rules* is to underplay and underappreciate the range of their effects, as we discuss below. Without 'confining' the effects of the avenues to the assessment of the applicable norms made by an adjudicator, therefore, it is nevertheless important to emphasise their role in decision-making.

In the previous chapter, we explained why we eschewed a definition of adjudication which looks to the formal content of a decision.[8] Such theories posit that adjudication is the process by which a predetermined standard is applied to a set of facts/dispute.[9] According to such a model there is no room for law-making in adjudication *strictu sensu*, although many of those who hold such a view as to the nature of adjudication would not deny that there is often judicial or other adjudicatory 'law-making'. They would simply state that these elements of the process are not adjudication. We do not attempt to draw a division of this type between adjudication and non-adjudication in the decision-making process.

However, these theories do hold an important lesson. In some cases there will be clear predetermined rules which are more or less close-textured. At other times, there will be clear and predetermined rules which are very open textured. An example of this latter would be a requirement that a decision be, 'reasonable'.

[8] See ch 2.II.

[9] See eg B Cardozo, *The Nature of the Judicial Process* (New Haven, CT, Yale University Press, 1921) and the discussion in JM Zane, 'German Legal Philosophy' (1918) 16 *Michigan Law Review* 287 and HLA Hart, 'Positivism and the Separation of Law and Morals' (1958) 71 *Harvard Law Review* 593.

The standard to be applied is clear: its meaning is not so determinate. At the other end of the spectrum will be cases where there is no predetermined standard to be applied at all. This is not a case of an open-textured rule, but rather an absence of rules. In such cases, a court (and other forms of adjudicator) will be required to generate a rule, or reason from analogy, in order to resolve the dispute before them. The process cannot leave a dispute unresolved. Thus, we argue that the generation of such rules is part and parcel of the adjudication process, but we also recognise that both when generating such rules, and when interpreting and applying those relatively more open-textured standards, an adjudicator will engage in a different form of reasoning than when applying a clear and predictable predetermined norm.

Finally, in each adjudication process, the values 'in play' in any dispute will influence the approach taken by the adjudicator. Largely this will manifest itself in the interpretation of terms, especially those such as 'reasonable, 'significant' and 'harmful' where determining their very mean is necessarily an exercise in normativity and in assessments of gravity, fault and seriousness.

Whilst our experience of courts in England and Wales tells us that (at least judicial) adjudicators are often unwilling openly to discuss how values shape their interpretation, that does not mean that they are not doing so. The desire for an appearance of neutrality and impartiality as between competing values can obscure the roles that such values are playing. However, calls to rely on the environmental principles, a purposive approach, and even a literal or textual approach all contain consequences for the prioritisation of values within each decision. Plus, as we have explained, the interplay of the other two dimensions will direct when and how such values can be directly called upon as relevant.

The identification of these elements of adjudication is not new. Indeed, the idea that adjudication involves working with these three elements (at least on the definition we have utilised) is not especially illuminating. However, the point of articulating the contents of the 'elements' dimension has been, first, to sit as part of our analysis of the conceptual role played by the avenues, and secondly, to emphasise the mutually shaping relationship that exists between the dimensions. A change in balance or approach in one of the dimensions will have significant consequences on the other.

C. Techniques

Let us now examine the second of these dimensions. This is the dimension of 'technique'. What we describe here is one aspect of the phenomenon of legal reasoning. As such, it might be asked why we consider 'fixings' and 'exploration' as techniques rather than considering (as is more common in the literature on reasoning in environmental law)[10] the *styles* of such reasoning: deductive, analogical, purposive,

[10] E Lees, *Interpreting Environmental Offences* (Oxford, Hart Publishing, 2015).

textual, literalist, etc. Our justification is that the fixing/exploration approach is a necessary part of adjudication, whereas the style of reasoning adopted will vary according to context (both legal and factual). Whilst the styles of reasoning are obviously important, we see the *choice* of such styles as being a matter of combination of application norms and prevailing values. By contrast the techniques to which we refer here are a necessary element of reasoned adjudication. Critically, which stage is underway – fixing or exploration – affects the kinds of reasons and style of reasoning which will be employed. The techniques we identify are in this way logically prior to the secondary and consequential issue of style.

These different techniques, which we label 'fixings' and 'exploration', involve the invocation of different kinds of reasons. When an adjudicator 'fixes' an issue, she will make a decision which involves the narrowing of avenues of debate. The ultimate 'fixing' is the eventual determination of the dispute, assigning the status of winner and loser to the parties. However, as we shall see, fixings occur throughout decision-making steps making up the wider process of adjudication. Exploration, by contrast, is a more free-ranging form of reasoning whereby the range of considerations that can be brought to bear upon a question, within the parameters set by a fixing, are explored, weighted, interpreted and in some cases discarded. This kind of reasoning obviously occurs when an adjudicator first 'turns their mind' to a dispute, but it also forms an important part of the ways in which they reach their final determination of the application of the set of norms they are required to interpret, expound on and apply to the facts of the case before them.

The kinds of argument to which attention is given when an adjudicator is exploring an issue may not be applicable when they seek to fix the parameters of a debate. This results in a multiphase process. How do these techniques influence how adjudicators reason about the different elements of the dispute? It might be thought at first glance that fixings might be most appropriate when considering relatively narrow and determinate norms, whereas a decision-maker would 'explore' when discussing values and wider norms. But a brief consideration of the necessarily relevant value of environmental protection shows the importance that such fixings might have even when reasoning about the role of values within a decision. Environmental protection as a goal may appear simple but clearly it is not. Not only can a single action both harm and protect the environment depending upon how one defines the environment (wind turbines constructed in a beautiful landscape, affecting local birdlife, but helping to combat carbon emissions are an easy example), but the indeterminacy built into defining the environment itself, and particularly the relevance of humans to that definition, means that even in seemingly simple cases, if considering environmental protection as a tool for interpretation (for example), an adjudicator will have to fix a meaning onto environmental protection in order for it to assist in interpretation. This does not mean that a 'rule' as to what environmental protection means is thereby generated. Rather, the meaning is temporarily crystallised in the process of reasoning. Depending upon what other issues require to be resolved, it may later be rendered indeterminate again, whereupon its lack of concrete status may itself operate as a guide for the adjudicator in making some other decision or fixing.[11]

These different kinds of reasoning are not easy to spot. Nor is an adjudicator necessarily only doing one of these at any one time. The two approaches will operate simultaneously, but just like approaches to interpretation will change how norms are understood, the fact of trying to keep one aspect of the overall balance being struck 'fixed' has an inevitable impact on the other elements and how they are understood. In environmental law this especially true, and as we shall see in chapter six in particular, thinking about this helps to explain the treatment 'the environment' as a reason for any particular decision in the case-law and other reported decisions.

D. Avenues

The dimensions of adjudication are: elements of the dispute; techniques of reasoning; and avenues as translators between the broad constitutional norms and the specific. Rarely would anyone make a decision entirely de novo from first constitutional principles; and rarely is there an existing case or rule so precisely set down and so perfectly applicable that no interpretation or reasoning is required. This is where the avenues come in. We consider these avenues in detail in chapters four to seven, so only a brief summary is needed here. We examine the avenues of judicial review, statutory appeals, private law and criminal law, as pre-existing 'areas' of law that are utilised by both ad hoc and designed environmental norms as the means by which disputes are resolved. There is no action brought before a court or other decision-maker which does not either engage the inherent common law jurisdiction of the court (eg in private law), or the powers so assigned to an adjudicator through statute. Which of these routes is relevant to a dispute has an enormous influence obviously on outcome, but also on the process of reasoning, on the identity and powers of the decision-maker, and on the consequences in real life following the resolution of such disputes.

But we must not forget that the avenues were not designed and engineered to perform this, or indeed any, role. They have, for the most part, arisen through coincidence, and historical and accidental development. In some cases a conscious design decision might have been made by government to assign a particular kind of dispute to a particular avenue. These will normally be divided according to the identity of the parties and/or the sort of norms relied upon. The allocation decision is made on the basis of resources, or commonly on superficial similarity with other

[11] This approach shares some similarities with the concept of 'bagging' articulated in OW Pedersen, 'Modest Pragmatic Lessons for a Diverse and Incoherent Environmental Law' (2013) 33 *OJLS* 103, 123. See also J Dewey, 'The Development of American Pragmatism' in LA Hickman and TM Alexander (eds), *The Essential Dewey: Volume 1* (Bloomington, Indiana University Press 1998) 4 and H Putnam, *Pragmatism: An Open Question* (Hoboken, NJ, Blackwell 1999) 70–73.

kinds of disputes. Once a dispute is allocated to an avenue of resolution, however, the similarities will inevitably translate from superficial to substantive, as the same balance of values will be applied in the application of the norms. Administrative ease too may be a factor in allocation decisions. Or, as in relation to judicial review, there may be a decision to treat one element of the dispute as more significant than another. In judicial review, it is the identity of one of the parties that predominates, rather than, say, the subject-matter of the dispute.

The premise of our argument about multidimensionality is that the presence of so many elements in the adjudication process means that although it is not possible to precisely identify effects, or to predict them, we can identify their influence. Most importantly, as we explain in chapter four, the avenues affect the adjudicator's view of their own role: '[T]he integrity of the process in which the judge is engaged depends not only on distinctions which he may make reasonably, but also on his own belief in the legitimacy and decisiveness of these distinctions.'[12] The third dimension of the avenues of adjudication therefore also shapes and controls the other two dimensions as well.

E. Case Study – *Dover v CPRE Kent*[13]

It is perhaps useful at this point to concretise some of the arguments we present here with an example derived from the case-law. A useful recent case which shows these different dimensions at play is that in *Dover v Council for the Protection of Rural England-Kent (CPRE Kent).*[14] In very brief terms, the case involved judicial review of a decision of the local planning authority to go against the recommendation of its professional advisors concerning the number of houses in a development. More specifically, the case turned on whether the council was obligated to provide reasons for this departure. As Lord Carnwath summarised:

> When a local planning authority against the advice of its own professional advisers grants permission for a controversial development, what legal duty, if any, does it have to state the reasons for its decision, and in how much detail? Is such a duty to be found in statutory sources, European or domestic, or in the common law? And what are the legal consequences of a breach of the duty?[15]

In this case, the rationale for the conclusion that there was a duty to provide reasons for the grant of the planning permission emerges from a purposive reading of the Environmental Impact Assessment rules.[16] However, in the reasoning

[12] Levi, 'The Nature of Judicial Reasoning' 397.
[13] *Dover DC v Campaign to Protect Rural England (Kent)* [2017] UKSC 79, [2018] 1 WLR 108.
[14] ibid.
[15] ibid [2].
[16] Directive 2011/92/EU of the European Parliament and of the Council of 13 December 2011 on the assessment of the effects of certain public and private projects on the environment. Town and Country Planning (Environmental Impact Assessment) Regulations 2011, SI 2011/1824, regulation 24.

about the common law duty to give reasons we see the subtlety and dynamism that comes from the interaction of the dimensions of adjudication.

First, we see the elements of the case beginning to form. The facts were such that the local authority had decided to grant permission for the construction of a larger number of houses than was recommended by the planning officer. The motivation for the claim from CPRE Kent lay in the fact that the development was within an Area of Outstanding Natural Beauty (AONB) and as an NGO particularly concerned with the preservation of rural landscapes in England, the CPRE sought judicial review and had sufficient resources to bring such an action.[17]

Looking at the norms surrounding the dispute, and analysing these from the point of view of the pillars discussed above, given the identity of the parties (private party versus administrative body), the constitutional principles of sovereignty of Parliament, of delegation of duties to the executive branch, and of the maintenance of rule of law all become relevant. More narrowly, since the case was brought as a judicial review action, the case inevitably engaged the relatively hands-off, supervisory role of this judicial process. At its most specific, the case engaged the common law rules surrounding duties to give reasons, and EU law in respect of Environmental Impact Assessments. This latter fact also, in the symbiotic way emphasised above, affected the operation of the judicial review avenue given that review on the basis of EU law introduced a wholly different approach to legal accountability for public authorities.

As a starting point, furthermore, this case is already useful in demonstrating the significance that the particular facts have for the kind of generalisable rule that is generated. At its heart, this dispute was not really about whether the EIA Directive, some other statute or common law meant that the council had to give reasons for its decision to depart from its advisor's view. Rather it was a complaint by a local pressure group regarding the scale of the development.[18] The claimant would have been perfectly happy if the council had provided no reasons whatsoever if they had rejected the development outright (although there would of course have been irate parties generated by such an outcome). But, the way the facts had panned out meant that this claim was the only route through which the pressure group and its lawyers felt that there was a valid avenue of challenge, providing, as it were, a chink in the authority's armour. This factual background therefore colours the reasons and approach to reasoning in the case.

The range in specificity and applicability of norms, and the interplay of values, is demonstrated in the reasoning of the court:

> Where there is a legal requirement to give reasons, what is needed is an adequate explanation of the ultimate decision. The content of that duty should not in principle turn on differences in the procedures by which it is arrived at. Local planning authorities are under an unqualified statutory duty to give reasons for refusing permission. There is no

[17] *Dover DC v Campaign to Protect Rural England (Kent)* [2017] UKSC 79, [2018] 1 WLR 108, [4].
[18] ibid [2]. We also consider this case in chs 6 and 7.

> reason in principle why the duty to give reasons for grant of permission should become any more onerous.[19]

The court here, in exploring the precise content of the norms in play, engages with the values of reason giving – in respect of knowledge for the wider public – but also with the issues of public authority resources. We can also see in the above quotation the operation of fixings and explorations at work. The court fixes the rules about reasons for refusal of planning permission (although one would imagine that at the margins there will be cases where the operation of this rule is not entirely clear-cut, not least in the analysis of what constitutes sufficient provision of reasons), and then explores the consequences of this fixing for the question of reasons for the grant of planning permission. Similarly, this process can be seen in the consideration of the common law duty to give reasons and when it is activated: 'Public authorities are under no general common law duty to give reasons for their decisions; but it is well-established that fairness may in some circumstances require it, even in a statutory context in which no express duty is imposed.'[20]

Finally, in looking at the conclusions in this case, the role that the avenue of judicial review plays, and the norms and values (such as deference on democratic issues, a hands-off review of scrutiny with focus on legality rather than merit, etc) that it, as a wider constitutional construct, imports into the legal analysis is apparent, even if subtle. Lord Carnwath reasoned that:

> The answer … must lie in the relationship of the common law and the statutory framework. The court should respect the exercise of Ministerial discretion, in designating certain categories of decision for a formal statement of reasons. But it may also take account of the fact that the present system of rules has developed piecemeal and without any apparent pretence of overall coherence. It is appropriate for the common law to fill the gaps, but to limit that intervention to circumstances where the legal policy reasons are particularly strong.[21]

In other words, whilst the avenue of judicial review in the absence of a statutory provision to the contrary suggested deference to ministerial discretion, the overall role of the court as supervisor of administrative legality meant that the court was obliged to be aware of the potential for common law intervention when the values embedded in such legality are threatened.

The web of reasons that is generated by the interaction of these considerations is emphasised by Bell:

> [O]ne consideration was also apparently bolstered by another: the common law principle of open justice. To invoke that principle was an interesting move on the Supreme Court's part. The principle of open justice originated in the specific context of *judicial* decision-making. The idea signified by the principle was that, as a general starting

[19] ibid [41].
[20] ibid [51].
[21] ibid [58].

point, courts ought to make publicly available the information on which they make their decisions unless there are good reasons not to.[22]

In this we see how the dimensions of adjudication – the key elements of facts, pre-established norms and applicable values; the judicial techniques of fixing and exploration; and of the avenue translating between constitutional principles and specific rules – operate together to form the reasons sufficient to justify the court's conclusions.

F. Conclusions

In this section we have emphasised the multidimensional nature of environmental adjudication. Reasons for decisions, and the power structures that generate decision-maker authority, do not emerge from a single direction. The development of such is not simple or entirely predictable. The more determinate a specific norm, and the more simple the facts of any dispute, the harder it becomes to spot the dynamics at play. However, once we get to the realm of decisions in, for example, the Supreme Court, like that in *Dover v CPRE Kent*,[23] it becomes apparent that the dynamism generated by the presence of these different dimensions or facets of legal reasoning produces subtle but powerful forces in the overall process of legal reasoning.

In attempting to give a sense of the operation of this overall picture, we have also demonstrated that the avenues of adjudication as translators from the general and constitutional, to the highly specific, are not, as might immediately be thought, simply part of the picture of norms which surround an instant case. Rather, they have a content of their own, bringing values, techniques of reasoning, power-structures and approaches to remedies of their own. We explore these in chapters five to seven. Perhaps more fundamentally, however, as chapter four demonstrates, they also mould the purpose of adjudication, which is not static across the legal system. In appreciating, therefore, that these avenues form one dimension of legal reasoning in environmental adjudication, and in understanding how this dimension plays against the other dimensions we have identified, we can better understand how this social institution works in practice.

IV. Linearity and Inevitability

The way in which the outcomes of adjudication are analysed above might be thought to give a sense of both linearity and inevitability. If the adjudicator

[22] J Bell, 'Reflections on Open Justice and the Status of the General Common Law Duty to Give Reasons' (2018) 77 *Cambridge Law Journal* 240, 242.

[23] *Dover DC v Campaign to Protect Rural England (Kent)* [2017] UKSC 79, [2018] 1 WLR 108.

progresses step by step through the motivation and ability to bring a case, the establishment of the facts of a dispute, the clear and close textured rules which apply, and then the more nebulous reasons that persuade but do not demand a particular outcome, then the outcome of one or the other parties being the victor in a case would seem to be an inevitable result of following these steps. This is not the case. Adjudicatory reasoning does not progress in this step-by-step fashion. There are many places where an adjudicator is authorised by the institutionalised standards which apply to the situation to weigh competing reasons, none of which is determinative, to reach their own autonomous decision. Indeed, that this is a central element of the task of the adjudicator is demonstrated by the fact that there is a need for an adjudicator at all (rather than say a computer-generated formula). As Halper highlights:

> Regardless of one's skepticism toward legal rules, it is plain that decision-making is not simply a matter of deduction, and that consequently what logically may be required is not ipso facto legally demanded. That a body of rules exists, even in the form of a written constitution, does not abolish judicial discretion, since the judge might not apply them, nor does it prevent the decisive influence of non-legal considerations.[24]

It may be said that there is an implication in both our modular blocks analogy and in its mapping onto the legal phenomena which form the subject-matter of our discourse that the process will/must be following in this linear pattern. However, this is true neither for the blocks – it is perfectly possible to decide you want a yellow cube 2 × 2 in a 3 × 2 formation and decide only at the end to build it from large-scale blocks – nor for the legal process. In both cases, the decisions can be taken in any order. Rather the decision-making processes are both much more complex and iterative than this simplified theory makes it appear. The precise boundary lines between these different phases and forms of decision-making are not clear-cut. Our argument is not that this simplified picture necessarily represents a reality of how decisions are made, but rather that by simplifying some of the forms we can better understand this social institution as it manifests in practice.

Perhaps even more important than this emphasis on non-linearity, however, is to bring to the fore the degree to which the legal decisions made under this model are not inevitable. Just as in relation to the blocks – where for ease of explanation the parameters of our decision-making scope were kept deliberately narrow – there is an enormous amount of variety in the final block forms, in real life where there is a vast variety of decision-making options – in deciding precise interpretations of terms; of the boundaries between the reasonable and the unreasonable; in remedies awarded; in costs; etc – even if the rules and guidance are clear, the outcome is far from inevitable. The seriousness with which environmental protection goals are pursued, and the understanding of what that

[24] T Halper, 'Logic in Judicial Reasoning' (1968) 44 *Indiana Law Journal* 33, 36.

goal actually is, means that all else being equal, even if thinking only about the value of environmental protection, decision-maker discretion is important to outcome. This is why the power-broker function of the avenues, as discussed in chapter five, is so important.

A related but separate argument relates to the fact that there is a danger, one underplayed by our use of the blocks analogy above, of thinking of legal reasoning purely in mechanism and engineering terms. Thus, as Halper reasons:

> The net effect of this approach [a focus on method of reasoning as engineering] is often that of a Pontius Pilate, who constantly lets execution proceed, while exculpating himself from moral or social considerations with a simplistic doctrine of legal reasoning.[25]

This relates to Levi's point above about not losing sight of the outcomes of reasoning, but it also goes deeper and emphasises that both as a matter of legal analysis, and as a matter of morality, we ignore adjudicator autonomy, and the consequences of this, at our peril.

But there are also merits in this autonomy, in the value of experience. Thus, again per Halper:

> [B]ehind abstract regulations there is ordinarily the domination (and distortion) of familiar examples; and, frequently, statutory obscurantism conceals what the draftsman otherwise would have revealed. No statutes are so plain and unambiguous that they do not require interpretation to relate them to a context of language or circumstances; much of the judge's work consists in coloring transparent abstract terms with the rich lacquer of experience.[26]

It is critical not to underestimate the importance and value of adjudicator autonomy, but also not to forget, that as with the block builders, that autonomy is shaped by guidance. As we show, much of that guidance comes from the avenues of adjudication as translators of the constitutional to the specific.

V. Level of Law-Making Power

The level of law-making power is also clearly significant to the process of environmental adjudication. This emerges for two main reasons. First, at different points in the 'adjudicator hierarchy' there is a prioritisation of different questions (ie findings of fact at lower levels; legal analysis at higher levels). This produces variation in how the dimensions of adjudication interact. By focusing on these dimensions we do not suggest that the dynamics operate in the same way in relation to the same dispute regardless of level within the hierarchy. It is partly for this reason that in chapter five we emphasise the power-broker function of the avenues of

[25] ibid 35. For a different perspective, see D Howarth, *Law as Engineering: Thinking about what Lawyers Do* (Cheltenham, Edward Elgar, 2014).

[26] Halper, 'Logic in Judicial Reasoning' 37.

adjudication, including power as between adjudicators. We also consider precedent value in chapter five as an aspect of power vis-à-vis other adjudicators, of which judicial hierarchy is obviously a significant, although not the only, part. However, levels of law-making power also imply different degrees and kinds of experience, may manifest in a different approach to the guidelines, may produce guidelines, etc, and so we recognise that at this higher level the purpose and the role of adjudication shift.

Second, it is significant because of the freedom accorded to decision-makers at higher levels which is sometimes not present at lower levels (although not always – see the description of the powers of the FTT in appeals against the IC, where the Tribunal has a much wider range of powers than the High Court does in a typical judicial review case). When we look at an individual case, we must also be aware that whilst there is a significant degree of autonomy for decision-makers, the directions in which this autonomy can be exercised will vary according to the power of precedent. In analysing the practice of environmental adjudication, we do not focus in all cases on the significance of the levels of such power specifically. Partly this is because our focus is so much more on explaining the significance of the avenues as forces in environmental adjudication, and partly it is because the fact of where in the hierarchy any decision is made is, in part, often a matter, effectively, of coincidence, rather than design. Does the complex legal question of which the Supreme Court is likely to take notice happen to arise in the case where the stakes are sufficiently high and the parties sufficiently well resourced to justify pursuing a case to that point? But this does not mean that we are unaware of its importance in practice.

VI. Conclusions

This chapter has demonstrated our conceptual framework for understanding the operation of environmental adjudication as we have defined it. An adjudicator's task is to generate reasons for their decision from the interplay of the elements of a dispute formed from its facts (encompassing motivation and resources to conduct a dispute before the relevant adjudicator); the general and more specific norms which surround the dispute; and the values which are embedded in those norms and which are engaged on the facts of the case before the adjudicator. In order to generate sufficient reasons from these elements, the adjudicator will engage in a range of explorations and approaches in which some elements are fixed in order that other issues can be resolved.

This is a necessary facet of adjudicator reasoning given that there are so many 'moving parts', especially in the hugely varied and often ad hoc nature of environmental rules. But it also has consequences of its own, and is not 'neutral' in terms of the effects that judicial fixing might have on how they reason about other elements of a case. Therefore any firm conclusions reached have inevitable knock-on effects later in the case. Where such firm conclusions are considered to be appropriate and helpful, they will introduce a dynamic of their own into the process of adjudication.

Finally, the avenues of adjudication which translate wider constitutional principles into specific forms of action and adjudication are not normatively neutral either. The long-standing nature of these avenues, as we demonstrate in the next chapter, means that in each the conception as to the purpose and driving role of adjudication is subtly but importantly different. As a result, as we show in chapters five to seven, the avenues play a critical role in determining power, reasoning and outcome in environmental law. This chapter has been designed to highlight where the avenues sit within our wider conceptual understanding of environmental law adjudication as a whole, and what this means for each individual case and the generation of reasoning within it.

This chapter has also sought to emphasise that these dynamics do not produce linear or inevitable outcomes. There is a huge amount of room for decision-maker autonomy in these processes, and the dynamics are not susceptible to reduction to a formulaic application of more of less specific rules. Indeed, the operation of these dynamics, although guided by the avenues in a range of ways, also influences the 'guidance manual' provided each and every time a decision-maker must find their way through a particular dispute to its legal resolution. And this of course means that there is the possibility of error, and as a result of this, the effects of hierarchy in legal decision-making become all the more important. Different levels of the hierarchy have a tendency to take somewhat varied approaches to their own task, to the appropriate forms of reasoning which they might use and to the scope of their gaze. The consequence is that neither autonomy, nor the place of the adjudicator within the wider legal system as a whole, can be forgotten when we analyse the dimensions of adjudication.

4

Avenues of Environmental Law Adjudication

I. Introduction

Having defined the characteristics and challenges of environmental adjudication, this chapter focuses on the avenues through which environmental issues end up before an adjudicator. These avenues comprise the third dimension of the practice of environmental law, as explained in the previous chapter. We will demonstrate that environmental adjudication takes place under the auspices of a wide range of forms, expressed through sets of institutionalised modes of reasoning, and that these different 'avenues' are constructed by law, as it is enacted by law-makers, and through incremental developments in the common law. Often the adjudication takes place before courts but a characteristic of environmental adjudication is that it also takes place within a range of fora which are not necessarily judicial. Recognising this lack of homogeneity is an essential first step in unravelling the knot of techniques, values and principles which entangles environmental law adjudication as well as jurisprudence. The purpose of this chapter is to demonstrate the existence of these avenues and to explore their defining characteristics.

Environmental adjudication, we argue here, encompasses the application of existing (but sometimes also new) modes and structures and institutions of adjudication to problems emerging in the area of environmental law. As a relatively recent regulatory phenomenon, environmental law and environmental adjudication have necessarily (but not always) been forced to work within well-established disciplines and structures of law (such as administrative law and tort law), and within mature cultures and practices of law and adjudication. In many environmental disputes before the courts, claimants are consequently required to frame claims and environmental arguments against a background of rules, norms and practices that are not necessarily native to the discipline of environmental law. The constraints imposed by the application of environmental law to other disciplines of law results in, as Warnock argues, environmental disputes that do not necessarily fit into neat structures in terms of understanding the law.[1] Environmental law

[1] C Warnock, 'Reconceptualising Specialist Environment Courts and Tribunals' (2017) 37 *Legal Studies* 391.

is a legal discipline and practice with its own characteristics and expertise, yet its application in the context of adjudication often takes place against a background that is neither self-contained nor unique to environmental law.

Environmental law is, therefore, at once an 'applied' discipline and a source of idiosyncratic legal norms in and of itself, and in this confluence of technique lies the avenues of adjudication which we consider here. Much of what follows in this chapter therefore rests on the argument that environmental law is essentially an applied discipline of law. By applied we mean a legal discipline which – though it is often seen as being self-contained and as having its own foundational core – is in essence operating within, and therefore shaped by, the confines of other areas and practices of law.

The chapter thus argues that the institutional design of the adjudicatory spaces significantly shapes not only the processes of adjudication (ie who can bring a claim and at what cost) but also the substantive content of the law. To put this another way, where and how environmental adjudication takes place shapes that adjudicatory process and the legal result. First, we consider this institutional set-up (section II). In section III we explore the substance of these avenues, considering statutory appeals, judicial review, criminal law and private law, using examples to demonstrate the lack of homogeneity which we identify. In dividing the chapter thus, we of course recognise that the institutional set-up will vary across the substantive areas, as we indeed explain in section IV. However, more fundamentally, we explain that the modes of reasoning – the nature of the appeal to reasoned argument that is the very essence of adjudication – are moulded by the substantive question being asked of the judge in question.

The avenues described here are generic representations and systematisations of the main ways in which the adjudicators encounter environmental claims. They are simplifications of the law as it operates in practice. The focus here is on statutory appeals, judicial review, criminal law and what we broadly speaking term private law claims. The desire to model the different types of adjudication, like much of the rest of this book, stems from the interest in better understanding the processes involved with, and the incoherence of, adjudication in the discipline of environmental law. Much of what follows in this chapter is therefore somewhat general, although more concrete examples exposing the avenues of adjudication are used.

II. Functions and Institutions

In order to explain these avenues, representing judicial engagement with environmental law, it is, however, necessary to appreciate the functional role of not just the adjudicator and the courts in each, but also the functional role played by claimants and the government (in judicial review), the 'appellant' and the public authority (in statutory appeal), the defendant and the government (in criminal law), and the claimant and defendant (in private law tort claims).

That is, each of the four avenues identified in this chapter is a reflection and representation of the interactions between the parties in the (typically) tripartite relationships of adjudication.[2] As noted in chapter two, environmental adjudication is a social process in which different actors interact with one another most commonly in an attempt to resolve disputes (though there are, of course, other relevant reasons for engaging in adjudication). Naturally, these interactions in turn represent the functional roles played by each of the relevant participants in the relationship.[3] Just as the interactions between a tennis umpire and the players on the court are a reflection of the perceived roles each of them perform within the game – in terms of fair play, commitment to and application of the rules of the game, and perceived impartiality – the various avenues of environmental adjudication necessarily embody preconceived perceptions of who is doing what and for what reason in the relationship of adjudication. Having said that, it must be borne in mind that the attempt to conceptualise generic avenues of adjudication are just that: general representations. These avenues are not meant to be prescriptive blueprints for adjudication in the sense that they put forward an ideal notion of adjudication. This means that the avenues identified here might not be universally applicable within every single instance of adjudication performed under the relevant heading of, say, judicial review or criminal law. It necessarily follows that the avenues identified here do not minimise the importance of context and contingency, which play such an important role in adjudication.

Moreover, institutional design both facilitates and constrains different modes of reasoning. In this respect, the first point to make is that formal environmental adjudication in England and Wales has historically been the purview of the courts, with the primary decision-makers thus being a legally trained judge or, more rarely, a panel of laymen jurors (as opposed, for example, to an administrative or scientific expert as appears in some other jurisdictions).[4] Although this is no longer exclusively the case, it nevertheless has important implications. The institutional set-up for environmental adjudication contains embedded value choices that may restrict and/or authorize judicial action in environmental claims.[5] Not only does the fact that the courts are afforded a central role in environmental dispute resolution in England and Wales impact on the ways in which conflicts around environmental law are resolved as a matter of process, but it also serves to confine the groups of people who might be able to bring a claim as well as the type of challenges that might be brought, as we discuss in detail below.

[2] Fisher et al, 'The Legally Disruptive Nature of climate Change' (2017) 80 *Modern Law Review* 173.

[3] M Shapiro, *Courts: A Comparative and Political Analysis* (Chicago, University of Chicago Press 1986).

[4] As is the case, for example, in New Zealand and in some Scandinavian countries. See eg C Warnock, 'Reconceptualising the Role of the New Zealand Environment Court' (2014) 26 *Journal of Environmental Law* 507 and U Bjällås, 'Experiences of Sweden's Environmental Courts' (2010) 3 *Journal of Court Innovation* 177.

[5] EL Rubin, 'The New Legal Process, the Synthesis of Discourse, and the Microanalysis of Institutions' (1996) 109 *Harvard Law Review* 1396, 1397.

In the discussion that follows, we briefly explore a number of the institutional features (and, critically, variations) which exist across different mechanisms for environmental claims – statutory appeals, judicial review, the criminal law and private law – to highlight our central argument, namely that these avenues vary more than simply in terms of the source of the relevant rules. The discussion that follows is not comprehensive, but rather an indication of the general framework of the institutional set-up.

III. Statutory Appeals

One of the primary avenues of adjudication in environmental law is statutory appeals. In line with our definition of environmental adjudication developed in chapter two, we define statutory appeals as being the avenue of appeal to independent institutions expressly provided for in statutory environmental law regimes. To be clear, we are not thinking of the right that a person sometimes has in a statutory regime to request that an administrative authority conducts an internal review or reconsider its decision. Such rights are evidently not undertaken by an independent body. Instead we are thinking of the avenues of appeal to independent third parties scattered throughout the extensive regime of statutory environmental law. By way of example, the request to reconsider the refusal by a public authority to disclose environmental information under regulation 11 of the Environmental Information Regulations 2004[6] is not environmental adjudication. Conversely, the right to appeal such refusals to the IC under Part IV of the Freedom of Information Act 2000, as well as the right in Part V of the Act to challenge decision notices by the IC before the FTT would constitute adjudication as defined in chapter two.

One of the main characteristics of statutory environmental appeals is the sheer number of avenues through which judicial engagement is facilitated and the wide range of adjudicators and courts through which the appeals are heard. Statutory appeals are heard by a wide range of courts, including magistrates' courts,[7] the High Court[8] and the FTT[9] among others. But statutory appeals are also heard by non-judicial bodies such as the IC[10] and the Planning Inspectorate.[11] This diversity makes for a highly variable and diverse avenue, from which it is challenging to distil generic features except that, and as a result of which, the statutory context

[6] Environmental Information Regulations 2004, SI 2004/3391, regulation 11.

[7] eg Environmental Protection Act 1990, s 79.

[8] Town and Country Planning Act 1990, s 288, for example.

[9] Regulatory Enforcement and Sanctions Act 2008, regulation 34; Nitrate Pollution Prevention Regulations 2015, SI 2015/668, regulation 6; and Environmental Protection Act 1990, s 46D.

[10] Under the Environmental Information Regulations 2004, SI 2004/3391 and the Freedom of Information Act 2000.

[11] Town and Country Planning Act 1990, s 78, as delegated by the Secretary of State.

becomes highly determinative. An added challenge is that the review undertaken by an adjudicator when hearing a statutory appeal often, but not always, varies from that undertaken by a court in, for example, judicial review. In many statutory appeals, the adjudicator hearing an appeal will undertake a de novo examination of the underlying decision, including the merits of the case.[12]

The combination of a wide range of adjudicators and the wider scope provided for in many instances of statutory appeal helps in identifying the first main characteristic of the statutory appeal avenue. The first main characteristic of the statutory appeal avenue of adjudication is that the process of adjudication remains acutely anchored in and confined to a tightly defined statutory context. Although this seems obvious, the fact that the adjudicator is called into action as a result of its oversight being directly mandated and defined by statute has implications for the role performed by the adjudicator and thereby also for the avenue of adjudication on a conceptual level. In statutory appeals, an underlying reason for providing a direct route of appeal to an adjudicator who hears the appeal through a specific and directly designated procedure is to provide for an independent hearing, in which an adjudicator is able to resolve an administrative dispute, which is typically between public authorities and individual claimants. The role performed by the adjudicator in statutory appeals consequently takes the form closely aligned with the traditional perception of adjudication as it plays out in traditional court-like forums: as an independent arbiter resolving disputes between two parties.

Increasingly in a statutory appeal, the avenue of adjudication utilises tribunals and administrative adjudicators rather than ordinary courts. There is a certain efficiency in disputes arising out of the often-technical apparatus of the administrative state being resolved quickly, cheaply, informally and by institutions with particular expertise. This move towards hearing statutory appeals in a particular forum suggests that the role performed by an adjudicator in statutory appeals is fundamentally different from the role performed by a court in, for example, judicial review. In statutory appeals, the adjudicator is, figuratively speaking, more closely connected to the administrative organ whose decision it is overseeing by virtue of being able to undertake a full de novo examination of the decision and by being able to reach its own decision.[13] In statutory appeals, the adjudicator may consequently form part of the administrative state engaged in discrete decision-making as envisaged and expressed through the statutory regime.[14] This is fundamentally different from the environmental judicial review avenue in which a court often performs the role of a guarantor of constitutional rights and administrative principles available to claimants in the 'Plan B' scenario where the claimant has no one else to turn to (discussed later).

[12] We consider these powers in detail in ch 5.III.C.
[13] See ch 5.III.
[14] Shapiro, *Courts* 20.

This does not mean that the adjudicator hearing a statutory appeal lacks independence in the traditional meaning of the word. The increased reliance, for example, on tribunals in the statutory appeal avenue of adjudication witnessed in the last 20 years in the UK has specifically taken place against an understanding of the tribunal system forming a formal and organisational part of the judiciary. But as discussed below in the context of the judicial review avenue of adjudication, independence in this context often includes considerations other than a purely formal assessment of whether a court or a judge is biased for or against a given course of action. This means, arguably, that the statutory appeal avenue, where the statutory framework expressly envisages a decision-making role for the adjudicator, brings the adjudicator closer to the role performed by court-like administrators in other jurisdictions (such as, for example, in Scandinavia) where administrative and statutory appeals are heard not by ordinary courts but by administrative appeal boards chaired by a judge. In statutory appeals, the role performed by the adjudicator is therefore closer to the role performed by the initial administrative decision-maker, and adjudication and administration are consequently closely aligned.

An additional feature, which gives significant shape to the statutory appeal avenue, are the characteristics of the claimants bringing an appeal. Unlike in the judicial review avenue of adjudication (see below), the scope of claimants who are able to take a claim to the adjudicator is typically narrow in statutory appeal. This narrowness manifests itself in two factors. First, 'standing' in statutory appeal is ordinarily only afforded to individuals or organisations who are directly affected by the underlying administrative decision.[15] This may include claimants whose application for a permit has been turned down in whole or in part, or an applicant whose request to access to information has been turned down, but it does not include interested third parties.

The upshot of this is that, unlike in judicial review where a subset of cases are brought as a result of public interest, most of the claims brought in statutory appeal are brought as a result of individual actors having a particularly strong interest in bringing the appeal, typically for commercial, personal or proprietary reasons. A common example would be the business challenging the failure to award an environmental permit in whole or in part.[16] Consequently, the interests at stake in statutory appeal cases are likely to be of a private rather than a public nature.

Linked to this high degree of private interests in the statutory appeal avenue is the regime for cost protection available to claimants when the avenue of appeal takes the claimant to a court, which is ultimately less accommodating than the corresponding regime in judicial review.[17] As discussed below, the regime in place in the judicial review avenue effectively makes it cheaper for claimants to bring a case in environmental judicial review compared to other areas of administrative

[15] See eg Town and Country Planning Act 1990, s 288(1)(a) and (b).
[16] See eg *R (Blewett) v Derbyshire CC* [2004] EWCA (Civ) 1508, [2005] Env LR 15.
[17] See Criminal Justice Act 2015 costs rules.

law. In the statutory appeal avenue, however, the generous regime for cost protection is only available in claims that relate to the two first pillars of the Aarhus Convention,[18] ie in claims relating to access to environmental information or public participation. Where a statutory appeal does not engage questions of compliance with the Aarhus Convention, the rules for cost protection are found in the 'Corner House' principles,[19] which have a much stronger emphasis on public interests objectively defined. The implication for the statutory appeal avenue of adjudication before a court is thus that there is a much narrower access to the court in statutory appeal. Imagined visually, the statutory appeal avenue emerges is a 'reverse funnel' with a narrow entryway, which gradually broadens out (see Figure 4.1).

The avenue in statutory appeal is thus one in which the adjudicator performs a function closely aligned with a traditional understanding of adjudication, focusing on dispute resolution between two parties through the structured application of existing rules. And arguably the interests at stake in statutory appeals are less about wider public interest claims than they are about vindicating private interests. But the avenue is also one in which the adjudicator, by virtue of being afforded direct decision-making authority by a statutory framework, emerges as an institution whose role is at times closer to that of an administrative decision-maker than that of a traditional judge. Ultimately the avenue of statutory environmental adjudication is best presented as a 'reverse funnel' with multiple entryways, signifying the variety in the types of adjudicators (including courts) hearing statutory appeals, albeit from a relatively narrow entry point as access to the adjudicator is reserved for those with direct and specific interests. From the entry point of the 'reverse funnel', the avenue of adjudication opens up, however, to reflect the fact that when hearing statutory appeals, the adjudicator often has a wide scope of review at its disposal, allowing it to undertake a de novo examination of the appeal before it. Similarly, when it comes to providing remedies, the adjudicator will have at its disposal a wide range of options insofar as the adjudicator can typically replace the administrative decision under appeal with its own legally binding decision or it can choose to remand the decision to the administrative decision-maker.[20]

The importance of context is, however, highlighted by the fact that on some occasions adjudicators do approach statutory appeals as if they were judicial review claims.[21] In such cases, the 'broad brush' features of the statutory appeals avenue, as we have explained them, blur against those of the judicial review avenue. At the

[18] UNECE Convention on Access to Information, Public Participation in Decision-Making and Access to Justice in Environmental Matters 1998.

[19] *R (Corner House Research Ltd) v Secretary of State for Trade and Industry* [2005] EWCA Civ 192, [2005] 1 WLR 2600. See, amongst others, T Mullen, 'Protective Expenses Orders and Public Interest Litigation' (2015) 19 *Edinburgh Law Review* 36 and C Ormondroyd, 'Access to Environmental Justice' [2011] *Journal of Planning and Environmental Law* 251.

[20] See ch 7 for discussion of the outcomes of adjudicator decisions.

[21] This is particularly notable in planning law.

boundaries, the distinctive features of the avenues become less clear-cut. Many of the statutory appeals heard under the Town and Country Planning Act 1990 (TCPA 1990) are treated akin to judicial review claims as a result of the nature of decision-making involved in such decisions. Under section 288 TCPA 1990 a claimant cannot utilise the statutory appeal avenue to scrutinise, for example, the reasonable interpretation of planning policy or the weight to be attached to material considerations or matters of planning judgement.

Even within this single statutory regime, however, there is variation. The right of appeal afforded an applicant for planning permission under section 78 to the Planning Inspectorate is a right to appeal questions of facts and law as well as the merits of the decision. Similarly, a magistrates' court hearing a statutory challenge to the refusal by a principal litter authority to issue a permit to distribute free materials under Part IV of the Environmental Protection Act 1990[22] will evidently have a different job on its hands than a magistrates' court hearing a statutory challenge to a local authority's issuing of a notice against a private water provider supplying dangerous water intended for human consumption.[23] Simply as a matter of establishing the legal elements of the two decisions and the validity of the challenges the considerations that the adjudicator must take into account are very different, emphasising here the mutual interplay between the elements of a case and the effects of the avenues on how such elements are handled.

Whilst the basic principle of securing independent oversight of administrative decision-making underpins the creation of a statutory right to appeal in both cases, the weighing of the considerations in the latter example (pressing public health concerns against the commercial interest in supplying water) may well give rise to a higher level of deference to the administrative decision-maker than in the former example where the considerations at play might centre around standard administrative law considerations such as fairness and equality when it comes to treating applicants for leaflet distribution permits equally.

Nevertheless, even in cases where a similar approach to, and standard of, review are applied, differences are still to be found between environmental adjudication conducted through the avenue of statutory appeals compared to that conducted through the avenue of judicial review. One such difference is that statutory appeals are more likely to take the form of an *ex post* challenge to a specific administrative decision against which an individual is aggrieved, providing the court with a concrete set of factual circumstances to adjudicate upon. Judicial review challenges, on the other hand, increasingly take the form of *ex ante* challenges to general statutory programmes and policies in which claimants (as noted later) seek to change and influence the direction of government and administrative decision-making in the area of environmental law and policy.

The key point here is that environmental regulation as a corpus of law is riddled with examples like this which give rise to a highly contextualised process

[22] Environmental Protection Act 1990, s 94B and schedule 3A.
[23] Private Water Supplies Regulations (England) SI 2009/3101, part IV.

of adjudication. In respect of statutory appeals, we are dealing not so much with one avenue of adjudication as a long list of different sub-avenues, each requiring a court to consider uniquely different circumstances, questions and legal elements. Nevertheless, as we see in later chapters, these sub-avenues share sufficient fundamental features to sit together within our analysis. In this respect, underpinning the statutory appeal route to adjudication, we can fairly say that the principle rule of the game is fidelity to statutory limits and to the perceived intention as to the locus of decision-making power which a court will attribute to Parliament as sovereign legislature. This means that whilst there are guiding principles as to the interpretation of statutes, these are not the same principles that guide judicial decision-making when they engage their common law judicial review powers.

Figure 4.1 Statutory appeals

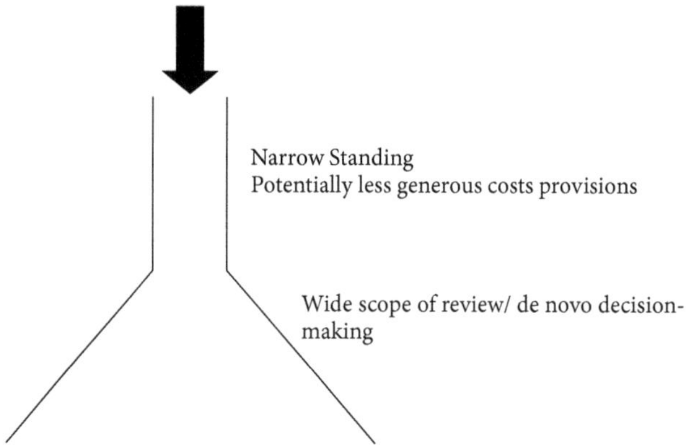

IV. Judicial Review

Another primary avenue of environmental adjudication is that of judicial review. Although judicial review is, to some extent, a statutory right of appeal provided for in section 31 of the Senior Courts Act 1981 (SCA 1981), we single it out as a separate avenue of adjudication precisely because the two avenues of adjudication have some important differences in terms of who can bring a claim, under what procedures and to what effect. Whilst statutory appeals and judicial review also share important similarities, we argue that the two avenues of adjudication also have more profound differences in respect of a number of important points. The most obvious difference is institutional. Judicial review is exclusively undertaken by judicial institutions, whereas statutory appeals are heard by a range of different adjudicators. This means that any claimant seeking to challenge government actions in judicial review will have to frame her claim in a way that 'fits' the rules and requirements of judicial review, developed against a background of a constitutional division of powers between the judicial and executive branches of government, as these are expressed in requirements of standing, grounds for review, scope of review and ultimately in terms of the remedy sought. This is basic stuff and not surprising. But it is also highly significant both formally and in substance.

In relying on the higher courts, judicial review mandates that the judiciary operates as an independent actor in the decision-making process with its own cultures, roles and responsibilities, and, as we will see, often with an emphasis on process over substance.[24] These roles are *not* defined by or unique to environmental law, but have instead emerged through a millennium of common law decision-making; through the historical enactments of hundreds of years of successive Parliaments; and through changing political, social and economic landscapes. The way judges act and reach their conclusions is as much a consequence of historical accident as it is of deliberate choice, and harnessing environmental decision-making to this judicial institution brings with it a lot of baggage. This need not be a negative – but it cannot be ignored. Where environmental judicial review claims come before the courts, such claims will necessarily have to play by the ground rules and practices of the adjudicatory system.

Fundamentally, judicial review is the vehicle used by certain types of claimants challenging actions or inactions of public authorities. Herein lies the first characteristic of the avenue insofar as judicial review challenges are only available where the decision-maker is a public authority. Although this is public law 101, it is worth reflecting on for the purposes of environmental adjudication as this seemingly obvious point highlights the wide access provided for in the judicial review avenue in environmental law. In environmental cases, the very definition of what constitutes a public authority is often broadened to include private for-profit companies delivering public environmental services of an environmental nature.[25] This means that the scope for taking judicial review claims against public authorities is potentially wider in environmental law than it is in other areas of administrative law, but that the constitutional paradigm nevertheless invoked is one of public administration and governance. Similarly, the Aarhus Convention[26] defines public authorities as any 'natural or legal persons having public responsibilities or functions, or providing public services, in relation to the environment'.[27] The potentially wider definition of what constitutes a public authority, and thereby whose actions and inactions are subject to scrutiny in judicial review, suggests that the avenue for environmental judicial review allows for scrutiny of a wide range of decisions. Critically, however, it does so by treating

[24] E Lees, 'Allocation of Decision-Making Power under the Habitats Directive' (2016) 28 *Journal of Environmental Law* 191.

[25] At least insofar as access to environmental information goes. See *Fish Legal v Information Commissioner* [2015] UKUT 52 (AAC).

[26] UNECE Convention on Access to Information, Public Participation in Decision-Making and Access to Justice in Environmental Matters 1998.

[27] ibid Art 2(2).

certain hybrid or private institutions *as though* they are public institutions for the purposes of approach to review. In this, we see the power of the prevailing culture of the avenue.

The wide access to environmental judicial review is broadened too when turning to the related issue of who can bring a claim against public authorities. Notwithstanding the 'Plan B' function of judicial review for litigants whose interests are not sufficiently accommodated in the mechanisms of statutory appeal (eg third parties and community groups), in reality the access to bring claims is wide.[28] Generally speaking, anyone with a 'sufficient interest' can bring a claim. In the abstract, the reference to 'sufficient interest' in the SCA 1981 does not tell us much about the ways in which the rules of judicial review interact with environmental claims. If, however, we consider the development and interpretation of the rules on standing and hold these against the characteristics of environmental adjudication identified in chapter two, we encounter one of the first important interactions between the rules of an already established avenue of adjudication and its implications in environmental law.

This is no surprise given the prominence afforded to judicial review in administrative law in general, emerging as it did in the latter half of the 20th century as the main mechanism for securing accountability of public decision-making.[29] With a gradual and substantive increase in the size and reach of the administrative state throughout the 20th century, independent oversight of the extensive 'new ephorate' of government becomes central as a matter of basic liberal constitutional commitment.[30] It is reflective of the importance of a generalised oversight even where statutory provisions do not explicitly provide for such. This need is arguably all the more pressing in the case of environmental law – the purpose of which on a very basic level is to govern contested collective action problems through the use of regulatory instruments. Much of the growth in the administrative state in the second half of the 20th century directly stems from the public desire to regulate environmental risks through executive and administrative decision-making.[31] The regulation of environmental risks – whether this is done to correct market inefficiencies, to maximise overall well-being, or by reference to the need to pursue certain social policies – as any other form of regulation, is highly controlling of individual behaviour. The need to secure independent oversight is therefore particularly important in the context of environmental decision-making.

To appreciate this interaction in the context of standing, we will need to bear in mind the role played by judicial review as a mechanism of independent oversight and scrutiny of executive decision-making and the ways in which this role has

[28] A Perry 'Plan B: A Theory of Judicial Review' (2017) Oxford Legal Studies Research Paper No. 66/2017.

[29] eg *Council of Civil Service Unions v Minister for the Civil Service* [1985] AC 374 (HOL), per Lord Diplock.

[30] M Loughlin, *Foundations of Public Law* (Oxford, Oxford University Press, 2010).

[31] See also D Robinson, 'Regulatory Evolution in Pollution Control' in T Jewell and J Steele (eds), *Law in Environmental Decision-Making* (Oxford, Clarendon Press, 1998) 29–72.

changed over time. Arvind and Stirton thus lay bare how the understanding of judicial review came to change towards the second half of the 20th century from one focusing on mediating between private individuals and public authorities, adjudicating claims essentially based in private rights, to one of supervising the pursuit of public interests.[32] That is, judicial review moved from what is elsewhere termed the 'private rights' avenue of adjudication to the 'institutional' avenue;[33] the former maintaining that the access of the courts to supervise administrative actions is contingent upon any illegalities violating the rights or interests of individuals or private entities, while the latter allows for a more general and wider access for the courts to review executive decisions. This wide access to review executive decisions in general is strongly mandated by the rule of law.[34]

The point of highlighting this development here is not so much to criticise the ways in which judicial review has evolved over the years, or to criticise what may be perceived as a juridification of public policy, but primarily to understand the relationship between judicial review and environmental law. In the judicial review avenue, judicial oversight of what has become an extensive administrative state providing for a wide range of environmental rules and statutes takes place against a background of historical and developing understandings of the relationship between the courts and the executive. Similarly, the analysis advanced here is not to be taken to suggest that the courts are somehow not sufficiently attuned to environment concerns. Such points of critique are generally too simplistic and fail to appreciate the layered and contextual nature of environmental adjudication as it takes place within well-established institutions and avenues. For example, one perhaps curious feature of environmental adjudication through the means of judicial review and the focus by the courts on process over substance has been a judicial willingness to hear claims from a wide range of interests, expanding the rules on standing.[35] The irony of this is that whilst the courts are willing to entertain claims based on non-private interests (which from an environmental perspective is surely a good thing), they have simultaneously declined to engage with the substance of these decisions, choosing instead to maintain a focus on procedural matters. The willingness of the courts, for instance, to entertain claims from a wider range of claimants against a narrow scope of review arguably also is a reflection of the changing nature of adjudication more generally. As highlighted by Arvind and Stirton, a central feature of judicial review in the 1970s and 1980s was an increased willingness of the courts to 'at once extend … the *availability* of judicial review, while limiting its *scope*'.[36] Such institutional behaviour must be

[32] TT Arvind and L Stirton, 'The Curious Origins of Judicial Review' (2017) 133 *LQR* 91.

[33] T Zwart, 'Overseeing the Executive: Is the Legislature Reclaiming Lost Territory from the Courts?' in S Rose-Ackerman and P L Lindset (eds), *Comparative Administrative Law* (Cheltenham, Edward Elgar, 2010) 148.

[34] ibid.

[35] *R (Edwards) v Environment Agency* [2004] EWHC 736 (Admin), [2004] 3 All ER 21.

[36] Arvind and Stirton, 'The Curious Origins of Judicial Review' 108 (original emphasis). See also R Rawlings, 'Modelling Judicial Review' (2008) 61 *Current Legal Problems* 95.

borne in mind when considering the appropriateness of a given institution's ability to provide a forum for environmental adjudication.

The strong influence of existing and historical rules does not mean, however, that environmental adjudication in the form of judicial review does not contain important unique features. In the context of costs of bringing judicial review claims, environmental claims benefit from a specialised regime, giving effect to the Aarhus Convention's provisions on access to justice.[37] Whilst the statutory regime for cost-capping serves to protect claimants against prohibitively expensive costs, it has two main effects. First, it puts in place a specific and detailed set of rules for the allocation of costs in environmental judicial review. This ultimately recognises the public interest (and thereby lack of incentive for private individuals to bring claims) of certain types of environmental claims, ie a so-called uniform low-stakes claim.[38] Second by providing specific levels of protection to environmental claimants, which is not necessarily afforded claimants in other areas of law, the costs protection regime puts in place a distinctive and unique system for environmental judicial review claims that stands apart from the rules and models found in the other models of adjudication. Consequently, where a claimant in environmental judicial review satisfies the court that the claim is a so-called 'Aarhus claim', a cost cap applies automatically and the court can only vary the cost cap where it is satisfied that doing so does not result in the proceedings being prohibitively expensive. Similarly, in environmental claims that are not 'Aarhus claims', the claimant may apply for a cost-cap order where the proceedings are public interest proceedings and where in the absence of an order, the claimant would withdraw the application for review (though such cost capping orders are also available to non-environmental claimants).[39] Taken together, this system creates a model where the courts are compelled to pause and consider the interests at play in environmental claims and, in some cases, beyond what would be the case in other non-environmental law claims for judicial review.

Moving on from the rules of standing and costs allocation to the substantive aspect of environmental judicial review claims, the adjudicatory avenue arguably moves away from making special accommodations of environmental claims. This change is most pronounced if, instead of considering the initial stages of judicial review, we focus on the way in which the courts scrutinise environmental claims. The first point to make in this context is, rather obviously, that judicial review does

[37] Found in the Criminal Justice and Courts Act 2015 (Disapplication of Sections 88 and 89) Regulations 2017, SI 2017/100 which disapply ss 88 and 89 of the Criminal Courts and Justice Act 2015 and Civil Procedure Rules, rule 54.41–5. It is worth noting that prior to the statutory changes, the application of the costs follow the event rule was in part limited in common law, cf *R (Corner House Research Ltd) v Secretary of State for Trade and Industry* [2005] EWCA Civ 192, [2005] 1 WLR 2600 albeit arguably unsatisfactorily. See eg *Morgan v Hinton Ltd* [2009] EWCA Civ 107, [2009] CP Rep 26.

[38] N Komesar, *Imperfect Alternatives* (Chicago, University of Chicago Press, 1995).

[39] See S Bell et al, *Environmental Law*, 9th edn (Oxford, Oxford University Press, 2017) 339–45 for a more detailed discussion of the rules.

not engage with the actual merits of a decision under review except for where the underlying statutory framework dictates a heightened level of scrutiny. In the judicial review avenue, the court famously undertakes a review, not an appeal, and the grounds for review are therefore limited to the traditional grounds of illegality, irrationality, procedural irregularity and legitimate expectations. This is well established and was highlighted in a recent decision:

> This Court is exercising jurisdiction as a court of judicial review. It is not an appellate tribunal with the power to take different views on the merits from the decision making body. It is not for this Court to determine whether a decision … was wrong on the merits. It may form a view on the process by which it was decided, or on whether the decision was made within the parameters of the relevant legal principles, but save for the exceptional case where a decision could be said to be irrational, this Court has no power to intervene in the decisions of a democratically elected decision maker for which is answerable at the ballot box.[40]

The strict focus on the legality of an underlying decision poses challenges for claimants who are in a sense forced to frame their disagreement about a given decision (or indecision) around a point of legality or irrationality. In certain types of environmental claims this problem is particularly acute – for example, EIA claims where what at times comes across as a challenge to the merits of a planning decision will have to be framed around the narrow focus of judicial review on illegality and irrationality.

The confined grounds for review and the narrow scope of review are also strongly related to the functions of the relevant parties reflected in the avenue of environmental judicial review. As noted earlier, a central characteristic of judicial review is the fact that claims are brought against public authorities. This means that often the court is invited to second-guess and scrutinise decisions of administrative agencies made against rules, procedures and policies drawn up and developed by those very same administrative agencies. Inevitably, this means that the decision-making power of the administrative agency is deeply embedded in the decision being challenged before the court.[41] In this situation, the court faces the relatively simple choice of accepting the decision-making power of the administrative agency, and in doing so, leaning towards finding in favour of the public authority, or rejecting the decision of the administrative agency. If the court chooses the latter, it necessarily runs the risk of having to second-guess the underlying decision (though this risk is often mitigated by simply annulling the decision, requiring the administrative authority to redo its initial decision).

For reasons of expertise and legitimacy, this is something that the court is often reluctant to do. In environmental judicial review a characteristic of the underlying law is often that it affords express decision-making authority to an administrative agency and requires the agency to draw up policies and guidance documents on

[40] *R (Dillner) v Sheffield City Council* [2016] EWHC 945 (Admin), [2016] Env LR 31, [94].
[41] Shapiro, *Courts* 33.

which to base its decision. Decisions made by, for example, local planning authorities are made against a backdrop of development plans drawn up by the local planning authority itself. Similarly, decisions made by the Environment Agency (EA), in the context of industrial pollution, are made against a background of environmental permits which the Agency has drafted and developed itself. Likewise, decisions made by the Secretary of State on whether to give priority to certain types of developments are made against the backdrop of a national planning framework which the Secretary of State has herself drawn up.[42] In this context, the function of the public authorities against whom an environmental judicial review claim is taken may gain a necessary advantage against a claimant as the decision subject to review is deeply embedded into a policy framework developed by the decision-maker itself.

The fact that in the avenue of environmental judicial review one of the parties is a public authority who has often had the benefit of being able to develop its own rules and procedures has acute implications for the way in which the avenue operates. In the absence of a clear-cut and outright illegality, the claimant in environmental judicial review claims consequently has a significant challenge on her hands. The combination of a wide access to review but a narrow scope consequently poses a dilemma for the court. The wide access to review and the potential that brings for policy-based and merit-based challenges run the risk of inviting the court into considering arguments and claims that it arguably would prefer not to get involved with. In response to this, the court develops a narrow set of grounds for review alongside a narrow scope for review as these are adopted in other areas of administrative law. From a societal perspective, this may seem counterintuitive and a waste of resources. Why invite claims from a wide range of claimants at low cost if they are unlikely to succeed? From the court's perspective, however, it makes sense, if, as highlighted above, the court's role is that of a supervisor of the government, aiming to ensure adherence to fundamental constitutional rules of proper administration. Hearing hundreds of planning disputes which seek to challenge the merit of an administrative decision adopted by a local planning authority, acting under specific statutory authority, would get in the way of the constitutional function of the court.

The purpose of this section is not to lay out the history of judicial review in environmental law. Rather, it is important to appreciate that the prominent role played by judicial review in administrative law *in general* necessarily shapes environmental adjudication. The shoe-horning of environmental claims into judicial institutions through the modality of judicial review is an example of environmental law being applied to a system of adjudication which was developed many years in advance of environmental law emerging as a legal discipline. This application of environmental claims within the existing regime of judicial review gives rise to challenges for those engaged in questioning administrative environmental

[42] Revised National Planning Policy Framework (MHCLG, London, 2019).

decision-making primarily because, as we will see, judicial review is the archetype of a process which operates with its own mode of reasoning.

One of the main challenges faced by environmental claimants when seeking to challenge administrative environmental decisions through judicial review is the primary focus on process rather than substance in judicial review proceedings. This is most prominently brought out in Lord Diplock's famous grounds for judicial review which, for our purposes, serve to restrain the bases on which a claimant can challenge an environmental decision (ultimately for very good reasons, although Lord Diplock's grounds of review were evidently not stated with environmental law in mind).[43] Consequently, a claimant not satisfied with government action in response to particular environmental problem will have to convince a court that the action is illegal, irrational, procedurally improper or fails to fulfil the legitimate expectations of the claimant. Of these four grounds, illegality and irrationality are the ones most commonly relied upon by claimants in environmental claims (procedural questions are enormously significant but usually procedural breaches are breaches of specific statutory provisions, ie giving rise to illegality, rather than relying on the generalised common law procedural standards).[44]

The reliance of the ground of illegality is in part linked to the fact that much of present-day environmental law is implemented in response to EU law which requires the government to implement certain standards. These underlying standards often underpin a claim to illegality. Similarly, the prominence of the ground of review of irrationality is arguably based on the fact that the majority of environmental decisions made by administrative agencies are contestable on a normative level (eg a claimant disputes the importance afforded to the need for environmental protection weighed against other considerations by an administrative agency) but are structured so as to involve a great deal of discretion for the agency in reaching their decision, making it very difficult to claim illegality in terms of a relative weighting of values and merits. As a result, contestation of environmental decisions is framed as claims of illegality and/or irrationality.[45] The result is that the avenue of judicial review produces a framing of challenges to an administrative environmental decision in terms of illegality or irrationality. The consequences of this are several.

[43] *Council of Civil Service Unions and Others Appellants v Minister for the Civil Service Respondent* [1985] AC 374 (HOL).

[44] Although there are examples of claimants advancing claims on issues of procedural unfairness, impropriety and legitimate expectations, eg *RWE Npower Renewables Ltd v Welsh Ministers* [2012] EWCA Civ 311, [2012] Env LR 29 and *R v Rochdale Metropolitan Borough Council* [1997] Env LR 100 (HC).

[45] See in general OW Pedersen. 'A Study of Administrative Environmental Decision-Making before the Courts' (2019) 31 *Journal of Environmental Law* 59; C Warnock and O W Pedersen, 'Environmental Adjudication: Mapping the Spectrum and Identifying the Fulcrum' [2017] *PL* 643; and R Macrory and M Woods, 'Modernising Environmental Justice: Regulation and the Role of an Environmental Tribunal' (Centre for Law and the Environment, UCL, 2003).

First, a claim of illegality or irrationality necessarily entails a detailed level of scrutiny of the underlying rules which form the basis for a contested decision. For example, in order to ascertain whether a decision permitting polluting activities is illegal or irrational, a court will have to scrutinise in detail the underlying statutory framework of that decision. This is pretty straightforward. The real issue, as highlighted in chapters two and three, is that when it comes to environmental law, this underlying statutory framework often requires courts to engage with open-textured rules, informed by underlying policy documents, giving force to EU rules which afford states a certain degree of discretion in implementing obligations. Ultimately, the regulatory framework against which many environmental decisions are taken is complex, multilayered and not necessarily 'exclusively legal'.[46] Often this combination gives rise to a significant degree of administrative discretion. One of the challenges faced by claimants seeking to impugn environmental decisions is that, whilst it is perfectly possible to frame a claim as fitting the grounds of review of illegality or irrationality, doing so inevitably invites the courts to scrutinise intimately the administrative discretion, and ultimately the judgement, of a regulatory agency. In the end, this invitation straddles a fine line between having to assess the merits of a decision and the legality of the decision, and courts are very wary of crossing that line.

A prominent example of this is the claim advanced in *Downs* where the claimant challenged the failure of the Secretary of State to apply mandatory no-spray zones in proximity to her property on grounds of a failure to properly assess the risks arising from the spraying of pesticides.[47] In order to ascertain the merits of the claimant's case, the Court of Appeal (and the High Court before it) was required to engage in depth with the risk assessment conducted by the Secretary of State and the underlying EU Directive against which the assessment was conducted. The challenges arising from the examination of the Secretary of State's decision are highlighted by the fact that the Court of Appeal reached a decision diametrically opposed to that of the Administrative Court,[48] finding that by criticising the Secretary of State, Collins J in the Administrative Court had ultimately substituted his own evaluation of the relevant evidence for that of the Secretary of State's.[49] In other words, Collins J had undertaken his own assessment of the risks, based on the evidence before him, rather than assessing

[46] *R (United Kingdom Renderers Association Ltd) v State for the Environment Transport & Region* [2002] EWCA Civ 749, [2003] Env LR 7 the primary point of contention was thus policy guidance issued by the Secretary of State and *R (Adriano) v Surrey CC* [2002] EWHC 2471 (Admin), [2003] Env LR 24 centred around a claim that local waste policy plans had been misinterpreted by the planning authority.

[47] *Secretary of State for Environment, Food and Rural Affairs v Downs* [2009] EWCA Civ 664, [2010] Env LR 7.

[48] *Downs v Secretary of State for Environment, Food and Rural Affairs* [2008] EWHC 2666 (Admin), [2009] Env LR 19.

[49] *Secretary of State for Environment, Food and Rural Affairs v Downs* [2009] EWCA Civ 664, [2010] Env LR 7, [76].

whether the Secretary of State's assessment was manifestly erroneous when held against the criteria set out in the Directive. In doing so, Collins J had crossed the line of the proper scope of judicial review. In the words of Sullivan LJ in the Court of Appeal, 'in a case such as this, involving complex questions of highly technical scientific judgment, the "manifest error" hurdle is a high one'.[50] That is to say, where scientific consensus is lacking and the relevant criteria of the EU Directive had been taken into account, the nature of judicial review dictates that deference is to be afforded to the decision-maker's risk assessment. Sullivan LJ is effectively saying that in environmental adjudication the bar for making a successful claim in judicial review is high because of the characteristics of environmental adjudication as these manifest themselves in terms of high levels of technicality and scientific judgements.

One may have legitimate concerns about the Court of Appeal's decision and whether, as a matter of cognitive and epistemological acrobatics, it is at all possible for a court to assess the legality of a risk assessment conducted by an administrative decision-maker by reference to the statutory criteria without to some degree engaging in a de novo assessment of the risks at hand, but this is beside the point. The real issue is that the institution of judicial review, as developed over time, mandates that a court maintains a focus on the process of the decision-making and not the substance. The claimant's disagreement as to the merits of this risk assessment (ie effectively a challenge of the merits of the decision) may be valid, but such objections do not fit with the parameters of judicial review. In judicial review, 'the court must rule only upon the legality of a decision and not upon its correctness; the court will concern itself with the manner in which a decision is reached rather than with the substantive merits of the decision'.[51]

These points are far from new and are well established. However, when it comes to environmental law and the contestation of environmental decisions through adjudication, there is reason to assume that such contestation arises not as a result of a claimant being dissatisfied with the process of a decision (though it does happen). Instead many environmental claims likely emerge because a claimant is challenging the substantive outcome of the decision either because this impacts on her private interests or because she is contesting the environmental impacts of a decision. The bottom line is, however, that judicial review proceedings do not entertain challenges grounded in substantive differences of opinion as to the environmental merit or quality of a decision even if therein lies the reality of the dispute.

Another area in which this problem is brought out, highlighting the challenges faced by those who seek to challenge administrative environmental decisions through judicial review, is in the context of adjudication of environmental impact

[50] ibid [43].

[51] Lord Irvine of Lairg, 'Judges and Decision-Makers: The Theory and Practice of Wednesbury Review' [1996] *PL* 59, 60.

assessment (EIA) claims.[52] In the context of claims arising against EIA decisions, the line between contesting the substance of a decision and the procedure through which the decision is made is particularly fine. And because of the nature of the EIA regime, the statutory framework has proved a particularly fertile ground for litigation. In EIA claims, contentious issues have centred on whether the discretion exercised by planning authorities in assessing, first, whether a proposed development impacts on the environment to the degree that it is subject to an EIA (screening); and, second, where this is the case, whether planning authorities have taken into account relevant impacts and struck a reasonable balance between competing interests. In response to an abundance of challenges, the courts have made it clear that the judicial engagement with such matters is confined by traditional doctrines of judicial review, including the grounds of illegality and *Wednesbury* unreasonableness.[53] A good example of this is *R (Bedford) v London Borough of Islington* in which Richards J (as he then was) observed:

> It is inevitable that those who are opposed to the development will disagree with, and criticise, the appraisal, and find topics which matter to them or which can be said to matter, which have been omitted or to some minds inadequately dealt with. Some or all of the criticism may have force on the planning merits. But that does not come close to showing that there is an error of law on the local planning authority's part in treating the document as an Environmental Statement or that there was a breach of duty in Regulation 3(2) on the local authority's part in granting planning permission on the basis of that Environmental Statement.[54]

In short, the claimants' disagreement with the planning decision is only relevant in so far as it meets the higher threshold of contestability in judicial review as defined through the grounds of review. Anything falling below that will be seen as going to the merit of a decision which is not a ground of review. A similar example is found in *Zeb v Birmingham City Council* where the claim that certain environmental impacts had not been properly considered by a planning authority were considered an attempt to challenge the merits of the decision rather than the actual process thereof.[55] Moreover, in *Dillner* the dichotomy between the perceived nature of the environmental claims advanced by the claimants (seen as being about respect for rights of participation in the context of environmental decision-making) and the rejection of this by the court is particularly stark. In *Dillner*, Gilbart J unequivocally

[52] Directive 2011/92/EU of the European Parliament and of the Council of 13 December 2011 on the assessment of the effects of certain public and private projects on the environment; Town and Country Planning (Environmental Impact Assessment) Regulations 2017, SI 2017/571.

[53] *Zeb v Birmingham District Council v Warwickshire County Council* [2009] EWHC 3597 (Admin), [2010] Env LR 30; *R (Jones) v Mansfield DC* [2003] EWCA Civ 1408, [2004] Env LR 21, [60], per Carnwath LJ; *R (Loader) v Secretary of State for Communities and Local Goverment & Ors* [2012] EWCA Civ 869, [2013] Env LR 7; and *R (Thakeham Village Action Ltd) v Horsham DC* [2014] EWHC 67 (Admin), [2014] Env LR 21.

[54] *R (Bedford) v London Borough of Islington* [2002] EWHC 2044 Admin, [2003] Env LR 22, [203].

[55] *Zeb v Birmingham District Council v Warwickshire County Council* [2009] EWHC 3597 (Admin), [2010] Env LR 30, [30].

rejected the claimants' argument that the local authority's plan to fell a substantial amount of local trees ought to have been subjected to an environmental assessment by finding that the matter before him simply centred on the local authority's statutory duties under the Highways Act 1980, duties which, to Gilbart J, were not affected by the issue of whether an environmental assessment ought to have been conducted.[56]

A final significant example of the subtle but profound ways in which the fact that judicial review as a mode of adjudication affects the substantive rules applied lies in the fact/law dichotomy and the way this has been applied in relation to environmental law questions. In judicial review the distinction between questions of fact and questions of law is enormously significant. Questions of law are for determination by a court, and are susceptible of a right or wrong answer. Questions of fact, by contrast, are determined by an administrative decision-maker and are not something that fall within the purview of the court, except as part of a broader reasonableness assessment. The critical issue therefore is determining when a dispute centres around a question of fact and when the focus is on a question of law.[57] This is a general issue for public law: it is not necessarily answered in a 'bespoke' way in relation to environmental law.

However, the very nature of many of the terms used in environmental law mean that they are particularly unsuited to this binary classification. Key examples can be seen in relation to words such as 'significant' and 'likely'.[58] Is the likelihood of an event occurring a question of law to be determined by a court, or a question of fact to be determined by a decision-maker? The courts have attempted somewhat to soften the dichotomy by stating that, in a sense, it is both.[59] The courts have responsibility for deciding what 'likely' actually means – the administrative body decides whether on the facts before it the test of 'likely' is met in an instant case. However, the challenge with this sort of approach, as neat as it appears in theory, is that it is not possible to express a likelihood test except in other, equally contentious, words. Thus, likely, meaning 'more likely than not' as a legal test, still provides for a great deal to be decided by the administrative authority. Similarly, where significance is presented as being simply more than de minimis, whilst a decision-maker will know what significance means in the context of the rule, that is little help in deciding whether an effect is or is not actually significant. This fact/law distinction, as we shall see, also has consequences elsewhere, for it is also relevant for criminal law action in terms both of what a jury is entitled to decide, and for the question of judicial review of a magistrates' decision (for example).[60]

[56] *R (Dillner) v Sheffield City Council* [2016] EWHC 945 (Admin), [2016] Env LR 31, [66], [75]–[77].

[57] E Lees, 'Allocation of Decision-Making Power under the Habitats Directive' (2016) 28 *Journal of Environmental Law* 191, 211.

[58] ibid.

[59] ibid.

[60] ibid.

None of these examples are to be taken to suggest that judicial review proceedings never yield an outcome in favour of a claimant challenging administrative environmental decisions (though environmental claimants in judicial review face lower rates of success than other types of claimants).[61] As noted above, context is determinative. Where the statutory framework underlying a particular decision is less flexible and confers less discretion on a decision-maker, the procedural nature of judicial review can work in favour of the claimant. In, *Birkett* for example, the Court of Appeal held that the wording of the underlying EU provisions on access to environmental information entailed an obligation to review the 'merits, both the factual and legal, of a decision … afresh'.[62] A similar conclusion was reached by the Supreme Court in *Evans* also relating to access to environmental information where Lord Neuberger held that the wording of the EU Directive[63] required a full merits review of the underlying decision beyond the scope of that traditionally afforded through judicial review proceedings.[64]

To summarise, the contestation of environmental law norms through the avenue of judicial review reveals a familiar picture: the courts maintain a focus on procedural concerns seemingly evading the real contentiousness of environmental claims. This picture is one that comes from the principles of judicial review and the choices these reflect in terms of the place of the judiciary within a decision-making process. Environmental decisions are funnelled into existing structures of adjudication and claimants are forced to reckon with the fact that their arguments receive short shrift if they resemble a challenge to the substance of an administrative decision. After all, 'the role of judges is to review, not to decide'.[65] In maintaining this distinction it may well be that law loses relevance, confers power on administrative decision-makers and in that process disempowers the judiciary, as Vermeule argues.[66] From the perspective of environmental law, these developments are not exceptional – environmental lawyers are used to the situation where the elements shaping the law are found outside the boundaries of its discipline. A main issue to arise from the application of environmental law challenges to well-established means of adjudication in the form of judicial review is that, as one of us has argued elsewhere, judicial review is not necessarily sufficiently nuanced to capture the governance relations of environmental law.[67] If this is the case, the high rate of deference found in environmental judicial review claims might be a positive development.[68]

[61] Pedersen 'A Study of Administrative Environmental Decision-Making before the Courts'.

[62] *Birkett v Department for the Environment, Food and Rural Affairs* [2011] EWCA Civ 1606, [2012] Env LR 24, [23].

[63] Directive 2003/4/EC of the European Parliament and of the Council of 28 January 2003 on public access to environmental information.

[64] *R (Evans) v Attorney General* [2015] UKSC 21, [2015] AC 1787, [104]–[106], per Lord Neuberger.

[65] A Vermeule, *Law's Abnegation* (Cambridge, MA, Harvard University Press, 2016) 7.

[66] ibid 7.

[67] Lees, 'Allocation of Decision-Making Power under the Habitats Directive'.

[68] Pedersen, 'A Study of Administrative Environmental Decision-Making'.

In addition to the narrow grounds and scope of review, an important characteristic of the environmental judicial review avenue is that where a court does find in favour of a claimant challenging an administrative decision, it has wide discretion when it comes to providing remedies. Not only is this well established as a matter of common law but it is increasingly recognised that this wide scope for remedial discretion applies in cases where a claimant's success is based on a point of EU law. This means that at the end of the process of adjudication, the court can choose from a range of remedies, from providing no remedy at all to issuing a mandatory order, a prohibiting order or a quashing order, to issuing an injunction.[69] As visualised below, this means that the avenue of environmental judicial review takes the form of two adjoining funnels with a wide opening at the early stage of the process, which narrows when the court moves on to consider the substance of the claim (Figure 4.2).

Following this narrow stage, the avenue widens again, at the stage at which the court considers whether or not to provide remedies. This does not necessarily mean that the avenue of environmental judicial review is static or remains the same. There is, for example, scope for changing the various parts of the avenue through developments in case-law and statute. The changes introduced by the Criminal Justice and Courts Act 2015, mandating the court to refuse relief where the court thinks it likely that the outcome for the applicant would not have been substantially different if the conduct complained of had not occurred, have the potential to narrow the wide opening of the avenue.[70]

As a result, in reality, the main function of the court in environmental judicial review claims is not so much that of an independent adjudicator resolving disputes. Similarly, there is relatively little actual law-making involved on behalf of the court (though in the type of claims where a claimant's interests are based on grounds of public policy as opposed to private interests, there is arguably a scope for the court to engage in the law-making function). Instead, the main function of the court in environmental judicial review proceedings is that of a facilitator and supporter of public policy as this is expressed in statutory rules and orders.

V. Criminal Law and Sanctions

Compared to the avenues of statutory appeal and judicial review, where the adjudicator performs a role of independent review and constitutional oversight, the role performed by the adjudicator in the criminal law and sanctions avenue is rather different. The role of the adjudicator when it comes to imposing sanctions against those committing environmental offences is to a large degree one of enforcer of

[69] See ch 7.

[70] See ch 7.III.C. Criminal Justice and Courts Act 2015, s 84 amended the SCA 1981 to include a new s 31(2A) mandating that relief be refused where no substantial difference would occur in outcome were the decision to be remitted to the original decision-maker.

Figure 4.2 Judicial review

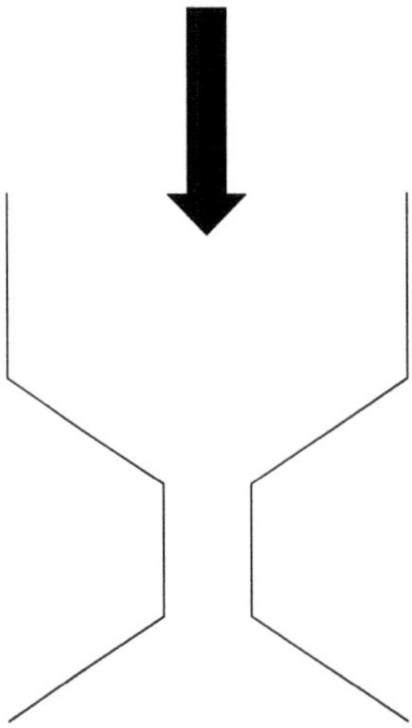

social policy. As discussed below, where an adjudicator is called upon to condemn criminal actions in the context of environmental law, the adjudicator often does so in a response to public policy, condemning particular criminal behaviour. Moreover, and somewhat akin to adjudication in the statutory appeal avenue, adjudication in the criminal law and sanctions avenue is undertaken by a range of different adjudicators and is not, as in judicial review, exclusively the purview of the courts. And as we will see below, the criminal law and sanctions avenue is, on one hand, the application of existing legal structures, rules and practices to the context of environmental law, whilst, at the same time, it exhibits unique characteristics not ordinarily found in other areas of law.

Initially, the criminal law and sanctions avenue, like judicial review, is an example of a well-established avenue of adjudication applied to a recent legal subject. Unlike the avenue of statutory appeal, the application of the criminal law and other sanctions to environmental issues consequently carries with it an entrenched system of rules, principles, structures and assumptions. These elements necessarily shape the avenue of adjudication, which emerges in the area of environmental crime. On one reading, the use of the criminal law in the context of environmental law is simply just another way of achieving a desired statutory objective. Although this argument is overly simplistic it is a useful starting point for considering the role performed by adjudicators in the environmental criminal law and sanctions avenue. For, if the attachment of criminal (and civil) offences to environmental law is, in simple terms, an add-on to the statutory regime aimed at strengthening the statutory objectives and condemning socially undesirable activities, then the role of the adjudicator will be confined by that statutory framework. As a result, the role of the adjudicator is that of an enforcer of norms found in the statutory regime which ultimately rests on social policy. Here we have an enforcer, who is called into action where the actions of a regulated entity have run afoul of the statutory regime and the administrative decision-makers have run out of regulatory options in the attempt to secure compliance. Support for this is found on two levels.

First, from very early on when encountering environmental criminal offences in the context of modern environmental law, adjudicators in the form of the courts readily accepted and applied the statutory 'instructions' provided by Parliament as these relate to the presence of strict offences in environmental law.[71] When encountering environmental criminal offences, the courts made relatively short shrift of the argument that the strict offences provided for by Parliament ought to be narrowly interpreted.[72]

A second example highlighting the role of adjudicator as an enforcer of social policy when adjudicating in environmental criminal matters is more recent and is found in the application of the courts of the sentencing guidelines for environmental offences enacted in 2014 by the Sentencing Council.[73] A full analysis of the guidelines is not warranted here apart from making the point that evidence suggests that the courts have readily applied the sentencing guidelines and the structure these sought to put in place in the sentencing of environmental offenders.[74] So much so that when sentencing certain offenders, the courts have in recent years handed down a series of record-breaking fines, rigorously applying the provisions in the guidelines relating to the size of fine by reference to the offender's annual turnover.[75]

The willingness of one type of adjudicator – that of the courts – to readily apply strict environmental offences when provided for by Parliament and sentencing guidelines when drawn up by the Sentencing Council, and in doing so performing a role as enforcer of social policy, is of course readily explainable by reference to the sovereignty of Parliament. However, this subsidiary role, rarely reflected on in the context of environmental law, contextualises the function of the adjudicator when adjudication is undertaken by the courts. As we saw in the context of the judicial review avenue, the role and function of the adjudicator was ipso facto

[71] eg C DuPont and P Zakkow, *Trends in Environmental Sentencing in England and Wales* (London, DEFRA, 2003); P Hampton, *Reducing Administrative Burdens – Effective Inspection and Enforcement* (London, HM Treasury, 2005); J Adshead, 'Doing Justice to the Environment' (2013) 77 *Journal of Criminal Law* 2015; and M Watson, 'Environmental Offences: The Reality of Environmental Crime' (2005) *Environmental Law Review* 190. See also E Lees, 'Environmental Law and Criminal Law' in E Lees and J Viñuales (eds), *Oxford Handbook of Comparative Environmental Law* (Oxford, Oxford University Press, 2019) 1119; A Brudner, 'Imprisonment and Strict Liability' (1990) 40 *University of Toronto Law Journal* 739, 740; R Lazarus, 'Assimilating Environmental Protection into Legal Rules and the Problem with Environmental Crime' (1994) 27 *Loyola of Los Angeles Law Review* 867, 882, citing M Kidd, 'The Use of Strict Liability' (2002) 15 *South African Journal of Criminal Justice* 23, 39.

[72] *Alphacell Limited v Woodward* [1972] AC 824 (HOL), 848–49.

[73] Sentencing Council, 'Environmental Offences: Definitive Guideline' (London, HMSO, 2014). See also Sentencing Council, 'Assessing the Impact of the Sentencing Council's Environmental Offences Definitive Guideline' (London, 2016).

[74] OW Pedersen, 'Revisiting the Role of Negotiation and Trivialization in Environmental Law Enforcement' (2019) *Journal of Law & Society* 29.

[75] See ch 7.II.D.

confined by the fact that much of the law upon which the court adjudicated was drawn up by the administrative agencies themselves, inevitably resulting in the balance of power tipping in favour of the public authority. In the criminal law and sanctions avenue, this balance of power is relevant on two separate, yet related, levels: it is relevant in the context of criminal adjudication before the courts, and it is relevant in administrative criminal adjudication. As discussed in detail below, the fact that the role of the adjudicator in the criminal law and sanctions avenue is closer to that of a social control function means that the avenue for environmental criminal adjudication is arguably different than the one found in other areas of criminal law that do not relate to the environment.

A. Judicial Criminal Adjudication

Ordinarily, the social control function of the court in criminal law adjudication carries with it important principles and assumptions, which shape the confines of adjudication. Because the very function of criminal adjudication is to apply potentially severe sanctions to offenders engaging in socially undesirable behaviour, the court necessarily wields a great deal of power (though that is to some extent always the case in adjudication). As a result, in criminal law adjudication, the court's potential to wield coercive power is at its highest insofar as the court has within its powers the means to incarcerate individuals and hand down severe fines.[76] Linked to this power is the fact that the court also operates as a check on the executive's ability to penalise individuals. Ultimately, the court serves in part to legitimise the authority of the state by ensuring that penalties are only applied where necessary. It might therefore be tempting to see the court as acting as an impartial arbitrator, which the state must convince in order to be able to impose severe sanctions. As a result of the values and principles embedded in the criminal law, however, the court is not necessarily performing the role of a neutral adjudicator.

This is because the criminal law recognises the inherent imbalance between the parties before the court. The power imbalance between the heavily resourced state, with its recourse to severe sanctions, pitted against an individual offender is limited by rules and principles central to the criminal law. These provisions include the need for the government to evidence beyond reasonable doubt that the defendant committed the offence, and the provision of a general presumption in favour of the defendant's innocence. Typically, in criminal law adjudication, in order to attach the label of the most severe offences, the state will also have to evidence that the offender committed the crime with some form of intent.[77]

[76] The Sentencing Guidelines specifically refer to fines up to £3 million, but the courts have discussed and handed down substantially larger fines, as we discuss in ch 7.II.D. Sentencing Council, 'Environmental Offences: Definitive Guideline' (London, HMSO, 2014).

[77] See Lees, 'Environmental Law and Criminal Law' and R Lazarus, 'Assimilating Environmental Protection into Legal Rules and the Problem with Environmental Crime' (1994) 27 *Loyola of Los Angeles Law Review* 867.

The general avenue of criminal law adjudication might therefore usefully be conceptualised as a process through which the state, by persuading the court (and it does not really matter for these purposes whether that is a judge or a jury), has to clear certain hurdles or barriers. These hurdles or barriers are not necessarily cumulative but the point is that failure to clear one of them is likely to imperil the prospect of conviction.

In environmental criminal law adjudication before a court, however, the avenue is slightly different and the balance of power is significantly modified. First of all, the hurdles or barriers which ordinarily are seen as tipping the process in favour of the defendant are altogether less influential. This is because in environmental criminal adjudication many of the criminal offences are strict liability offences. In practice, this means that the burden of proving, for example, that a defendant possessed the requisite mens rea to commit a given offence is absent. Instead, the requirement is simply that of proving that a defendant committed the actual offence, which is often a relatively straightforward exercise. The result of this is that the ordinary rules and principles of a criminal law avenue of adjudication are severely relaxed in environmental criminal law adjudication.[78]

The loosening of the barriers ordinarily found in criminal law adjudication is not just at play in the multitude of strict liability offences found in environmental law. It is worth bearing in mind that criminal offences in environmental law include so-called two-step offences where the actual criminal offence is parasitic upon the failure to comply with an administrative order or permit.[79] In these two-step offences, there is typically, as with strict liability offences, no requirement that the defendant possesses any particular mens rea as the actual offence pertains solely to the failure to comply with the administrative permit or licence.

Similarly, the scope for discretion when it comes to the court sentencing an offender has been restricted in the environmental criminal law avenue of adjudication as a result of the sentencing guidelines being brought in. As far as sentencing goes, however, the result of the sentencing guidelines has arguably been to bring sentencing of environmental offences into line with sentencing in ordinary criminal law insofar as sentencing guidelines exist for a wide range of offences.[80] Up until 2014, when the sentencing guidelines for environmental offences were introduced, the lack of guidance in environmental criminal law was arguably an outlier. Consequently, the avenue of environmental criminal law adjudication, as far as sentencing goes, is seemingly aligned with sentencing for other types of offences and does not vary in the same way it does in respect to establishing the defendant's guilt.

[78] See RJ Lazarus, 'Meeting the Demands of Integration in the Evolution of Environmental Law: Reforming Environmental Criminal Law' (1995) 83 *Georgetown Law Journal* 2407.

[79] Lees, 'Environmental Law and Criminal Law'. Consider also M Faure, 'The Revolution in Environmental Criminal Law in Europe' (2017) 35 *Virginia Environmental Law Journal* 321.

[80] A list of which can be found at www.sentencingcouncil.org.uk/crown-court/.

The direction of administrative preferences for sentencing of environmental offences through the sentencing guidelines effectively operate as a 'feed-forward' signal issued by the administrative state to the courts.[81] Where this is the case, as Rubin argues, the role of the courts in this context is different from what we ordinarily perceive it as being. Instead of having a firm delineation between the administrative state and the independent judiciary on the premise of the rule of law, the network model identified by Rubin suggests that when it comes to specific avenues of environmental adjudication in criminal law, a strong link is in place between the courts and the government. We will return to the implications of this relationship in the conclusion below, but the main point to make here is that this high level of engagement between the different branches of government is possibly more pronounced in the adjudication of environmental offences than in some of the other avenues discussed in this chapter.

A particularly strong example of the network between the administrative state and the courts which plays out in the avenue of environmental crime is found in the actual adjudication of environmental offences by the courts. As discussed in more detail by one of us elsewhere, the approach taken by the courts to the adjudication and interpretation of environmental offences is primarily one that gives force to the purpose of the law.[82] That is, when engaging with environmental offences, the courts have by and large opted for an interpretive approach anchored in the strict liability approach favoured by Parliament, and have repeatedly stressed that the purpose of avoiding environmental harm justifies the imposition of criminal convictions even where an offender shows little intention to cause harm.[83] As Lord Salmon memorably put it in *Alphacell*:

> If this appeal succeeded and it were held to be the law that no conviction could be obtained … unless the prosecution could discharge the often impossible onus of proving that the pollution was caused intentionally or negligently, a great deal of pollution would go unpunished and undeterred to the relief of many riparian factory owners. … The legislature no doubt recognised that as a matter of public policy this would be most unfortunate. Hence section 2 (1) (a) [of the Rivers (Prevention of Pollution) Act 1951] which encourages riparian factory owners not only to take reasonable steps to prevent pollution but to do everything possible to ensure that they do not cause it.[84]

It is moreover worth highlighting that there is otherwise very little scope for the defendant to disprove his guilt.[85] The only real scope there is for challenging the

[81] EL Rubin, *Beyond Camelot* (Oxford, Oxford University Press, 2005) 61. See also Loughlin, *Foundations of Public Law.*

[82] E Lees, *Interpreting Environmental Offences* (Oxford, Hart Publishing, 2015).

[83] eg *Walker & Son (Hauliers Ltd) v Environment Agency* [2014] EWCA Crim 100, [2014] 4 All ER 825, [36], per Lea HHJ noting: '[S]trict liability in environmental regulation was "a deliberate choice … made in order to secure higher environmental standards," and … that there is no longer a defence based on the exercise of due diligence to avoid the commission of this offence.' See also *Taylor Woodrow Property Management Ltd v NRA* [1995] Env LR 52 (DC).

[84] *Alphacell Limited v Woodward* [1972] AC 824 (HOL), 848–49, per Salmon LJ.

[85] The challenge that this creates for traditional criminal law theory is considered in A Brudner, 'Imprisonment and Strict Liability' (1990) 40 *University of Toronto Law Journal* 739.

imposition of a criminal sanction before a court in environmental law is effectively at the stage of sentencing. Consequently, a defendant is likely to put forward mitigating circumstances as these relate to, for example, assisting authorities with clean-up activities, or, in the absence of that, to challenge the classification of the offence as this underpins the court's findings as to the severity of the offence as put forward by the EA. Specifically in the context of putting forward mitigating circumstances, it has been a well-established principle that, even prior to the adoption of the sentencing guidelines, the defendant's actions towards limiting the harm caused by an offence and the defendant's assistance in terms of clean-up will be taken into account when sentencing.[86] Similarly, where a defendant, following a guilty plea, has made voluntary payments of reparations to, for example, local environmental causes, the courts has held that fines ought to reflect such donations.[87] These considerations have now been formally incorporated into the sentencing guidelines.[88]

All of this is not to say, of course, that the power balance in criminal environmental adjudication before the courts favours exclusively the prosecution. Some balance is found in the administrative system which shapes criminal prosecutions prior to prosecutions making it before a court. The decision to bring criminal charges against an alleged polluter is, as one would expect, shaped by the Agency's internal policies, including the Enforcement and Sanctions Guide and guidance drawn up by the Crown Prosecution Service (CPS), such as the Code for Crown Prosecutors as well as the Director of Public Prosecution's Guidance on Charging.[89] The former is expressly created with the environmental offences in mind, whereas the latter are general guidance documents for all prosecutors irrespective of what offences they are prosecuting. This latter point is important, as the Code for Prosecutors obliges prosecutors to take into account certain principles and considerations prior to prosecuting that are of general relevance to the criminal process. These principles include, for example, the 'full code test' which requires a prosecutor to establish that there is sufficient evidence to provide a realistic prospect of conviction (the evidence stage) and whether prosecution is in the interest of the public (the public interest stage). In this sense, the criminal law avenue is perhaps less 'random' in its self-selecting effects than is the litigation arising in the other avenues explored here, which rely on private interest for their initiation.

[86] *R v Anglian Water Services Ltd* [2003] EWCA Crim 2243, [2004] Env LR 10.
[87] *R v Thames Water Utilities Ltd* [2010] EWCA Crim 202, [2010] 3 All ER 47.
[88] Sentencing Council, 'Environmental Offences: Definitive Guideline' (London, HMSO, 2014).
[89] Environment Agency, Enforcement and Sanctions Guide (2019) www.gov.uk/government/publications/environment-agency-enforcement-and-sanctions-policy/environment-agency-enforcement-and-sanctions-policy (accessed 8 January 2020) and Crown Prosecution Service, The Code for Crown Prosecutors (2018) /www.cps.gov.uk/sites/default/files/documents/publications/code_2013_accessible_english.pdf (accessed 8 January 2020) and Crown Prosecution Service, Charging (the Director's Guidance) (2013) www.cps.gov.uk/legal-guidance/charging-directors-guidance-2013-fifth-edition-may-2013-revised-arrangements (accessed 8 January 2020).

Although these 'pre-litigation' procedures are, strictly speaking, not substantive rules of law but more akin to administrative directions, they are important in order to understand the ways in which the courts get involved with environmental issues in criminal law. This is particularly so considering that the majority of (though far from all) environmental offences are strict liability offences. On that basis, one would perhaps expect that prosecution of environmental crimes (for want of a better term) would be abundant and a matter of administrative course. In reality, however, the application of the evidence and public interest tests act as a restraint on the assumption towards criminal prosecution of strict liability offences. As the Code for Prosecutors states: 'It has never been the rule that a prosecution will automatically take place once the evidential stage is met.'[90]

Similarly, considerations which may constrain the decision to prosecute what might seem a straightforward case thus include the seriousness of the offence, the level of the defendant's culpability, the impact on the community, and whether prosecution is deemed to be a proportionate response to the offence committed.[91] Consequently, the shaping of a given case arising from an action of environmental harm takes place in a space which is heavily influenced by principles and considerations which are part and parcel of the toolbox of criminal prosecutors. These principles and considerations have been developed as a result of a decade's worth of prosecutorial experience from parts of the criminal law unrelated to environmental law and legal obligations, including those of the Human Rights Act 1998 and the European Convention of Human Rights. As with the other avenues discussed above, the application of environmental law to the process of criminal prosecution results in environmental law being shaped and moulded by – or made to fit into – the procedure of criminal prosecution through the established rules, principles and practices of that process. And a significant part of this shaping and fitting takes place in the administrative system of a regulatory agency even before a charge is formally brought before the courts.

The importance of the administration of the criminal process prior to formal adjudication is perhaps best highlighted by a series of examples. Although there are no available data indicating the rate of criminal prosecutions versus the total number of environmental offences committed in England and Wales, the evidence suggests that the role played by criminal prosecutions in the enforcement of environmental law is small relative to other types and methods of enforcement and, moreover, that this role is diminishing. The EA's own data indicate that the number of prosecutions has dropped from over 300 in 2007 to around 60 in 2015.[92] This drop has to be set in the context of an overall drop in serious

[90] Crown Prosecution Service, The Code for Crown Prosecutors (2018) 8.

[91] ibid 7–11.

[92] Environment Agency, 'Pollution Evidence 2015 Summary' (2016) available on https://assets.publishing.service.gov.uk/government/uploads/system/uploads/attachment_data/file/651707/Pollution_incidents_2015_evidence_summary_LIT_10487.pdf. There is a methodological limitation in making this point, arising from the classification of offences by the Environment Agency as 'serious

pollution incidents in the same period. The main point, however, is that the relative use of prosecution as a means of enforcement has dropped when compared to other means of enforcement, such as enforcement notices and enforcement undertakings, which have both been used with increasing frequency in the same period.[93]

The willingness of the courts to apply the sentencing guidelines is, thus, another example of the way in which guidelines adopted by administrative agencies impact on the process of adjudication. This response by the courts to administrative instructions suggests a proximity and connection between the administrative state and the courts when it comes to the actual adjudication of criminal proceedings. This connection is different from the situation discussed above where administrative enforcement decisions not to prosecute an environmental offender – taken by reference to a reliance on principles and ideals of criminal process as these are manifested in the evidence and public interest tests – effectively preclude judicial involvement. Naturally the broad-brush description of judicial engagement with criminal offences put forward here disguises a lot of finer detail in the ways in which cases are prosecuted and the ways in which the judicial engagement varies from offence to offence.[94] The main point is that in the avenue of criminal law, we encounter a direct link and engagement between the courts and the administrative apparatus when it comes to the interpretation of offences and application of sanctions. Second, this interaction is different from what takes place in some of the other avenues of environmental adjudication where, in some cases, the rules and procedures of a given avenue serve to maintain a distance between the courts and the administrative state.

B. Administrative Criminal Adjudication

Partly in response to the imbalance of power present in the criminal law and sanctions avenue when adjudication takes place before the courts, ie partly in response to the fact that imposition of criminal sanctions is comparatively speaking easier in environmental law, a range of administrative and non-judicial sanctioning tools have been developed. The best example of this is the creation of the civil sanctions regime created by the Regulatory Enforcement and Sanctions Act 2008. This regime effectively moves some of the enforcement activities away from the courts and into the administrative system where regulatory agencies instead become the

pollution incidents' in accordance with its common classification scheme rather than classifying incidents as offences by reference to specific regulatory regimes. Presumably any incident classified as a 'serious incident of pollution' is likely to be a criminal offence (though the Agency might choose to take no formal enforcement steps) whereas the reverse is not necessarily the case in so far as not every criminal offence need be a 'serious pollution incident'.

[93] Pedersen, 'Revisiting the Role of Negotiation and Trivialization in Environmental Law Enforcement'.

[94] See Lees, *Interpreting Environmental Offences*, for a more detailed account.

adjudicator, which imposes sanctions and condemns undesirable activities. This regime of sanctioning maps onto our definition of adjudication developed in chapter two insofar as the use of civil sanctions by the EA entails the application of pre-existing standards and procedures, albeit newly enacted ones, through a defined mode of reasoning, based on arguments, reasons and proof, which gives rise to winners and losers.

Consider, for example, the process through which the EA, which is for these purposes an adjudicator, accepts an enforcement undertaking, to date the most widely used civil sanction. Typically, upon becoming aware of an offence having taken place, the EA will assess the gravity of harm caused by the offence and the offender's culpability.[95] This initial assessment will determine whether the EA deems it appropriate to offer an enforcement undertaking or will decide to prosecute the offender before the courts (in which case we find ourselves in the part of the avenue which relates to judicial imposition of sanctions). Once the EA decides that an enforcement undertaking is an appropriate response to the offence, the offender and the EA will commence negotiations on the content of the undertaking, ie the legal obligations which the offender undertakes to deliver. This negotiation, whilst flexible in nature, takes place against a background of established procedures, including standards which prevent the EA from prosecuting offenders for offences for which the undertaking was entered (except for where the offender fails to comply with the undertaking) and publication of details on the undertaking, as well as the need for the EA to verify compliance with the undertaking prior to issuing a certificate of compliance. Similarly, where the enforcement undertaking is not entered into as a result of the EA making the offer but because the offender proactively comes forward to offer an undertaking, the processes for assessing whether an undertaking is the appropriate response and for negotiating the undertakings are largely identical.[96]

Consequently, whilst fundamentally different from a criminal sanction, the use of enforcement undertakings nevertheless takes the form of adjudication as we have defined that in chapter two. It is a form of adjudication which, in many ways, serves the same purpose as the imposition of criminal sanctions by a court: that of condemning socially undesirable activities although the civil sanction arguably maintains a stronger focus on the need to secure future compliance rather than imposition of penalties. Nevertheless, the imposition of sanctions, not by a court but by a regulatory agency, is an important form of adjudication.

The picture which emerges of criminal law and sanctions avenue is therefore one that has a strong element of social control attached to it insofar as a main role of the adjudicator is to impose sanctions in order to condemn socially undesirable practices. The fact that, in reality, administrative agencies make increasing

[95] Environment Agency, Enforcement and Sanctions Guide (2019).

[96] Environment Agency, 'Enforcement Undertaking Offer Form' available on https://assets.publishing.service.gov.uk/government/uploads/system/uploads/attachment_data/file/460813/784_14.pdf (accessed 8 January 2020).

use of civil sanctions instead of traditional criminal sanctions simply just means that the forum of adjudication has shifted from the courts to the administrative agency. A significant influence on the form and content of environmental law emerges not only from the application by the courts of established structures and doctrines (as in judicial review), but also from the administration of the criminal law by regulatory agencies. In environmental criminal law, a significant influence is thus derived from the administrative decisions made by the regulatory agencies in terms of whether to take enforcement actions against an alleged offender and, moreover, what specific enforcement steps to take as noted above. The avenue of criminal law and sanctioning in the context of environmental law is thus one that varies significantly from the avenue found in 'traditional' criminal law avenues. The main feature of the criminal law and sanctioning avenue in environmental law is that the hurdles a prosecutor and regulator ordinarily need to climb are lower (as a result of the nature of offences) (Figure 4.3).

Figure 4.3 Criminal law

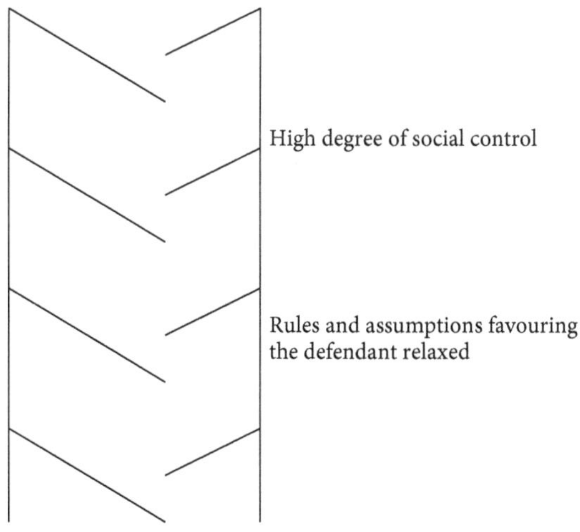

VI. Private Law

So far, the avenues explored here have been broadly speaking in the area of public law (defined as the situation where the state remains an influential party to the adjudication either because a decision made by a public administrative agency is contested, or because the government itself takes steps to contest the actions of individuals by seeking to sanction actions through the criminal law). Public law contestation aside, avenues of environmental adjudication are also found in private law where a dispute takes place between two private parties (or, on a rare occasion, against a public authority and a private individual, seeking civil law remedies).[97] The main focus here will be on the scenario where private legal action is, broadly speaking, taken in respect of environmental harms through tort actions in nuisance, trespass or negligence. In saying this, it must of course be appreciated that the application of the label 'private' to any of these disciplines of law is somewhat misleading if for no other reason that the application of 'private' does not necessarily suggest the state is entirely sidelined and has no influence over the law (public nuisance is a case in hand here), or that actions in private law are entirely set aside from statutory rules and frameworks. Nor does the application of the prefix 'private' to, say, private property suggest that definition of and the rules governing private ownership of property are not shaped or understood partly through prisms of public interests.

Historically, however, the avenues of private law – in particular in the form of private nuisance – have played a prominent role in adjudicating environmental disputes and the character of such disputes is markedly different from those considered above. The reason for this is clear when we consider the purpose of, in this case, private nuisance, and the relatively late onset of environmental regulation.[98] On a very basic level, private law provides individuals with actions and remedies against harmful activities by others. Private nuisance, for example, provides claimants with an avenue to contest the alleged harmful behaviour of others to the extent the harmful behaviour interferes with the claimant's right to enjoy her land.[99] On this reading, the legal relevance of private nuisance for environmental law is evident. The point is not so much, however, to discuss whether rules in nuisance are relevant or effective as means for environmental protection. The main consideration here is to reflect on the ways in which the forms of private law adjudication in tort shape the treatment of environmental claims.

It is clear that this avenue is significantly different from the other avenues of environmental adjudication. These differences reflect the fact that the function and role of the adjudicator when adjudicating in private law claims is fundamentally different from the functions exercised by the adjudicator when adjudicating in any of the other avenues. The first main characteristic of environmental adjudication under the private law avenue is that it resembles very closely a traditional understanding of adjudication as being a tripartite relationship between two parties and an independent adjudicator.

Adjudication in the private law avenue is closely aligned with an understanding of adjudication that emphasises resolution of disputes between two private parties who appeal, as we saw in chapter two, to the independent adjudicator

[97] See D Howarth, 'Environmental Law and Private Law' in J Viñuales and E Lees (eds), *The Oxford Handbook of Comparative Environmental Law* (Oxford, Oxford University Press, 2019).

[98] eg J Steele 'Assessing the Past: Tort Law and Environmental Risk' in T Jewell and J Steele (eds), *Law in Environmental Decision-Making* (Oxford, Clarendon Press, 1998) 107–38 and S Coyle and K Morrow, *The Philosophical Foundations of Environmental Law* (Oxford, Hart Publishing, 2004) ch 4.

[99] *Hunter v Canary Wharf Ltd* [1997] AC 655 (HOL).

through the use of predetermined procedures and vocabularies. Unlike in some of the other avenues of adjudication, each of the parties enjoys equal status in practice before the adjudicator in their attempt to persuade the adjudicator (which is most commonly a court).

Neither of the two parties benefit from the advantage of having his/her prior decision, act or rule-making forming the basis of adjudication as is the case in judicial review and statutory appeal. This balance is a reflection of the dynamics of private law environmental adjudication where, at its core, the adjudicator is called upon to resolve conflicts between competing rights (often property or contractual rights) between private individuals. Ultimately, when resolving these disputes, the adjudicator assigns legal rights and legal wrongs between two parties competing on an equal footing to persuade the court.

The strong presence of the dispute settlement paradigm in private law environmental adjudication is linked to the fact that, unlike some of the claims brought in judicial review, private law adjudication is usually retrospective.[100] Obviously retroactivity is a prominent feature in many types of adjudication but it is particularly prominent in the private law avenue. This is because up until the point of adjudication, the parties in the conflict have maintained a mutual understanding of the rules governing their relationship. This relationship, however, has at the point of adjudication broken down. The determining factor in explaining why an adjudicator finds herself deciding in a private law claim is therefore that the relationship between the two parties has broken down and the adjudicator is called into action to resolve this. That is to say, the decision by an adjudicator effectively ends up regulating the relationship between the two parties.

This regulatory function highlights that, in the private law avenue, the court inevitably takes it upon itself to engage in a degree of law-making which is not present to the same degree in some of the other avenues. The law-making function of the court in the private law avenue does not just come about because the two parties to a conflict are uncertain about the legal rules governing their relationship but also because of the high degree of retroactivity involved in adjudicating in private law matters. It follows that where the two parties effectively call upon the adjudicator to declare what legal rules govern their relationship, the adjudicator will have to do two things. First, it will have to engage in an assessment of what the law actually is, both on a general level and in the context of the specific relationship of the two parties. Second, the adjudicator will have to apply this exercise of 'discovering' the law to the factual circumstances of the conflict between the two parties. Taken together, these two undertakings lead to a predominance of the law-making function in the private law avenue. Of course, any adjudicator and court to some extent will always 'discover' law and ascertain the factual circumstances of a conflict when adjudicating. That is

[100] See also ch 7.II.C.

the very essence of adjudication: applying novel factual circumstances to legal rules and in response to that, through the application of precedent, distinguish a claim from previous cases or settle it in accordance with existing doctrine. The point is, however, that in the private law avenue, the two parties to a dispute cannot agree on what the legal rules governing their relations are, nor do they agree on to what the factual circumstances surrounding their dispute actually amount. For the institution adjudicating the dispute, this means that it will have to engage in a full assessment of the facts as well as the law. This in itself is an important characteristic of the private law avenue as the necessity of the adjudicator to engage in an assessment of the facts is different from some of the other avenues of adjudication where matters of fact are ordinarily not examined in depth.[101] In this respect, it may well be said that much of the dispute before the adjudicator is about facts rather than law. Are, for example, the actions of a defendant unreasonable to the degree that they give rise to responsibility in law? Answering this question necessarily requires a deep scrutiny of the factual circumstances surrounding the claim, and where that is the case, it might be assumed that the adjudicator's focus is to a larger degree on the facts rather than on the law. Whilst this no doubt is true, the main feature of adjudication as defined here is that the disagreement between the parties in respect to factual circumstances only ends up before the adjudicator because the two parties seek a resolution to their disagreement through an independent third party. And once the parties go down that path, their disagreement will have to be framed and contextualised against legal claims and vocabularies in order to fall within the jurisdiction of an adjudicator.

Taking this together, the pursuit of environmental claims through the law of private nuisance gives rise to a set of unique challenges and considerations. Whilst the procedures and structures of judicial review that result in environmental claims being made to 'fit' judicial review are in part linked to the constitutional role performed by the courts, the characteristics of the law of tort similarly result in environmental claims taking on particular characteristics. In the private law of tort, the role of the courts is thus to act as the ultimate arbiter and enforcer of rights held by private individuals and corporations. Central to conflicts and claims in tort therefore are not prima facie claims to environmental protection but claims to private rights and in private nuisance to property rights. The protection of the environment achieved through this is consequently incidental.[102] This incidental relationship highlights the challenges faced by claimants seeking to pursue environmental claims in private law. Appeals to the law of tort in the attempt to achieve environmental protection have 'been tempered' by the way the courts have

[101] See ch 5.II.A.
[102] Coyle and Morrow, *The Philosophical Foundations of Environmental Law*, 112.

received and conceptualised such claims, focusing instead on maintaining key characteristics of the law of tort.[103]

Not only must a claimant possess an interest in land in order to be able to bring a claim in private nuisance – an approach which the courts have been eager to maintain[104] – but a claimant must also grapple with the challenge of foreseeability, showing that the harm caused by a defendant was foreseeable.[105] Related to this, those seeking to furnish an environmental claim in private law must be able to evidence causation between the relevant activities and alleged harm.[106] The implication of this is that when it comes to the avenue of private law, environmental law claims will be judged from the mode of reasoning which is so well established in the law of tort. This is not in and of itself a novel discovery but serves the purpose of highlighting the general point made throughout this chapter that adjudication of environmental claims inevitably takes place against a background of procedures and reasoning which is not necessarily anchored in environmental law itself. This means that environmental adjudication (and thereby also environmental law as an applied discipline of law) necessarily takes the form of other disciplines of law.

The avenue of private law environmental adjudication is thus one in which the adjudicator's functions are closely aligned with traditional ideas of dispute resolution between two parties whose access to the independent adjudicator is defined by the very nature of their relationship (Figure 4.4). This means that access to the adjudicator in the private law avenue is ordinarily only afforded to those who, in the case of private nuisance, have a proprietary interest in land, and, in negligence, where a claimant is owed a duty of care and in contract law only parties to a contract can bring a claim. Again, this highlights the inherently private nature of the avenue; unlike that of, for example, judicial review, where claims with a high degree of public interest are more likely to emerge. The entryway to the adjudicator in the private law avenue is therefore best conceptualised as being somewhat narrower than in the other avenues, instead taking the form of two independent funnels. From there, the scope of the court to engage in an assessment of facts as well as the law results in an avenue that is, compared to judicial review, wider insofar as the adjudicator's review is all encompassing and entails a comprehensive law-making power. This wide scope of assessment is, moreover, maintained when it comes to the remedial stage where the adjudicator has, akin to judicial review, wide discretion either to issue an injunction or reward compensation.[107] Consequently, the relative narrowness of the entry point in the avenue is reversed

[103] Steele 'Assessing the Past' 126–27.

[104] Compare the decision of the Court of Appeal in *Hunter v Canary Wharf Ltd* [1996] 1 All ER 482 (CA) with that of the decision of the House of Lords above.

[105] *Cambridge Water v Eastern Counties Leather Ltd* [1994] AC 264 (HOL).

[106] eg *Corby Group Litigation v Corby DC* [2009] EWHC 1944 (TCC), [2010] Env LR D2.

[107] See ch 7.

when it comes to the ultimate decision-making by the adjudicator where it enjoys a wide discretion.

Figure 4.4 Private law

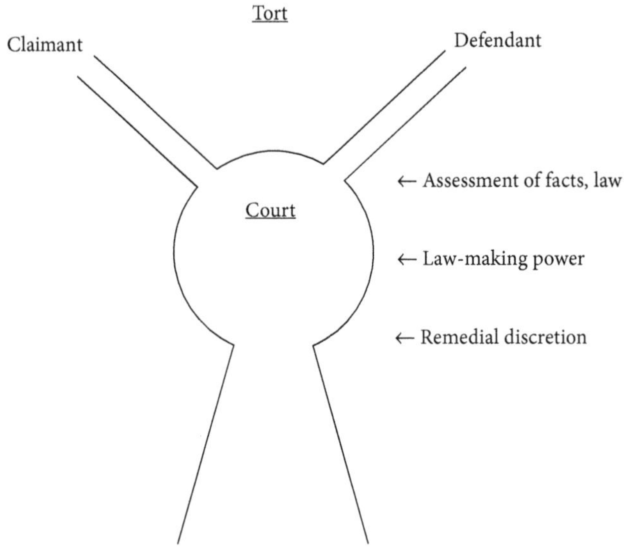

Characteristics:

- Traditional tripartite dispute resolution
- High degree of judicial law-making
- High degree of retroactivity
- Based on private interests
- Court assigns rights/wrongs

VII. Conclusions

Thus far, in considering the different avenues of interaction between law and environmental problems, we have through our structure implied that questions of form – of the rules surrounding the practice of adjudication – can be sensibly separated from those substantive rules and principles which are applied as a result of the wider context within which a dispute arises. Such is not the case. Indeed, the two will tangle together to influence a dispute at different points. By way of example, we can consider the role of time limits in relation to nuisance actions in the law of tort, and of the nature of environmental harms and how these issues interact in respect of the substantive rules that emerge. One of the criticisms often directed at tort law as a source of redress for environmental harm is that it is by definition reactive – the action is brought as a consequence of harm having been suffered, rather than proactively to prevent such harm. However, as is well known in the case of environmental damage, such harms may only come to 'fruition' many years after the occurrence of the polluting act. Indeed, when we consider encroachment of substances on neighbouring land, for example, it may take decades for a polluting substance to migrate from its source onto the affected neighbouring property. The significance of this rests in the time limit given for the action. In tort law generally – and for very good reasons – the action only becomes available once a harm has actually materialised, rather than when simply the risk of a harm becomes apparent.

This rule was developed in relation to mesothelioma cases, where those exposed to asbestos were unable to bring an action against their employer merely for having developed pleural plaques (a harmless consequence of asbestos exposure, but which was evidence of an increased risk of developing asbestos-related cancers).[108] A first glace this may seem like a harsh restriction, but it was introduced to prevent the cases where mesothelioma did emerge being outside the relevant time limits. If pleural plaques had been enough to found an action, then in some cases if cancer did develop, the claimant would be time barred, a wholly undesirable outcome. If we translate this to the environmental context, however, we can see that this means that even where it is perfectly apparent that within a relatively short period of time a harmful substance will migrate, and it is significantly easier to ensure clean up prior to that occurring, an action will not lie in the tort of nuisance since at that point, although it would be inevitable, an action had not accrued. We see in this the consequence not only of the 'baggage' which arises from the applied nature of environmental law, but also of the close and intractable relationship between form and substance as a process of decision-making. The substantive rule in this case was a consequence of procedural limitations on action, but it has a hugely significant role in shaping the sorts of harms which can be remedied under the law of tort.

Similarly, in respect of standing, the consequence of a limited class of claimants – ie those genuinely aggrieved, or with a legitimate interest – being entitled to bring an action will have a very profound influence on the kind of arguments that are raised in the court hearing, and therefore on the sorts of precedents that will emerge through the system of common law. By privileging a certain kind of person in a legality challenge in relation to administrative action, we deliberately or otherwise privilege a certain kind of *reason* for upholding or dismissing that claim.

Rules relating to costs have a similar effect. The consequence of a 'loser pays costs' rule, even with a cost-capping order, is that a claimant has to be strongly motivated to bring a claim. In some cases this motivation may indeed emerge

[108] eg *Fairchild v Glennhaven Funeral Services* [2002] UKHL 22, [2003] 1 AC 32.

from their personal values and views about the situation at hand, but more often it would emerge from either a threat to their own commercial interests, or to their property and home life. As a result, there is much more likely to be a series of cases which consider, for example, the impact of a waste plant on neighbouring property in terms of smells or amenity, than the impact that such a plant might have on the interests of a displaced or homeless community within the affected areas. Even though such persons might be able to establish standing through a legitimate interest, the lack of resources vesting in such persons, and of economic and social interests to protect, mean that they will be unable or unwilling to bring an action for fear of costs, thus meaning that their voice – and the sorts of reasons for a decision which such persons represent – will not be heard in court and will not therefore start to form part of the corpus of the substantive rules fleshed out and reasoned with by the common law courts.

The importance of appreciating the role of institutional design in the context of adjudication and the impact this has on the content of environmental law itself goes to the overarching theme of incoherence and its prominent presence in environmental law. In the absence of a 'grand masterplan' for environmental adjudication, a central point which follows from the analysis of the avenues and institutional backgrounds of environmental adjudication is, not surprisingly, that institutional context is determinative. The adjudicatory context ultimately shapes the content of the law.

In the chapters that follow, we explain that this means in turn that environmental adjudication does not result in a coherent structure of doctrine which gives rise to a systematic concept of law (let alone a coherent discipline of law). Instead environmental adjudication, and ultimately the law following from the adjudicatory process, is necessarily the product of a disjointed process. If environmental adjudication is conceptualised as the application of environmental problems to existing avenues, structures and cultures of law, then it follows that this application necessarily alters the discipline of environmental law. Often this alteration goes beyond what claimants, commentators and scholars might traditionally perceive environmental law as being. That is, the application of environmental law to other disciplines and structures through various avenues leaves an imprint on environmental law: an imprint which resembles the discipline into which environmental law is applied. Making this claim is not a critique of the institutions engaged in environmental adjudication nor is it an attempt to argue for a more coherent solution (eg in the form a one-stop specialist tribunal). Similarly, it is not an attempt to draw up a coherent theory of adjudication. It is simply a modest attempt to explain what goes on in environmental adjudication and on the back of that to argue that a lack of coherence is necessarily a prominent feature of environmental law.

The contestation of environmental law decisions takes place across a range of different avenues. Often these different avenues give rise to a specific and unique set of procedures and challenges for those who seek to contest environmental decision-making. The main reason for this is the fact that the avenues of adjudication are in a sense alien to environmental law. This is because the avenues of adjudication originate in areas of law which do not necessarily have much in common with environmental law. Consequently, the adjudicators often end up having to 'fit' environmental claims into existing avenues where, as a result, environmental claims are shaped by the mode of reasoning that is central to the respective avenue in which they are applied. The main explanation for this is that in England and Wales adjudication predominantly takes place within the institutional set-up of the courts. That is, the strong reliance on the courts – a well-established institution – when it comes to resolving environmental disputes naturally results in environmental claims being controlled by existing cultures, structures and modes of reasoning.

Having said that, it necessarily follows that the application of environmental claims to existing avenues of adjudication and modes of reasoning varies from avenue to avenue. In some, eg the criminal law, the relative proximity between the adjudicators and the administrative state results in an almost network-like avenue where the formal adjudication is significantly shaped by administrative decision-making. In others, eg judicial review, the constitutional role played by the courts and the development of judicial review as an institution of supervision results in a rather different sets of dynamics. It also means that the dynamics of claims being pursued in each avenue vary drastically. On the one hand, we encounter the type of cases that law and economics scholars see as a uniform high-stakes claim where a relatively small number of participants bear a high stake.[109] These types of cases arise, for example, in private nuisance and statutory appeal claims. In contrast to this, there are the types of cases in which there is not necessarily a discernible private interest at stake but in which a claimant instead seeks to vindicate a public interest against regulatory action or inaction, causing a risk to a dispersed range of individuals. In this latter case, the contestation is aimed much more at public policy choices and a claimant seeks to direct the ways in which a 'government policy or program[me] shall be carried out'.[110] These type of cases arise more readily in, for example, a subset of judicial review claims and arguably also in a subset of specific types of environmental claims (eg in EIA claims). Altogether, this in a sense gives rise to an adjudicative fragmentation across environmental law: a fragmentation that takes place across a range of avenues with each of their own modes of reasoning and sets of procedures. In some the adjudicators serve to supervise and review administrative actions by reference to constitutional norms and narratives, whereas in other avenues the adjudicators perform an entirely different role of arbiter of private disputes of land rights.

[109] N Komesar, *Imperfect Alternatives* (Chicago, University of Chicago Press, 1995).

[110] A Chayes, 'The Role of the Judge in Public Law Litigation' (1976) 89 *Harvard Law Review* 1281, 1295.

5

Avenues of Adjudication as Power-Broker

I. Introduction

Adjudication is defined by institutionalised decision-making.[1] It involves the resolution of a dispute between parties in such a way as to create relative winners and losers, as well as generalisable rules, on the basis of reasoned argument and proof in such a forum. In the institutional element of an adjudicatory system, we therefore see an essential component of its character. With, and through, socially constructed institutions comes power. Adjudication is thus an exercise of power: power to resolve disputes; power to determine facts and evidence; power to make new rules and to interpret old ones; and power to allow or deny access to the adjudicatory fora. Consideration of how adjudicators examine the powers they have been given, and their relationship with the powers of others, allows a deeper understanding of the adjudicatory role. These powers determine the relationship between the parties themselves; between the parties and the adjudicator; with higher and lower adjudicators within the system as a whole; and with the wider administrative state. In this sense, the avenues through which adjudication takes place become power-brokers.

The previous chapter demonstrated that the significance of the avenues of adjudication lies, in part, in the role that they play in shaping the *purpose* of adjudication within each of these avenues. These purposes ranged from the resolution of private disputes to the exercise and enforcement of social control. This chapter examines how these purposes mould the above facets of adjudicatory power in practice; how the purposes themselves are shaped by the avenues which funnel environmental adjudication; and what role wider constitutional principles have to play in striking this balance.

What becomes apparent is that there are two forces at play here. On the one hand, the 'scale' of the power of an adjudicator is a function of the purpose(s) (including environmental protection) behind the specific avenue in play and its position within the wider legal system. On the other hand, it is a consequence of legal norms that sit without the avenues and govern institutionalised

[1] See the discussion in ch 2.II.

decision-making as a whole. Thus the characteristics of each avenue colour how the power of an adjudicator is conceived, but these sit in tension against the generalised principles as to the role of independent third parties in resolving disputes and creating and interpreting new norms. This is seen when we examine the general principles that shape normative legal power in the UK constitutional set-up, and how these are balanced and shaped within the individual avenues. The precise calibration of this balance varies.

This chapter will demonstrate this by, first, in section II, explaining in more detail the relationship between the institutionally created social institutions of adjudication, and power through law. In section III, we examine the most fundamental adjudicator power – the power to resolve disputes. We consider both the scope of this power in relation to the parties themselves, and in relation to other adjudicators. In doing so, we engage with discussion of the overarching guidance of the principles of parliamentary sovereignty, and of upholding private rights, and how these interact with the specific adjudication avenues. In section IV, we examine the consequences of the powers which are established in respect of fact-finding and the rules of evidence, and how control over interpretation of past events shapes the power structures in play. In section V, we explore how this dispute resolution function begins to expand into the creation of more fundamental norm structures in the process of norm interpretation and creation. This encompasses both statutory interpretation, and the development of common law rules. Section VI then considers the power-allocation functions of access to justice, in respect of both standing rules and costs provisions, and how these are understood by the adjudicators themselves. Of course, the precise nature of each adjudicator's jurisdiction varies enormously, not only within different legal contexts within each avenue, but also within the hierarchy of adjudication, but certain trends can nevertheless be seen.

II. Adjudication and Power

Before we commence our discussion of environmental adjudication in practice from the perspective of power, it is useful here briefly to explain our perspective on adjudication as a constructor of power. The argument is simple. In providing a forum in which a dispute between parties can be resolved, adjudication as a social institution privileges the position of one of these parties over the other in outcome, in mode of reasoning, and in narrative as to the operation of the world. This is an exercise of power. This power, although often developed by individual legal norms, is more fundamentally constructed by the approaches which adjudicators take to their own task. In this sense, the relationship between the *content* of a legal norm and the power relationships between those applying and developing those norms is a mutually reinforcing one. As Sypnowich explains: 'If law both mirrors and distorts the realities of power, it is power, not principles of legality, which tells us what law is.'[2] Even if one does not subscribe to an understanding of law *as* power structures, understanding the operation of law in practice will nevertheless require some analysis of who is able to make decisions, and about what.

This is explained further by Kennedy in the context of judges specifically, but it applies across our field. The following passage explains the frontiers in which adjudicator power may be developed, and we explore these further below in the specific realm of environmental adjudication. The specific examples given here are less significant than is the overall lesson of the self-determined nature of institutional authority.

> What this means is that judges, not the legislature, typically decide in the first instance whether a new technology or a new resource is 'property' or not, whether a new contract clause is enforceable, and so on. In other words, in cases where it is obvious to everyone that there is a gap, or a conflict or an ambiguity in the system, the judges resolve it. But it also means that it is up to the judges to decide when to change the rules of the complete pre-existing system even in the absence of a gap, conflict or ambiguity. Again, I knew that judges overrule cases, but I had not absorbed the importance of the fact that the rules about when to overrule are judge-made rules.[3]

This chapter explores the consequences of the fact, as Raz argues, that in order for a legal system to exist there must be a relevant primary institution charged with application of legal norms and that this institution is tasked with explaining its own role.[4] Since these institutions are necessary for the legal system to exist, their defining characteristic is power. To say that the ways in which such primary institutions operate creates power structures is therefore merely acknowledgement that a significant (and necessary) part of legal systems are the institutionalised power structures created through the necessary primary institutions. Raz, in explaining the necessity of authority in adjudication (linking therefore to our definition of adjudication in chapter one), gives the following useful analysis:

> Primary organs are concerned with the authoritative determination of normative situations in accordance with pre-existing norms. Consider judicial bodies. Courts and tribunals have power to determine the rights and duties of individuals. But cannot any person do the same? Cannot John determine whether he owes £100 to Alan or whether Paul owes money to Jack? He may be ignorant of the facts but like a court he may investigate them. He may be ignorant of the law but like a court he may study it. The difference between a court and a private individual is not merely that courts are provided with better facilities to determine the facts of the case and the law applying to them. Courts have power to make an *authoritative* determination of people's legal situation. Private individuals may express their opinion on the subject but their views are not binding.[5]

[2] C Sypnowich, 'Law and Ideology', https://plato.stanford.edu/entries/law-ideology/ (first published 2001, amended 2019 – accessed 14 August 2019).

[3] D Kennedy, 'The Stakes of Law, or Hale and Foucault' (1991) 15 *Legal Studies Forum* 327, 350.

[4] J Raz, *Authority of Law: Essays on Law and Morality* (Oxford, Oxford University Press, 1979, online edition 2012).

[5] ibid 108.

Authority here is the key to the institutional establishment of the adjudicator. Indeed, even a short reflection on the reality of most legal systems in practice, and the way that adjudication proceeds, demonstrates that understanding the adjudicator's attitude to power is essential to understanding power as constructed through that system.

One need not subscribe to either a postmodernist or a critical legal theory approach to recognise that there are power structures created through legal rules and through the process of litigation. Such recognition does not necessitate a conclusion of legitimacy or illegitimacy, but it does require acknowledgement that findings of evidence, the creation and application of standing rules, and the like, are systemic allocations of power. The argument upon which this chapter is premised – that environmental adjudication is in part an exercise of power through social institutions – is, in this sense, both a modest and an obvious one. Our interest therefore lies not in proving that litigation and adjudication do involve exercising power per se, but rather to explore the forms of power structures which are built through theses processes in the context of environmental law.

Furthermore, it is also not necessary to find despair or opposition to the possibility of adjudication in the presence of such power. Fish explains the position of Fiss in relation to the relevance of power to adjudication:

> In the absence of absolute constitutional values, that is, of values that are accepted by everyone no matter what his perspective, 'adjudication is not possible, only power'. By power Fiss means 'mere' persuasion as opposed to the more legitimate assent that would be forthcoming if adjudication were grounded in some extra-interpretive principle.[6]

We do not explore the legitimacy or otherwise of such power. However, the relationship between it, and values, and the consequences for coherence, are our concern (see chapter eight).

In this chapter, the goal is to explain the patterns that emerge. It is useful to return to the argument developed in chapter three, that in the fundamental elements of adjudication, the rules which apply are built upon three pillars (see Figure 5.1): the general constitutional ordering of relationships between parties; the avenues of adjudication native to environmental law which provide a contextual but still generalised shaping influence on the power structures; and the specific norms applicable to the instant case. These pillars, as we explained there, encapsulate the content of environmental adjudication as a whole, but we can also use them as a lens through which to examine power.

There are multiple frontiers across which power structures are created through adjudication: categorisation of new situations under existing norms; the significance given to private arrangements; analysis of the presence of ambiguity in existing norms; and the power to 'move the law on' are all powers open

[6] S Fish, 'Interpretation and the Pluralist Vision' (1981–82) 60 *Texas Law Review* 495, 497, citing O Fiss, 'Objectivity and Interpretation' (1982) 34 *Stanford Law Review* 739, 763.

Figure 5.1 Pillars

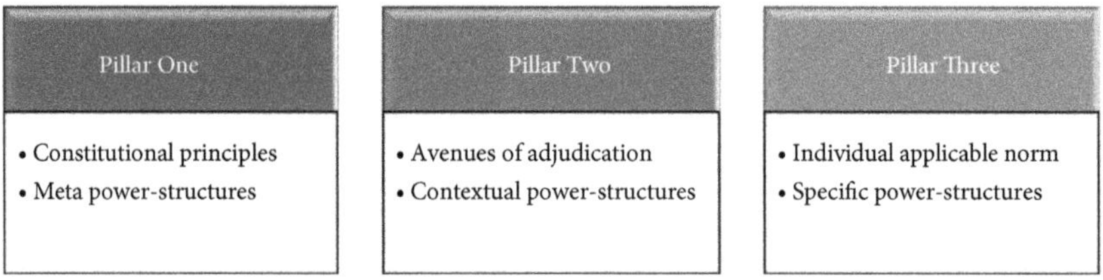

to adjudicators in ways that are *not* generally managed through statutory rules. Rather, the adjudicator themselves constructs and reasons within these parameters. This process occurs within each of the three pillars. These rules, which affect how judges can exercise their power, are the 'ground rules' of the game, as we discussed in the previous chapter.

It is also important in this section to explain what different facets of the adjudication system we envisage as shaping these power structures, whereas the subsequent sections demonstrate this construction of power at work. We envisage the power structures to be constructed of four blocks: jurisdiction; scope of fact-finding; interpretation and creation of norms; and conferral of access to adjudicator (Figure 5.2). At the heart of this sits jurisdiction and the fundamental question of who has the power to resolve the dispute at hand, but this is not the end of the picture.

Figure 5.2 Elements of power

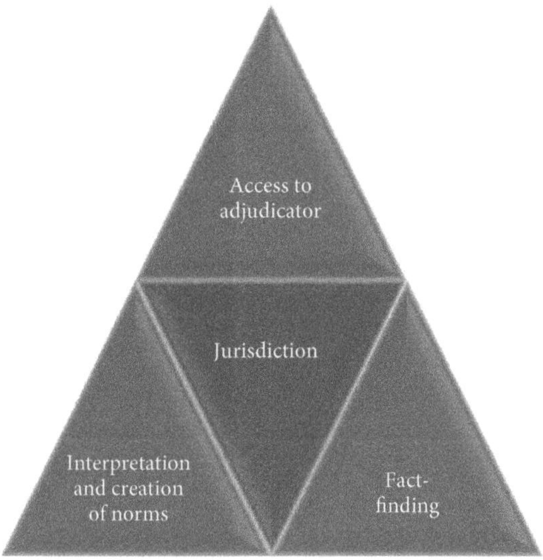

Our conception of these other elements requires some explanation.

A. Fact-Finding

In explaining fact-finding power, we commence with some analysis as to what the purpose of findings of fact is within the judicial process. Essentially, whichever burden of proof is applied, once a finding of fact is made, for the purposes of dispute resolution, a concretisation of the factual background occurs, and the facts as found by the adjudicator become 'truth' for the purposes of the remaining legal questions. It should be acknowledged here that not everyone accepts that such a finding of truth is possible. As such we should be keenly aware of the 'hidden' goings-on in assertions of findings of truth. As Farber explains, 'judge[s] … traditionally defined their roles on the basis of concepts like evidence, proof, and truth. Whatever else may be said on the subject, these concepts can no longer be taken for granted.'[7] As such, findings of fact are, as much as development of norms, interpretation of existing norms and defining jurisdictional scope, potentially political questions.[8] In the following chapter we consider how adjudicators, in the different avenues, regard their own legitimacy in reviewing and handling scientific and expert evidence, but it is useful to highlight here that there is an intimate relationship between findings of fact as framing power; as seeking or rejecting the possibility of a non-politicised 'correct' answer; and of confirming the purpose of adjudication in general. Whilst in part 'the question is whether the litigation process can claim the goal of establishing truth',[9] the more important question is really: who decides when the truth has been found?

One of the purposes of litigation therefore is to assign the task of determining the truth for the purposes of decision-making. Without subscribing to a wholesale postmodernist critique of the possibility of finding an objective truth through the review of historical evidence, we can nevertheless say that litigation, in moving from an open-ended analysis 'on the balance of probabilities', to a position where established facts become sacrosanct, elevates the level of certainty present in that evidence when it comes to the task of applying the law to the facts. One power of fact-finding is therefore a power to fix the historical truth of what has occurred, and to operate even in the face potential uncertainty, as though that uncertainty is overcome. The decision about when such uncertainty can be overcome is, obviously, a significant one. Adjudication therefore gives the

[7] DA Farber, 'Adjudication of Things Past: Reflections on History as Evidence' (1998) 49 *Hastings Law Journal* 1009, 1010.

[8] It is useful to think of an analogy with history here, as discussed by Farber. He reasons that, 'even the greatest believer in objective historical truth must admit that there are limits to historical knowledge. As a practical matter, there are some events whose true facts will forever remain debatable because of the ambiguities in the historical record, and some facts whose import will always be subject to conflicting interpretations. Thus, everyone seems to agree that it is possible to "know" some things about the past, and that there are other things that cannot be definitively resolved', ibid 1027.

[9] ibid 1020.

power of 'fixity'[10] and litigation as a tool for truth-finding becomes an exercise of government power.[11]

If this is accepted, then the secondary question becomes one of whether the approach to how facts are found and made sacrosanct is one dictated to the adjudicator by the statutory provisions conferring power upon them, or whether it is self-defined. Can adjudicators answer for themselves, 'with what attitude should we approach inquiry into past events?'?[12] This secondary question is a question not about the scope of adjudicator power to determine facts, but the meta-question of who determines whether the adjudicator can determine facts. Often the ultimate arbiter of such questions will in fact be a 'higher adjudicator' in the hierarchy of courts. In acknowledging the need for such a contextual (and institutional) understanding of how facts are constructed, we recognise, as Fish argues:

> Facts can only be known by persons, and persons are always situated in some institutional context; therefore facts are always context relative and do not have a form independent of the structure of interest within which they emerge into noticeability.[13]

Our inquiry is into this 'structure of interest' and how it is constructed.

B. Interpretation and Creation of Norms

It is obvious to state that the abilities to interpret and create norms are expressions of power within an institutional set-up. An ability to create a new norm to resolve a dispute is of course an exercise of state power. It is perhaps less evident that interpretation equally involves such an exercise, but in interpreting a norm an adjudicator's understanding of what the rule in question means becomes prioritised within the system. As with a fact-finding, their understanding of something that is inevitably ambiguous becomes sacrosanct for the purposes of the resolution of the dispute. The creation of new norms and interpretation of old ones does not just change the rules as applicable to a dispute. It also fundamentally changes the relationship between the parties themselves, and between the parties and the other potential members of the decision-making bodies around them.

The process of interpretation, in our secondary 'meta' form, is perhaps more significant, as when an adjudicator decides the proper approach to the question of interpretation, not only do they influence the actual norm applied going forward, but they affect the proper technique of interpretation for other adjudicators, and

[10] MJ Osiel, 'Ever Again: Legal Remembrance of Administrative Massacre' (1995) 144 *University of Pennsylvania Law Review* 463, 630.

[11] Graham conceives of litigation as a tool to find truth is indeed an exercise of government power. Farber explains that '[h]e castigates inductive logic as a tool of government power'. Farber, 'Adjudication of Things Past' 1033, citing K W Graham, Jr, '"There'll Always Be An England": The Instrumental Ideology of Evidence' (1987) 85 *Michigan Law Review* 1204, 1233–34.

[12] D A Farber, 'Adjudication of Things Past: Reflections on History as Evidence' (1998) 49 *Hastings Law Journal* 1009, 1027.

[13] S Fish, 'Interpretation and the Pluralist Vision' (1981–82) 60 *Texas Law Review* 495, 497.

other questions of law. In deciding not, 'what does rule *x* mean?', but rather, 'what are the rules by which I decide what rule *x* means?', the adjudicator sets up and alters the structures of power within the system (by, for example, showing more or less deference to parliamentary intention,[14] prioritising the values of procedural and substantive fairness, and the like).

C. Access to Adjudicatory Fora

By access to adjudicatory fora here we mean standing. The standing rules are critical in allowing not only a particular form of action to be heard by an adjudicator, but by *this claimant* being able to bring this claim. As with the above, this changes not only the position of the claimant, but of all other actors within the process. It is not only possible for a decision to be challenged, but for the decision to be challenged *by this particular person*. This can result in change in the assessment of the likelihood of challenge, and the likely content of the grounds of challenge. The content of the standing rules and the ways in which they shift the anticipated role of adjudication were explained in detail in the previous chapter as these rules mould the avenues of adjudication as shown there. What is important for this chapter is how the rules about standing are themselves understood, applied and interpreted by the adjudicatory fora applying them. There are two questions about standing rules: who has standing in a particular avenue (discussed in the previous chapter)? And who has the power to decide who has standing, and how do they reason about that standing as part and parcel of the power structures within the administrative and adjudicatory institutional set-up (discussed here)?

***

In summary, when these component parts of the landscape of power conferral created by adjudication through the avenues of environmental adjudication are taken together, we build a highly complex picture. It is one in which the central importance of the *avenues* of adjudication as power-brokers becomes apparent. There are four building blocks of this power: jurisdiction; fact-finding; norm interpretation and creation; and access. Within each of these blocks we have a substantive question – do I have jurisdiction? Can I make a finding of fact? Can I interpret and create norms? Can I confer access to this forum? – and a meta-question – what approach do I take to answering the substantive question, and who decides what approach is legitimate? In answering both the substantive and the meta-question, an adjudicator must look to the three pillars of rules – general and constitutional rules, the rules of the avenue of adjudication, and the specific contextual rule. We now examine how these questions and approaches play out in practice in environmental adjudication.

[14] For a very useful analysis of this concept, and what it might mean for interpretation of norms, see A Rosen, 'Statutory Interpretation and the Many Virtues of Legislation' (2017) 37 *OJLS* 134.

III. Power to Resolve Disputes

First we consider jurisdiction – the power to resolve disputes. In this section we explain how adjudicators reason about their power and their relationship with both the parties themselves and other decision-makers, broadly defined. Mostly this takes place in the context of parliamentary processes authorising and establishing jurisdiction, but we also see inherent and common law jurisdictional power at play. Again, keeping in mind the importance of institutional authority, the starting point for the creation of the relevant institutional framework is the constitutional set-up which establishes separation of powers between the executive and independent adjudicatory systems (with the courts at the centre); between private parties and the administrative state; and between private parties themselves. Thus at the foundation of adjudicatory power constructs, we find the concept of the institutional decision-maker as primary institution, applying norms.

A. Constitutional Principles and Jurisdiction

At the fundamental core of this set-up in English and Welsh law lie the principles of parliamentary sovereignty, of liberty absent prohibition for the private citizen, and of the inviolability of legal rights. In all avenues, these principles affect how adjudicators see their role, but what is critical is that the effects that they have operate in different ways in the face of the adjudicatory model established within each avenue. Furthermore, when we keep in mind that environmental law engages a large amount of discretion in interpreting more or less value-laden norms; often involves interpretation of 'cloudy' evidence; and requires balancing and prioritisation of competing goals, it is clear that the locus of power even in respect of the relatively 'mundane' task of resolving an instant dispute is critically important. Who decides, matters.

We can take as our launching pad the impact that sovereignty, as the fundamental principle of our (explicit) constitutional set-up, has on how dispute resolution power is divided up amongst institutions. This is the bedrock of the first pillar explained above. The effect of this principle is, of course, central. It operates to shape adjudicator jurisdiction, in more or less subtle ways, within the corpus of environmental adjudication. In statutory appeals, as we shall see, the emphasis is on parliamentary authorisation being given to go beyond what might be termed a 'reviewing' but inherent jurisdiction, to a specific, merits or de novo jurisdiction. The consequence is that in conferring the power to resolve disputes *in this way*, Parliament has demonstrated its intention for an adjudicator to operate differently from the 'paradigm' adjudicatory model in the context of administrative law, ie judicial review. There has been a deliberate move, in effect, from a legality-focused approach to public law control carried out by an independent observer, to what appears more like 'quality control'. In judicial review the opposite is true. Sovereignty is explained as the principle separating what is 'appropriate' judicial oversight, and what should be left in the hands of 'democratically assigned' administrative bodies. Sovereignty shapes adjudicator reach.

Second, there is an emphasis apparent on how statutory provisions shape the relative relationships between adjudicators. We see this in discussions in the courts regarding the higher courts and their interaction with decisions of the Planning Inspectorate – which is both an adjudicatory and a de novo forum – and in the relationship between the First Tier Tribunal (FTT) and the Information Commissioner (IC) – which are both adjudicatory and de novo decision-makers. The role of sovereignty as explanatory force for power structures is not limited to hands-off or hands-on reviewing power.

Furthermore, focus on sovereignty very clearly shapes cases involving judicial review in terms of the level of scrutiny deemed appropriate, where it is derived from the inherent jurisdiction of the courts. Although a highly hands-off approach is taken in cases where parliamentary authorisation has left the development of detailed policy rules to administrative bodies, in cases where there is a clearer statutory rule, the court will simply apply that without reference to deferential decision-making. We see this playing out in the context of the distinction drawn between questions of fact and questions of law. On its face, this question appears to be a decision about what sorts of question are susceptible to a 'right/wrong' assessment rather than a reasonableness assessment. However, it is really a tool by which decisions are allocated amongst decision-making bodies dependent upon their democratic legitimacy (or perceived democratic legitimacy) and their relative expertise. In this sense, the fact–law distinction forms an important part of the division between juridical and expert power.[15]

Even in judicial review cases however, Parliament is not always 'king'. This can be seen in *Spurrier*,[16] where the court discusses the standard of review to be applied under the broad umbrella of reasonableness:

> For reasons which by now will be apparent, we consider that the degree of scrutiny required by any challenge before us will be dependent upon, amongst other things, the strand of policy which is under review. However, although Parliament scrutinised and approved the content of the ANPS as later designated, generally we do not consider that the main grounds of challenge in these proceedings raise issues in respect of which Parliamentary approval is an especially weighty matter in relation to the appropriate degree of scrutiny, particularly when the nature of the grounds of challenge are considered.[17]

It is unsurprising that the constitutional principles surrounding adjudication in general, and judicial review in particular, bend to the context of the decision being made. This is what we would expect. However, as this section and subsequent chapters will show, in the environmental context the contingency effect is a particularly

[15] See the discussion of G Gutting and J Oksala, 'Michael Foucault', https://plato.stanford.edu/entries/foucault/ (first published 2003, amended 2018 – accessed 14 August 2019).
[16] *R (Spurrier) v Secretary of State for Transport* [2019] EWHC 1070 (Admin), [2019] JPL 1163.
[17] ibid [166].

complex one. On the one hand, the fact-sensitive nature of many decisions, their value-laden content, and the expertise involved in balancing a wide range of such considerations results in an attitude, at least in the courts, of hands-off deference. Expert decision-makers are allowed to carry out those decisions constitutionally allocated to them, without interference from a neutral outside observer. As we explained in chapter two, adjudication is always treading a tight line between experts remaking decisions which they are particularly well equipped to consider, and neutral arbiters ensuring that when exercising their judgement, experts are not led too far astray from the principles of legality, of equal treatment before the law, of fair process and of reasonableness. *Spurrier* is a good example. Courts will construct the constitutional power structures in a contingent and reflexive manner when exploring the limitations of their own power.[18]

Where we move into those avenues (criminal and private law) where courts (there is a much narrower range of adjudicator 'options') see their role as being more central to ensuring good governance, the attitude towards parliamentary intention shifts. The wider principles of criminal law alter how statutory interpretation is carried out. More fundamentally, fidelity to the constitutional principle of parliamentary sovereignty takes a back seat to the principle of operating in favour of a defendant in cases of doubt. Similarly, in private law, the focus is on the relative rights and obligations of the disputing parties. There is little focus on the ways in which the norms establishing their rights and obligations came to be, except where ambiguity arises as we consider in relation to the 'mischief' rule of interpretation.[19] Partly this is a result of the common law source for many of these rules – one thinks here in particular about tort – but it is also a result of the fact that the central concern in private law, the parties themselves and their negotiations, actions, mutual conduct and relationship, takes centre stage.

When we move into other adjudicatory avenues, therefore, the principle of the inviolability of individual liberty and rights starts to become predominant. This has consequences for the interpretation of norms, and for the creation of new rules. But it also has implications for the power of dispute resolution. Indeed, the starting point that individuals are at liberty to behave as they wish without a specific legislative prohibition, or absent the competing right of another, is central to how adjudicator power is conferred and managed in the context of environmental law through these avenues.

Let us consider here, for example, contract law. The resolution of contract law disputes, whatever the context, lies in the content of the contract. In this contract we see the institutionalised determination of the mutual rights and obligations

[18] ibid.

[19] The mischief rule approach to interpretation is well established in common law, *Sussex Peerage Case* (1844) XI Clark & Finnelly 85, 8 ER 1034 (HOL), 1057 (although it is treated narrowly in criminal law, *Dyke v Elliott* (1871–73) LR 4 PC 184). The decision in *Pepper v Hart* [1993] AC 593 (HOL) and subsequent interpretation of how Parliamentary intention should be understood has perhaps morphed how the mischief rule is understood. For more information, see S Vogenauer, 'A Retreat from *Pepper v Hart*? A Reply to Lord Steyn' (2005) 25 *OJLS* 629.

of the co-contracting parties. The power to determine who is able to resolve disputes, therefore, lies primarily with the parties themselves. They may include a mandatory arbitration clauses, which would be a way of avoiding state-centred institutionalised dispute resolution mechanisms as far as possible (although it is clear that the Arbitration Act 1996 means that arbitration is not wholly without the wider institutionalised state). In such cases, the private parties are able (within limits) to reject the institutional authority of state-backed adjudicators and to opt instead for a private arrangement. However, underpinning this option lies the 'threat' of enforcement of the contractual obligation to go to arbitration by the courts themselves. Thus, even in the context of a deliberate decision by parties *not* to engage adjudication as we have defined it, it is the threat of such adjudication and the associated principle of the inviolability of legal rights created through contract that allows for this option.

In criminal law too, the principle of individual liberty has hugely significant impacts upon who is able to resolve disputes. The answer is simply that only the (traditionally conceived) courts can do so. This is in recognition of the importance of liberty when weighed against the consequences for the individual of the dispute being resolved against them. Some element of this reasoning is present in the decision of the Court of Appeal in *Ideal Waste*.[20] The Court accepted that it is troubling (to say the least) in the context of criminal law sanctions, for a judge to be unable to explain, in comprehensible terms, to a jury, what some of the key terms in the relevant offences mean.[21] To counter this – which is significant in itself – the Court requested the Environment Agency, as administrative 'interface', to work with waste operators to ensure clarity. Thus:

> In saying what we have, of course, we do not rule out the possibility of co-operation between the Environment Agency and operators in this field to the mutual benefit of the public interest and the interest of the operators. In the end it is for the courts to apply the law. But we see scope for co-operation which will assist operators in knowing what they can reasonably expect to do without enforcement action being taken against them.[22]

In effect, the Court was reasoning that whilst the power to decide whether an offence has been committed lies with the adjudicatory forum, it would be a more satisfactory position, given the uncertainty, if a degree of cooperation from the regulator and the regulated could provide a practically predictable position in the face of linguistic uncertainty.

In summary, when we consider adjudicator reasoning in respect of their own power, conferred within the avenues, but constrained by the nature of their institutional formation, statutory appeals and judicial review sit on one side. Here, parliamentary fidelity triumphs. Criminal law and private law sit on the other,

[20] *R v Ideal Waste Paper Co Ltd* [2011] EWCA Crim 3237, [2012] Env LR 19.
[21] ibid [42]. The reported comments of counsel are also thought-provoking in this regard, [21].
[22] ibid [47].

where the focus is on courts as upholders of rule of law and of private rights and obligations. The avenue is critical in shaping how adjudicators see their role, and consequently their power to resolve disputes. However, we can break down this argument further into two distinct questions: first, how is power shaped vis-à-vis the parties themselves? Second, how is power shaped vis-à-vis other adjudicators, within the avenues of environmental law?

B. Power Vis-à-Vis the Parties

First, we consider statutory appeals. Given its statutory underpinning, it is no surprise that the adjudicator's attitude to the *source* of their power (ie statute) will be critical in shaping how they reason within this avenue. Even in the context of a full merits review of a decision, it is clear from the reported decisions that there is a focus on the powers of the adjudicator as constrained by a parliamentary authorisation.

The establishment of power vis-à-vis the disputing parties is clearly a consequence of the conferring statute. It is important to note at this point, however, that there is a distinction to be drawn between (in some cases) the parties as named in a dispute. For example, in relation to the Environmental Information Regulations[23] (EIR) before the FTT, ostensibly the parties will be the applicant and the IC. The 'real' locus of the dispute in such cases is nevertheless between the public authority refusing to disclose the requested information and the applicant.

Whoever the parties are though, we can clearly see that the starting point will always be the statute itself. This was emphasised in the decision in *Evans*[24] (a case concerned with interpretation of the Freedom of Information Act 2000 in the context of environmental information). The focus of the adjudicating court was on the statutory provisions themselves, albeit that this analysis of power was not all one way. The 'sovereignty-centric' approach can be seen most clearly in the dissenting judgment of Lord Hughes. Here, even what we might refer to as the cardinal ideology of judicial reasoning[25] – compliance with the rule of law – is contextualised through sovereignty.

> The rule of law is of the first importance. But it is an integral part of the rule of law that courts give effect to Parliamentary intention. The rule of law is not the same as a rule that courts must always prevail, no matter what the statute says. I agree of course that in general the acts of the executive are, with limited exceptions, reviewable by courts, rather than vice versa. I agree that Parliament will not be taken to have empowered a member of the executive to override a decision of a court unless it has made such an intention explicit. I agree that courts are entitled to act on the basis that only the clearest

[23] Environmental Information Regulations 2004, SI 2004/3391.

[24] *R (Evans) v Attorney General*, [2015] UKSC 21, [2015] AC 1787.

[25] E Lees and E Shepherd, 'Morphological Analysis of Legal Ideology: Locating Interpretive Divergence' (2018) 10 *Journal of Property, Planning and Environmental Law* 5.

language will do this. In my view, however, Parliament has plainly shown such an intention in the present instance.[26]

In other words, the very underpinning of the possibility of judicial or quasi-judicial challenge to administrative action, ie the upholding of the principle of rule of law, is not itself an absolute. Rather, it is a contextual principle which is driven by the statutory provisions underlying the legal context. But there are limits to this. In this limit, we find the balance the Court strikes in terms of the power in this context. In the majority judgment, a desire to hold public authority to account was superior to the principle of sovereignty at all costs (given at least almost plausible ambiguity in parliamentary instructions). As Khushal Murkens explains: '[T]he UKSC emerges [in *Evans*] as "dialogical partner" and "public reasoner" that challenges the political branches to engage with its reasons and arguments based on certain community promises that have stood the test of time.'[27] Thus, where the institutional power structures come into conflict with the requirement of reasoned argument, reasoned argument, at least in this context, wins out.[28] It is indeed ironic that the Court, in this statutory context, felt so able to move beyond its 'inherent jurisdiction' in the form of judicial review, notwithstanding the fact that the *specific* statutory provisions did not appear, at least at first glance, to give the it the power to take on such a role. However controversial the decision in this case, it is significant in demonstrating how the core elements of what adjudication *is* can come into conflict. Power and reason do not always sit together comfortably.

Furthermore, the general emphasis on the power-conferring nature of the statutory provisions does not mean that discussions regarding the scope of jurisdiction will always be simplistic. The conferral of decision-making power is not an all-or-nothing process. The FTT in *Warren v Natural England*[29] (a case concerning the Regulatory Enforcement and Sanctions Act 2008 (RESA)) explains this tension in the context of civil sanctions relating to environmental harm.[30] In particular, the tribunal judge was anxious to examine their role as de novo but non-expert (comparatively speaking) decision-maker versus the initial and expert decision-making powers of Natural England (NE). Thus, the judge:

[N]ote[s] that the Tribunal is not required to undertake a reasonableness review of the Respondent's decision to serve the Stop Notice, but instead to decide whether it would

[26] *R (Evans) v Attorney General*, [2015] UKSC 21, [2015] AC 1787, [154].

[27] JE Khushal Murkens, 'Judicious Review: The Constitutional Practice of the UK Supreme Court' (2018) 77 *Cambridge Law Journal* 349, 366.

[28] We consider the importance of reasoned argument in adjudication in the next chapter.

[29] *Warren v Natural England* [2018] UKFTT NV_2018_0006 (GRC).

[30] The jurisdiction of the FTT (General Regulatory Chamber) requires some elaboration here. The RESA provisions establish an alternative, in effect, to criminal enforcement of certain environmental law norms. They allow the regulator to apply a range of civil sanctions to an offender, including fixed monetary penalties and enforcement undertakings. The decision to use the RESA sanctions – rather than to proceed to formal prosecution, or vice versa – is not susceptible of appeal, although it may be subject to judicial review. However, the Act establishes FTT competence to hear appeals in respect of the enforcement of some of the civil sanctions approaches.

> itself issue the Stop Notice on the evidence before it. The Tribunal has no supervisory jurisdiction.[31]

However, she also emphasises the 'primacy', in a sense, to be given to the initial decision of NE.[32] This attitude is mirrored in many instances where an adjudicator is required to take account of scientific information regarding conservation, as we see in chapter six.

The tribunal in this case also emphasised that there is no 'inherent jurisdiction'[33] vesting in the tribunal, in contrast to the courts. Recognition of this fact encouraged the tribunal to depart from a line of jurisprudence developed by the courts. Judge McKenna reasoned:

> I note that the line of authority to which I was referred may readily be distinguished on the basis that the judgments were given by courts able to rely on their inherent jurisdiction. By contrast, the Tribunal is a creature of statute and may not do that which Parliament has not given it an express power to do.[34]

This demonstrates that the focus on Parliament as the source of adjudicatory power is not limited to questions of jurisdiction, but also substantively affects the kinds of decisions, and the kinds of reasons, which the adjudicator in question feels legitimate in exploring. We see this pattern repeated in the discussion in chapter six in the contrast which exists in relation to handling of scientific information by de novo decision-making adjudicators, as opposed to the courts in their role in judicial review.

Significantly, the Upper Tribunal in *Warren*, whilst rejecting in very clear terms the FTT's approach to handling scientific information, did not find issue with Judge McKenna's assessment regarding jurisdiction. The subtlety of the division between the tribunal as adjudicator and NE as administrative body is captured in the Upper Tribunal's response to the question of whether the FTT was itself directly bound by the provisions of the Habitats Regulations. Judge K Markus QC reasoned that:

> Even though the First-tier Tribunal in a stop notice appeal stands in the shoes of the regulator and makes a fresh decision for itself, it is not suited to or even capable of carrying out a scientific assessment as envisaged by Article 6(3) and regulation 63.[35]

She emphasised the importance on maintaining a degree of separation between the role of adjudicator and regulator, even where the distinction in powers is a fine one:

> Natural England's submission mischaracterises the tribunal's role, which was to adjudicate on the dispute between the parties. It suffers from the same objections as in

[31] ibid [11].
[32] ibid [12].
[33] ibid [82].
[34] ibid [83].
[35] *Natural England v Warren* [2019] UKUT 300 (AAC), [64].

relation to 'competent authority', in confusing the role of the tribunal and that of the regulator.[36]

This focus on the legislatively assigned nature of the adjudicatory role is also emphasised in the decisions emerging from the FTT in relation to information requests under the EIR. Unlike in relation to RESA, there are large numbers of appeals to the FTT under these regulations. These actions themselves take the form of a review against the decision of the IC, herself an independent adjudicator.[37] The FTT acts not only as adjudicator, but also as a further appellate authority, albeit that they are given the power of de novo decision-making. The ways in which the tribunal expresses its approach to this task are telling and emphasise the point made by Kennedy above,[38] namely that whilst statutory provisions may express the limits of adjudicator power, it is in the hands of the adjudicator how they interpret the limitations on their own power. In this respect, in the FTT decisions, there emerges relatively early on in its jurisprudence a 'stock phrase' paragraph, appearing in the majority of FTT judgments, and explaining the jurisdiction of the tribunal.

> The Tribunal's remit is governed by section 58 FOIA, as incorporated by Regulation 18 EIR. This requires the Tribunal to consider whether the decision made by the Commissioner is in accordance with the law or whether he should have exercised any discretion he had differently. The Tribunal may receive evidence that was not before the Commissioner, and may make different findings of fact from the Commissioner.[39]

Whilst it is clear that the FTT in such cases has power vis-à-vis the IC *as adjudicator*, they also develop, as a result, power in relation to the 'original parties' (ie the public authority and the applicant) because they are in a position to ask for, rehear and reanalyse, evidence – and, as we explain in chapter seven, they are also in a position to *remake* the original decision. In this sense the degree of power over the parties is extensive.

It is also important to note that the FTT has, on a number of occasions, examined its own role by reference to the judicial review powers of the higher courts, and as a result attempts to articulate how its relationship with administrative decision-making bodies shifts as compared with a court undertaking judicial review. In this we see analysis of the principles of jurisdiction present in the two avenues, and the consequences of how power is constructed in these differing contexts. In both *Gaskin v Information Commissioner*[40] and *Leeds CC v Information Commissioner*,[41]

[36] ibid [75].

[37] Freedom of Information Act 2000, s 47.

[38] D Kennedy, 'The Stakes of Law, or Hale and Foucault' (1991) 15 *Legal Studies Forum* 327, 350.

[39] This particular citation comes from *Anthony Lavelle v IC* (Environmental Information Regulations 2004) [2011] UKFTT EA_2010_0169 (GRC), [23].

[40] *Susan Frances Gaskin v Information Commissioner* [2012] UKFTT EA_2011_0101 (GRC), [23]. For further steps in this litigation, see *Gaskin v Information Commissioner* [2018] UKFTT 2017_0147 (GRC); and *Gaskin v Information Commissioner* [2018] UKFTT 2018_0035 (GRC) (15 August 2018).

[41] *Leeds City Council v Information Commissioner* [2013] UKFTT EA_2012_0020 (GRC).

the FTT examines its role in respect of reasonableness assessments. In the former case, the Tribunal is clear that *Wednesbury* reasonableness is not a standard which it is mandated to apply. The Tribunal reasons that, '[i]n respect of the Appellant's final contention that the Commissioner's response and or Decision Notice is *Wednesbury* unreasonable, the Tribunal does not undertake judicial review'[42] and is therefore neither mandated nor indeed permitted to carry out a reasonableness assessment of the decision-making of the Commissioner (or the original public authority).

However, in the latter decision, the relationship between the Tribunal's powers and the standard-of-reasonableness review appears to be more nuanced. Whilst in that case the Tribunal's conclusion in respect of the level of charge imposed by the council for access to information meant that it was not necessary for them to reach a conclusion on the meaning of reasonableness, the FTT nevertheless highlighted that, 'the approach to be taken in respect of whether a charge was reasonable should be based on public law principles rather than an objective approach'.[43] The tribunal does not entirely eschew the approach taken to reasonableness to be found in public law generally, even though that reasonableness standard is calibrated to reflect a reviewing and supervisory jurisdiction, not a de novo jurisdiction. Thus whilst a judicial review court is governed clearly by these public law principles and the governing consideration of reasonableness, the FTT, despite its more 'lowly' status, is not (always), and that is directly a consequence of the nature of the statutory conferral of power.

This tension between recognition that an adjudicator is *not* a first-instance, primary decision-maker, and the desire to ensure 'correctness' in administrative decision-making, is most clearly demonstrated in the judicial review avenue. Here, the distinction between questions of fact and questions of law takes centre stage in a way that is not necessary in statutory appeals cases[44] (given the statutory circumscription of adjudicator power in such cases). In different ways, however, the distinction is relevant in relation to the other avenues, representing as it does the division of labour between judge and jury in criminal cases, for example.

Returning to judicial review, however, the meaning of the fact/law distinction is, referring back to Kennedy above,[45] not under the purview of the legislature. Rather, it is determined by the courts. Here we have a classic example of

[42] ibid [10].

[43] *Leeds City Council v Information Commissioner* [2013] UKFTT EA_2012_0020 (GRC), [101].

[44] The possible exception to this is the judicial jurisdiction under s 288 Town and Country Planning Act 1990, where the courts themselves have consciously drawn a parallel between their jurisdiction under this section and judicial review. In particular, in *Tesco Stores v Dundee City Council* [2012] UKSC 13, [2012] JPL 1078, it was held that the power to determine the meaning of policy is a question of law, and therefore under the auspices of the courts, whereas the power to determine whether a particular application *meets with* that policy is a question for the planning authority. In this specific context, therefore, there is a clear parallel drawn with judicial review. It is not a concern present in the other statutory appeals context, however, and does not 'dominate' questions of jurisdiction within that avenue to the same extent as it does in relation to judicial review.

[45] D Kennedy, 'The Stakes of Law, or Hale and Foucault' (1991) 15 *Legal Studies Forum* 327, 350.

an adjudicator self-defining the scope of their jurisdictional reach. This is particularly significant when the content of the test is examined. It is particularly unsatisfactory in an environmental context because of the rule that where a term is an 'ordinary' word of English language, the definition of a key term will be a question of fact (and therefore susceptible to a reasonableness assessment only), rather than a question of law.[46] Endicott comments on this approach to treating definitions as questions of fact:

> This is an unstable test – not because there is no such thing as ordinary words with ordinary meanings, but because ordinary words can be used in special senses, and the question can always arise whether that is what Parliament has done.[47]

When we look at environmental legislation and terms such as 'deposit', 'harm' and indeed even 'environment', whilst we can say that these terms are indeed ordinary words, the breadth of the 'penumbra' surrounding words such as these means that treating them as questions of fact is as much a grant of power to administrative bodies (and an abdication of responsibility by the adjudicator) as it is a decision regarding the appropriate meaning of key terms. Justifying such an approach on the basis of sovereignty is, therefore, a use of the constitutional principle to shape the power structures in play.

We noted above that the principle of sovereignty is much less important in the context of private law. This does not mean that it is irrelevant. Indeed, one of the most significant lines of cases in the tort of nuisance is concerned with the role of planning permission in private law.[48] We see the courts grappling with the conflict that has emerged between the governing concerns of private law and those of the administrative state. The courts attempt to navigate the conflict of power that comes from a clash between public decision-making in the context of a planning permission, and private rights. This plays out as consideration by the courts as to whether they have the ability to provide remedies in the context of a nuisance where the act constituting the nuisance has otherwise been authorised by a planning authority (or in the case of *Barr v Biffa Waste*,[49] by an environmental regulator). It is trite law that a statute can prevent an action from being a nuisance where it otherwise would be, but only where that action is an inevitable consequence of the statute (*Coventry v Lawrence*,[50] *Allen v Gulf Oil*[51]). The statute removes from a private law court the ability to strike the balance of give and take between neighbours, and in addition to shaping their mutual rights and obligations, therefore also has consequences for legitimate scope of the adjudicator's gaze. Sovereignty has a role to play in determining the power of an adjudicator

[46] E Lees, *Interpreting Environmental Offences* (Oxford, Hart Publishing, 2015).

[47] TAO Endicott, 'Questions of Law' (1998) 114 *LQR* 292, 299.

[48] See the lines of cases culminating in *Coventry (t/a RDC Promotions) v Lawrence* [2014] UKSC 13, [2014] AC 822.

[49] *Barr v Biffa Waste Services Ltd* [2012] EWCA Civ 312, [2013] QB 455.

[50] *Coventry (t/a RDC Promotions) v Lawrence* [2014] UKSC 13, [2014] AC 822.

[51] *Allen v Gulf Oil Refining Ltd* [1981] AC 1001 (HOL).

in the private law avenue, but its role in the balance of considerations to be taken into account is less potent. As the Court of Appeal emphasised in *Barr v Biffa Waste*:[52]

> The common law of nuisance has co-existed with statutory controls, albeit less sophisticated, since the 19th century. There is no principle that the common law should 'march with' a statutory scheme covering similar subject-matter. Short of express or implied statutory authority to commit a nuisance …, there is no basis, in principle or authority, for using such a statutory scheme to cut down private law rights.[53]

However, the scope of public decision-making to limit the jurisdiction of the courts is again in the hands of the adjudicator themselves, for it is they who decide whether the statutory authorisation necessitates that there be no action in nuisance. Furthermore, it is only in cases of statutory permissions that the courts will refuse to engage in the adjudication of the facts on the basis of nuisance. In cases involving planning permission, it is clear that the decision-making power of the planning authority does not extend to power over private rights and the parties will be able to defend these rights thanks to the confirmation of the courts in cases such as *Coventry v Lawrence* that the planning permission does not limit the scope of the tort of nuisance,[54] and therefore does not limit the reach of the courts.

In summary, this section has revealed a number of different elements of the power structures made concrete through the ability of an adjudicator to have jurisdiction in respect of a particular question. It has focused on the relationship between the adjudicator and the position of the parties to the disputes. We have shown, first, that the principle of sovereignty, so important above, has specific consequences for how adjudicators explain and reason about their own power in relation to parties to a dispute, but the ways in which sovereignty is invoked as a reason for or against adjudicatory power vary across the avenues. Second, it is clear that in respect of scope of jurisdiction, those limiting 'rules', such as ambiguity and the fact/law distinction, are themselves within the power of the adjudicator to decide. The analysis here has confirmed the argument of Kennedy above that a significant element of understanding how adjudication works is to recognise that the principles which shape its power are self-determined. To recognise the significance of these arguments, however, we must return to the purpose and role of adjudication in general.

C. Power Vis-à-Vis Other Adjudicators

This second dimension – ie the effect that constitutional principles in general, and the contextual factors generated through the avenues of adjudication, have

[52] *Barr v Biffa Waste Services Ltd* [2012] EWCA Civ 312, [2013] QB 455.
[53] ibid [46].
[54] *Coventry (t/a RDC Promotions) v Lawrence* [2014] UKSC 13, [2014] AC 822.

on the relationship between adjudicators within the different avenues – is also very important in charting the structures of power thus constructed. Here we examine not the jurisdictional reach an adjudicator has in respect of resolving the dispute between the parties themselves, but rather the reach they have when considering whether the decision of an earlier independent party is right or wrong, acceptable or unacceptable, immune from challenge or vulnerable to it. As is to be expected, the position is considerably more complicated than simply an assessment as to whether a decision can be appealed or not. Rather, it depends on complex relationship between different kinds of decision and different kinds of decision-maker.

This is amply demonstrated by the comments in *Adlard*.[55] The court emphasised that the power of any adjudicator in terms of adjudicator 'choice' is also first and foremost a reflection of a legislative allocation of power. It also means, as highlighted above, that which side of the very thin boundary line that exists here between adjudicator and administrator a decision falls on is primarily decided by Parliament:

> It was not the intention of Parliament that the function of the Secretary of State should be to make good any shortcomings in the process undertaken by the planning authority. Parliament intended that applications for planning permission would usually be dealt with at local level by local planning authorities; but that, exceptionally, they could be dealt with by the Secretary of State if he decided to call them in.[56]

In other words, Parliament characterises the Secretary of State (in the form of the Planning Inspector) as *primarily* an adjudicator, and only secondarily an administrative decision-maker, except where there has been a calling-in decision.

When referring to statutory appeals, the underpinning in statute means that Parliament becomes the ultimate arbiter as to the whereabouts of decision-making power amongst adjudicators. Nor can the parties themselves decide that they would prefer to bring their dispute before a different kind of forum. In this sense, in the 'realm' of statutory appeals, the ability of a claimant to bring an action inevitably becomes a question of Parliament as power-broker. This is amply demonstrated in the comments of Judge K Markus QC in *Warren*. In considering how to dispose of the appeal, the UTT considered whether it should itself remake the decision, and the make-up and statutory footing of both itself and the FTT influenced the Tribunal in limiting its own powers. In so doing, it examined the subtle differences between its role and that of the lower tribunal. Thus:

> I am clear that it is not appropriate for the Upper Tribunal to remake the decision. There will need to be a complete rehearing involving extensive expert and factual evidence. That is a task pre-eminently suited to the First-tier Tribunal rather than the Upper Tribunal. In the Upper Tribunal the case would be decided by a single judge with no

[55] *R (Adlard) v Secretary of State for Transport, Local Government and the Regions* [2002] EWHC 7 (Admin), [2002] 1 WLR 2515.

[56] ibid [49].

possibility of appointing a member with experience in environmental matters, unlike the position in the First-tier Tribunal. I consider that this case would benefit from the experience of such a member. Moreover, a party aggrieved by a decision of the Upper Tribunal would be subject to the much more limited right of appeal (see section 13(6) of the 2007 Act and the Appeal from the Upper Tribunal to the Court of Appeal Order 2008, SI 2008/2834) as compared to the right of appeal under section 11(1) from a decision of the First-tier Tribunal. In my view the Upper Tribunal should be cautious about taking on what is in essence a first instance decision-making function in the light of the consequence for the losing party's appeal rights.[57]

The statutory provisions, their relative assignment of tasks and the overall structures put in place to deal with disputes arising from the exercise of NE's authority to control activity on protected habitats sites influenced how the Upper Tribunal both viewed the powers of the adjudicator below it, but also the scope of its own powers.

The strongest elaboration of this principle can be found in *R (Great Yarmouth Port Co Ltd) v Marine Management Organisation*.[58]

A person aggrieved by an administrative decision cannot opt to bring judicial review proceedings rather than pursue a statutory appeal on a whim, or simply because he believes he can persuade a judge of this court that he or she will do as good a job in as short a time as the statutory appeal tribunal might do. That is not the test. Nor is it sufficient that the main, or only, issues to be determined in a particular challenge are legal. Such a person must persuade this court that there are exceptional circumstances that justify this court interfering with the statutory appeal procedure fixed as generally obligatory and exclusive by Parliament. Such circumstances may include cases in which the decision-maker has acted in obvious abuse of his power, or where a statutory appeal is in the circumstances clearly unsatisfactory. But I respectfully agree with those who have made this clear before: the cases in which such a test will be satisfied will be rare.[59]

Again, however, even where there is a specific legislative allocation of power, adjudicators are conscious of an implicit need to respect or at least to practically prioritise 'lower-tier' decision-making if only because of relative resources, time and the likely complexity of decisions which are successfully 'challenged' on more than one occasion. We see this in relation to the EIR. The degree to which the FTT will utilise its de novo and evidence-reviewing powers is telling. The FTT's willingness to undertake such decision-making is shaped by the fact that it is acting as appellate jurisdiction. As such, there is, clearly, on occasion, a feeling that the Information Commissioner should be undertaking the primary responsibilities associated with needing to make extensive findings of fact. Thus, per the FTT in *Andrew Plumb v Information Commissioner*:[60]

The Tribunal strongly recommends that the Commissioner take steps to ensure compliance, including an analysis of the disputed bundle as against the proposed application

[57] *Natural England v Warren* [2019] UKUT 300 (AAC), [189].
[58] *R (Great Yarmouth Port Co Ltd) v Marine Management Organisation* [2013] EWHC 3052 (Admin).
[59] ibid [56].
[60] *Andrew Plumb v Information Commissioner* [2011] UKFTT EA_2011_0067 (GRC).

> of exceptions and redactions. It should not fall to the Tribunal, essentially unassisted, to address whether a large bundle of documents falls outside of the terms of the appeal and ought properly already to have been disclosed.[61]

It is clear from this that the Tribunal, whilst comfortable with the scope of its decision-making power, does not regard itself as having been assigned the same role as the primary decision-maker.

Nevertheless, the importance of this fact-finding jurisdiction is highlighted when one considers again that this is really an appellate jurisdiction not from the primary decision-maker, but from a separate independent adjudicator who has already considered the issue at hand. In *Dunne v Information Commissioner*,[62] the FTT expresses that '[i]n our view the evident purpose of questioning the Commissioner's consideration … includes seeing whether the Commissioner arrived at the right answer'.[63] This is critically different from the approach taken by the higher courts in judicial review, and by the High Court in relation to its jurisdiction under the planning appeals process, as we explain shortly. The FTT in *Leeds City Council v Information Commissioner*[64] also highlights what role the rules relating to evidence play here, and what consequence a different fact finding may have:

> The Tribunal, having considered the evidence (and it is not bound by strict rules of evidence), may make different findings of fact from the Commissioner and it may consider that the Decision Notice is not in accordance with the law because of those different facts.[65]

However, that does not mean that the FTT is keen to overturn decisions of the Commissioner. Indeed, the evidence of *Rattray v Information Commissioner* suggests quite the reverse:

> We note with some consternation that our understanding of the statutory framework seems incompatible with the Commissioner's written case. … This divergence has caused us anxiously to examine our thinking afresh. Having done so, and with diffidence, we stand by it. We regret that we were not able to explore these matters with the parties face-to-face. The disadvantages of deciding disputes like this without an oral hearing have been commented upon at a higher level.[66]

The dismay shown here at departing from the decision of a previous adjudicator produces discussion very different in tone from that which we might see in respect of departures from decisions of local planning authorities, for example. The relationship between adjudicators, even where such adjudicators are very closely aligned with the administrative state, is different to that between public authority and adjudicator.

[61] ibid [16].
[62] *Richard P Dunne v Information Commissioner* [2013] UKFTT EA_2012_0257 (GRC).
[63] ibid [10].
[64] *Leeds City Council v Information Commissioner* [2013] UKFTT EA_2012_0020 (GRC).
[65] ibid [16].
[66] *Gavin Rattray v Information Commissioner* [2019] UKFTT 2018_0219 (GRC), [20].

Planning law is a hugely significant part of this discussion about relative adjudicator powers. In the following chapter we consider the degree of scrutiny that is brought to bear between the courts and Planning Inspectors. In many ways, this is a substantive question of the test being applied, not the logically prior question of jurisdiction. But if we examine the useful 'summarising' comments of the court in *Preston New Road Action Group*,[67] there is a very thin dividing line between jurisdiction and scrutiny. In this case, the court emphasises the division of labour between themselves and the planning decision-makers, particularly in terms of the content of policy. The judges effectively withdraw their lens entirely from the application of policy where it is clear that policy has been properly understood.[68] The significance of this is that Planning Inspectors, although adjudicators in our sense, are treated in many ways as both original decision-makers and *administrative* decision-makers, thus blurring the institutional lines and affecting the relationship between themselves and the courts.

> The court must remember that planning policies should not be construed as if they were provisions in a statute or a contract. … Its role here is limited. … It risks exceeding that role if it neglects the basic distinction between discerning the meaning of a planning policy – read in its 'proper context' and with common sense – and bringing public law principles to bear on the application of that policy in a planning decision. It must not step too far in interpreting policies written for planning decision-makers, in language intended to inform their exercise of planning judgment, not for judges considering the lawfulness of a planning decision when challenged.[69]

In respect of criminal law, it is useful to remember that in terms of adjudicator interaction, appellate authority rests in a limited number of directions. It is of course possible to appeal against a conviction, and these appeals tend to be conducted along familiar lines. In the context of our consideration about relative adjudicator power, therefore, the much more interesting discussion relates to appellate jurisdictions and sentencing. This is because the sentencing position in relation to environmental offences is heavily constrained by the Sentencing Council's Sentencing Guidelines, which are in effect binding statements of policy but couched in highly ambiguous terminology.[70] As a result, as was made clear in *Thames Water*, the task of an appellate court in relation to sentencing is not as simple as a de novo decision-making process.[71] Rather, as the Court of Appeal emphasised:

> The task of this court is to determine whether a sentence in any given case was manifestly excessive or wrong in principle. That task is not made easier if a judge fails to

[67] *Preston New Road Action Group v Secretary of State for Communities and Local Government* [2018] EWCA Civ 9, [[2018] Env LR 18.

[68] Similar comments can be made about the court's attitude to the Marine Management Organisation. See *Powell v The Marine Management Organisation* [2017] EWHC 1491 (Admin).

[69] *Preston New Road Action Group v Secretary of State for Communities and Local Government* [2018] EWCA Civ 9, [2018] Env LR 18, [14].

[70] Sentencing Council, 'Environmental Offences: Definitive Guideline' (London, HMSO, 2014).

[71] See also ch 7.II.D.

follow a structured approach to sentencing. Equally, such a failure does not invalidate the sentence.[72]

The determination of a sentence is treated here in the same way as the application of planning policy, and the power between adjudicators is determined by this complex interplay between the definition of policy as a legal question, the application of policy as a factual question and the levels of scrutiny applied.

Similar approaches apply within a private law appeal process. Although the higher courts are authorised to remake in its entirety the *legal* analysis of the situation, they are not authorised to reconsider the facts. This is partly a question of capability given that private law disputes will be heavily dependent upon facts. Therefore, it is critical for whoever is making a decision about the factual background to be able to see the evidence directly in front of them.

In summary, what this review reveals is that the relationship between adjudicators in environmental law is determined not only by official hierarchy in terms of routes of appeal, but also by a subtle range of rules relating to the interpretation of policy, questions of fact and law, deference to expertise, and legality. The operation of these rules is particularly significant in a context where the line between administration and adjudication is very fine, and the policies and rules in play are often vague, rely on subjective judgment and contain broad-brush statements of intention with little specificity as to method.

D. Conclusions

The purpose of this part of this chapter has been to demonstrate the landscape of power constructed around the seemingly simple question: who decides whether the actions of person A are acceptable or unacceptable in law? This is the question of jurisdiction. If we accept from the outset that *someone* within the institutional state is authorised to answer this question, then the issue as to who gets to decide becomes hugely significant. Different actors within this state have different pressures and concerns shaping the kinds of reasons which they take into account when answering this question; different kinds of powers for remedying it; and different powers to investigate and generate norms in providing an answer. Thus the identity of who will adjudicate a dispute is a critical first step.

In the environmental law landscape, the identities of the adjudicators which might possibly be called upon to resolve environmental law questions is vast – Planning Inspectors, the IC, the EA, NE, tribunals, the higher and lower courts – are all tasked in various places with applying environmental norms through the resolution of disputes. However, and most significantly, whilst Parliament has clearly had an enormous role in allocating up such decision-making power, the interpretation and real-world development of this allocation

[72] *R v Thames Water Utilities Ltd* [2019] EWCA Crim 1344, [22].

is left in the hands of the adjudicators themselves. This section has demonstrated (some of) the means by which they carry out this task of self-determination. First, they rely upon wider constitutional principles to provide a guide as to how they should reason about the scope of their own power. Second, they then look to the governing characteristics of the 'kind of law' they are doing (that is to say, the avenue of adjudication in which they find themselves). Finally, they will look at the specific rules of the case before them, but these rarely give concrete articulation of the precise boundaries of decision-making power.

IV. Powers of Evidence and Fact-Finding

Thinking only in terms of scope of jurisdiction is, however, to conceive too narrowly of how power is constructed in this legal landscape as discussed above. Once one delves into the range of actual questions which are answered through the dispute resolution process, it becomes clear that different *kinds* of decision-making authority produce different patterns of power within the avenues. Thus, beyond 'do I have the power to resolve the dispute between the parties?' an adjudicator will also ask themselves whether they have the power to make a determination of fact; to create and interpret new norms; and to hear the dispute in the first place from the particular claimant. In this section we consider this first question: can the adjudicator make a finding of fact, and how do they decide if they are so able?

In the chapter which follows, we consider how the courts in the different avenues are legitimised in reviewing and handling scientific and expert evidence,[73] but it is useful to highlight here that there is an intimate relationship between findings of fact as framing power; as seeking or rejecting of the possibility of a non-politicised 'correct' answer; and of confirming the purpose of adjudication in general. To put this another way, whilst the kinds of evidence which are seen as relevant to a dispute is obviously critical, the power to make a determination of the truthfulness of that evidence is equally significant. The decision-maker who controls findings of facts controls the framing of the dispute, and therefore directs the ways in which the law is applied to those facts.

It is often thought that a fact-finding process is 'neutral' in the sense that determining the state of facts in a case is not itself a substantive resolution of a dispute (see the discussion regarding 'truth' in evidence above).[74] Rather, the argument runs that dispute resolution occurs when the relevant norms are applied to the facts. However, in many cases, it is the resolution of factual issues that is the very heart of the dispute. In criminal law and in the 'run-of-the-mill' private law cases,

[73] ch 6.VI.
[74] ch 5.II.A.

it will be fact-based arguments that dominate the attention of the court. But in environmental law the position is enhanced by the fact that slightly different characterisations of factual evidence, particularly scientific evidence, will alter the balance of values at play in any dispute.

It is useful to commence this discussion with an analysis of what a fact-finding jurisdiction actually is. Intuitively, we know that a finding of fact is a decision made as to the state of play 'in the real world', as opposed to analysis of the meaning, scope or applicability of a legal rule. However, the boundary line between findings of fact and norm interpretation is not clear-cut. This plays out most clearly when we consider the limiting function that the fact/law distinction plays in relation to judicial review which we discussed above.[75]

In judicial review, the ability of the court to even hear evidence as to factual questions is very limited. Certainly, except in a very narrow class of cases it will not be possible for a claimant to bring new evidence before the court which was not available or put to the original decision-maker (in line with the principle that judicial review involves interrogation of the original decision, not the making of a new one).[76] A new factual position which emerges after the original decision is unlikely to be taken into account by the court. Furthermore, a judicial review court has very limited jurisdiction to *hear* expert evidence[77] (although it may of course consider the expert evidence as presented to the original decision-maker – something we explore in the next chapter).[78] The circumstances in which expert evidence is permitted in judicial review actions is limited, largely, to cases where a court requires expert evidence in order to understand the nature of the dispute. As Blundell explains, the judicial review process

> allows the admission of expert evidence if its purpose is, in a technical field, to explain a process and its significance where the same is in issue before the court. More fundamentally, the reason a court will admit such evidence is to enable it to perform its function. Its purpose is to assist the court by explaining matters within the expert's expertise, about a process or its significance, which the court needs to understand to reach a 'just' conclusion on the case.[79]

This approach to factual, and particularly expert, evidence in judicial review proceedings is confirmed by the Court of Appeal in *Mott*,[80] where it was made very clear that such litigation is not the place where conflicting expert evidence should be reviewed and interrogated. Rather, the original decision-maker is tasked with reviewing such evidence, and unless their conclusions on such were irrational

[75] ch 5.II.A.
[76] *R v Secretary of State for the Environment ex p Powis* [1981] 1 WLR 584.
[77] *R (Mott) v Environment Agency* [2016] EWCA Civ 564, [2016] 1 WLR 4338, [69]–[75].
[78] ch 6.VI.
[79] D Blundell, 'Of Evidence and Experts: Recent Developments in Fact-Finding and Expert Evidence in Judicial Review' (2018) 23 *Judicial Review* 243.
[80] *R (Mott) v Environment Agency* [2016] EWCA Civ 564, [2016] 1 WLR 4338.

or unreasonable in a *Wednesbury* sense, then the court will not further probe such evidence or the conclusions reached on the basis of it.

But this hands-off approach to evidence and fact-finding is not the norm for environmental adjudication. Even in cases involving the administrative state, where a statutory appeal is brought under, for example, the EIR, the adjudicator will be very willing to interrogate the factual position for themselves and to make factual assessments. This is of course very much the nature of judicial review, but it is significant that it is not the *public law* character of the dispute which dictates that evidence should not be reviewed by the adjudicator, but the particular characteristics of the judicial review avenue. Indeed, in the vast majority of both criminal and private law actions, and in a large proportion of statutory appeals without the planning process, adjudicators will be faced with the task of reviewing factual evidence to a greater or lesser extent.

An effective exercise of such power, however, demands the ability to make findings of fact which are reliable, and it is here that the adjudicator's attitude to and powers in respect of evidence become hugely significant. Whilst the judicial fora we consider are bound by the rules of evidence, and a criminal court will of course be bound by even more stringent rules, the other adjudicators are not so constrained, for good and for bad. For example, the FTT is not bound by the civil evidence rules, and is able therefore to take evidence from parties much more 'randomly'. This may help both sides, and certainly may avoid the need for costly and very time-consuming disclosure exercises, but it should be noted that these evidence rules have been developed without a clear purpose in mind. They are there to ensure that parties have a fair chance to openly contest the characterisation of the factual situation alleged by the other side. A lack of parity in this respect may speed up decision-making and make it less costly, but that does not mean that the process is necessarily improved.

Furthermore, if we look again at the power of the FTT in relation to both environmental information and civil sanctions, it is particularly interesting that the FTT is given this fact-finding role, given the nature of its adjudication processes (ie usually conducting hearings on the papers). The question of fact which the FTT is regularly required to decide in respect of environmental information is whether or not a public authority holds any information that falls under the scope of the request for information made by the individual concerned. This piece of factual information is likely to be within the knowledge only of the public authority itself. It might be supposed that the only way for an adjudicator to reach a conclusion on this question would be at the very least to see evidence from relevant individuals in person. However, very often the FTT will make its decision on paper, and must, as a result, essentially 'take the word' of the public authority (except where it is so manifestly unlikely that they would not hold such information that it can be inferred that the authority is not being entirely transparent). It seems strange, given this, that the FTT has been given the power to reconsider the facts, as it is not well equipped to make assessments in relation to these sorts of factual questions.

How this tension is managed by the FTT is demonstrated in *Cleminson v Information Commissioner*, where the FTT reasons:

> We have, in the course of making this decision, reviewed the evidence for ourselves. … We have reminded ourselves that the burden of proof in showing that the Information Commissioner's decision was wrong rests with the Appellant. In all the circumstances we are satisfied that the Commissioner correctly directed himself to the correct legal test and that it was reasonable for him to rely upon the evidence presented to him by the Council.[81]

The test therefore employed by the FTT here is a complex mixture of an assessment of the reasonableness of the Commissioner's 'faith' in evidence presented to her by the local authority, and a relook at the evidential basis for the decision, and the burden of proof, to produce a compromise between the ostensible jurisdiction of the FTT and its actual ability to review evidence in relation to factual questions.

We can contrast this approach to findings of fact with that of both the courts in relation to private law, and in relation to criminal law, where one of the most significant roles of the adjudicator is to make a determination as to the factual state of affairs and to reason accordingly. In order to undertake this task they are given the ability to interrogate the evidence given by witnesses in cross-examination. The trustworthiness of information is, for such an adjudicator, not a question of whether an earlier decision-maker was 'reasonable' upon relying on it.

In concluding this section on the resolution of factual questions, it is also critical to emphasise that as well as determining the relationship between the parties to the dispute, the boundaries as to how factual evidence can be handled, and the scope of the adjudicator's gaze in respect of facts, also shapes the relationship between adjudicators. We can consider this in cases where there is an appellate jurisdiction but one with powers to re-find actual evidence and to re-make decisions (as, for example, in relation to the FTT), and cases where there is no fact-finding jurisdiction in an appellate forum. This is the case for courts in general, not only in judicial review cases. Thus whilst we explained above that courts in private law and criminal law cases are centrally concerned with the resolution and clarification of the facts underpinning the dispute, this is not the case where a court is operating as an appellate forum. In such cases, unless there is a manifest error of law, given that the appellate court will not have had the benefit of hearing witnesses, of being party to any cross-examination, etc, they will be reluctant to undermine factual conclusions. This much is trite law when considering appellate courts, but when we look at the breadth of the field of environmental adjudication, it becomes an important determining factor in the shape of any appellate jurisdiction.

[81] *David Cleminson v Information Commissioner* [2012] UKFTT EA_2011_0192 (GRC), [21].

V. Power to Interpret Existing Rules and Create New Rules

As we move along the 'power spectrum' from the personal – in the form of instant dispute resolution – to the generalisable, we find the power to interpret existing rules in a manner that is binding upon, or relevant to, future adjudicators, either generally, or of specific types, and to create new rules. The process of interpretation and judicial 'legislation' is, of course, the subject of much analysis. Indeed, the prevailing approaches to interpretation of statutory provisions in the context of environmental law[82] – that of purposive or teleological interpretation, sitting alongside but in tension with an apparent fidelity to parliamentary intention as expressed through textual approaches to interpretation – are a hugely influential factor in the practical operation of environmental law rules. However, this section focuses not on the rules that govern interpretation per se, but rather on the adjudicator attitudes to such rules across the avenues, and to their own role in carrying out such interpretation.

It should also be emphasised, as we have highlighted so far throughout this work, that the process of interpretation and norm-creation is highly contextual. It is particularly significant that where a question of environmental law involves an EU law dimension, the jurisprudence of the CJEU means that a purposive approach to interpretation is adopted. This can be seen in a wide variety of contexts and has as its consequence a focus on environmental harm and its prevention in the process of interpretation. Interpretation across adjudicators in environmental law has a distinctive flavour compared with what we might find elsewhere. However, this does not mean that approaches to interpretation and norm creation are *homogenous*. Reliance on context implies variation. Even within avenues, we can see how the different attitude to interpretation questions can vary. Context becomes the driving force.

An excellent example of this contextual approach is to be found in the recent decision in *Boots v Severn Water*.[83] The case involved the question as to how different categorisations of water should be interpreted. The question was relevant because of the statutory powers accorded to Severn Water as a statutory undertaker, but also formed part of the contractual arrangement between Boots as a customer and the utility company. Interpretation of the relevant terms in this case involved interpretation both of statutory provisions and of contractual provisions. In this mixed context, the Court of Appeal looked primarily at the public law approach to statutory interpretation, rather than the private law approach to contractual interpretation, even though in part this was a contract law dispute.[84] This point about context and the blurriness at the edges of the avenues should be kept in mind through the following discussion as it is

[82] E Lees, *Interpreting Environmental Offences* (Oxford, Hart Publishing, 2015).
[83] *Boots v Severn Water* [2018] EWCA Civ 2795, [2019] 3 All ER 371.
[84] ibid [24].

here, more than anywhere else, that we see malleability in the power structures predominating in environmental adjudication.

Significantly, thanks to the purposive approach to which we referred above, we see a much greater attention on 'the environmental' than we do in relation to questions about jurisdiction and evidential powers. This makes sense given that interpretation of norms is a more 'substantive' question. Nevertheless, it should be noted that environmental considerations are driving not only the actual interpretation given to a norm, but also the perceived legitimacy in creativity in such interpretation. The fact that a case involves an environmental question affects the technique of interpretation as much as the outcome. This can be seen most clearly in the series of cases concerned with waste legislation.[85] However, there are limits to the degree to which the fact of a case being environmental will be relevant. In *Patersons of Greenoakhill Ltd v Revenue and Customs Commissioners* the court was required to interpret the word 'material' for the purposes of making assessment for landfill tax.[86] The process of interpretation largely involved focus on fidelity to the language, but also took account of the environmental context within which the decision was required to be made. As the court reasoned:

> As this is a taxing statute, it must be assumed that Parliament enacted a provision that would be certain at that point in time. If 'material' means the material in the form it may exist at any time, then it would be uncertain.[87]

However, the court emphasised that the central purpose of the statute, ie the reduction of waste, ought not to be determinative in this context. Purpose should take a back seat to statutory terminology in cases involving taxation. The precise effect of the rule for individuals was a more important consideration than the environmental outcomes. A traditionalist approach to interpretation was therefore adopted in this case.

However, this does not mean that the principles of statutory interpretation traditionally understood are the only relevant factors in evidence. Indeed, the environmental principles are clearly having a subtle but important role to play here. This can be seen in the reasoning of the Upper Tribunal in *Forager*,[88] a case concerned with the RESA sanctions. The Tribunal reasoned as follows:

> We consider that the expression 'serious harm' falls to be given its ordinary meaning. In deciding whether there is present a significant risk of serious harm it is plainly relevant

[85] See, amongst others, DEFRA, 'Guidance on the Legal Definition of Waste and its Application' (London, DEFRA, 2012) www.defra.gov.uk/publications/files/pb13813-waste-legal-def-guide.pdf, and Joined Cases C-418/97 and C-419/97 *ARCO Chemie Nederland Ltd v Minister van Volkshuisvesting, Ruimtelijke Ordening en Milieubeheer and Vereniging Dorpsbelang Hees, Stichting Werkgroep Weurt and Vereniging Stedelijk Leefmilieu Nijmegen v Directeur van de dienst Milieu en Water van de provincie Gelderland* [2000] ECR I-04475, [51] and [64]; C-206/88 and C-207/88 *Criminal proceedings against G Vessoso and G Zanetti* [1990] ECR I-01461, [12] and [13].

[86] *Patersons of Greenoakhill Ltd v Revenue and Customs Commissioners* [2016] EWCA Civ 1250, [2017] 1 WLR 1210.

[87] ibid [42].

[88] *Forager Limited v Natural England* [2015] UKFTT NV_2015_0002 (GRC).

> to have regard to the nature of the object which is contended would be so harmed. The greater the importance of the object (as recognised by both domestic and international legislative criteria) the greater will be the scope for applying the 'precautionary principle' in determining whether activities should be regarded as posing a material or significant risk of serious harm.[89]

The environmental principles changed the attitude of the adjudicator to the meaning of 'significance' in the statute. These principles will not always be of assistance, however. As *Powys CC v Price*[90] shows, in some cases adjudicators will conclude that the environmental principles cannot themselves be the subject of interpretation by the courts in appropriate cases. Thus:

> However, to my mind [the polluter pays principle] does not assist in determining the outcome of the present appeal. The principle is dependent on determining who is the polluter. If the transfer of liabilities under the 1994 Act and the 1996 Order is used to support a submission that Powys was the polluter, the argument based on the 'polluter pays principle' becomes circular. Furthermore, as the *Transco* case itself shows, the means selected by Parliament to give effect to this new regulatory regime when combined with provisions governing succession may give rise to gaps in the scheme of responsibility. However, as Lord Neuberger pointed out, at para 33, whether, and if so, in what circumstances and on what basis, it would be right to extend the concept of a polluter paying is a matter of policy for the legislature, not for the courts.[91]

Finally, if we consider the spectrum of forms of power an adjudicator may have, the ability to create new norms represents the furthest reach of adjudication as a social institution. Of course, all adjudication, in effect, creates a more or less generalisable rule. In some contexts though, the scope of jurisdictional power is so narrow that in effect no new substantive norms can be created. Furthermore, many adjudicators do not have power in terms of precedent to create norms which are formally binding on subsequent decision-makers (although of course they may be followed through the persuasive nature of the principle of consistency in general, or through the good sense and sound reasoning that any particular decision in fact represents). When we consider this aspect of adjudicator power, therefore, we must look beyond the formal expressions of precedent value and examine also the *practical* ability of an adjudicator to create new norms as well.

One of the main ways in which environmental adjudication experiences the creation of new norms is in adapting to modern environmental conditions and understandings. The common law jurisdictions which largely make up private law represent the most fertile ground for such development, given that there is no limitation on the conduct of the court in a governing statutory code. We can see this form of creativity in *Coventry v Lawrence*,[92] where the Supreme Court was

[89] ibid [109].
[90] *Powys CC v Price* [2017] EWCA Civ 1133, [2018] 1 WLR 1717.
[91] ibid [45].
[92] *Coventry (t/a RDC Promotions) v Lawrence* [2014] UKSC 13, [2014] AC 822.

willing to adapt its approach both to remedies in nuisance cases (as we discuss in chapter seven), but also to explore novelties in terms of the development of land law rights.[93] Here, the court was willing to entertain the possibility that an easement to create a noise could be created through prescription, thus acting, in effect, as a defence to nuisance in the form of long use. This was significant in the context of noise, since it had not previously been considered a possibility in the context of other noise nuisance cases. From an environmental perspective this is particularly important for wind farms. If long use can indeed provide a defence to future neighbour claims about noise, then this will provide a degree of insulation for wind farms against future challenge. In the words of Lord Neuberger:

> Given the property-based nature of nuisance, and given the undesirable practical consequences if the benefit and burden of the right to emit a noise would not run with the relevant land, it appears to me that both principle and policy favour the conclusion that a right to create what would otherwise be a nuisance by noise to land can be an easement.[94]

It is interesting to note here that it is the land-based element of the rights surrounding the tort of nuisance which prompts the development of the new rule, along with the public interest in allowing noise to emanate from one property to another. By focusing on the rights and obligations of the parties in a nuisance action, in the form of their proprietary interests, the court emphasises the fundamental underpinning of the new rule, and ties it to the purpose of adjudication in this context.

In this private law context, especially when dealing with Supreme Court judgments, we can clearly say that there is a high degree of norm-creating power. Even in this situation, however, there are limits, as can be seen in the famous decision of *Cambridge Water v Eastern Counties Leather*.[95] Here, Lord Goff highlighted that, in respect of the contamination of land by polluting substances, their Lordships did not feel able to fill what was a genuine lacuna in the law by judicial invention, but rather statutory action was required.

This sort of norm generation is relatively rare. There are few areas where there are genuine legal lacunae which need filling. However, interpretation of rules going beyond that which was previously understood, and most importantly, of policy, occurs regularly in the different avenues of environmental adjudication. This occurs in the planning law context. As *Tesco v Dundee*[96] makes clear, the *meaning* of policy is a question for the courts, not administrative authorities (being, a question of law). As a result the courts (in judicial review and statutory appeals) and the Planning Inspectors (in statutory appeals) effectively create new rules and engage in a policy-making exercise, through the determination of what policy as drafted means.

[93] See ch 7.II.C.
[94] *Coventry (t/a RDC Promotions) v Lawrence* [2014] UKSC 13, [2014] AC 822, [34].
[95] *Cambridge Water Co Ltd v Eastern Counties Leather Plc* [1994] 2 AC 264 (HOL).
[96] *Tesco Stores v Dundee City Council* [2012] UKSC 13, [2012] JPL 1078.

It is also critical to note, however, that even where there is no formal precedential value in a decision, the goal of consistency in decision-making will always act as a reason to follow a previous decision, even if there are stronger, countervailing reasons to depart from it. We can see this in the recent planning decision in *Baroness Newick of Cumberlege v DLA Delivery*[97] in which the Court of Appeal emphasised the importance of consistency in decision-making. In this case, the Secretary of State had failed to take account of his own earlier decision in reaching a planning conclusion, and as such, both the High Court and the Court of Appeal concluded that his decision should be quashed given the central importance of consistency. As a result, whilst the Secretary of State did not himself have the power to create rules binding upon himself, the value of deciding like cases alike is so inherent in a system of law that the courts demanded that he indeed take account of his own decision, even if he was not bound to follow it if there were strong countervailing reasons that could distinguish the situation at hand from the one in which he made his earlier decision.

In the words of the court:

> First, because consistency in planning decision-making is important, there will be cases in which it would be unreasonable for the Secretary of State not to have regard to a previous appeal decision bearing on the issues in the appeal he is considering. … Secondly, the court should not attempt to prescribe or limit the circumstances in which a previous decision can be a material consideration. It may be material, for example, because it relates to the same site, or to the same or a similar form of development on another site to which the same policy of the development plan relates, or to the interpretation or application of a particular policy common to both cases. … Thirdly, the circumstances in which it can be unreasonable for the Secretary of State to fail to take into account a previous appeal decision that has not been brought to his notice by one of the parties will vary. But in tackling this question, it will be necessary for the court to consider whether the Secretary of State was actually aware, or ought to have been aware, of the previous decision and its significance for the appeal now being determined.[98]

In this, therefore, there is a combination of the importance of rule of law values as understood by the courts (consistency, and equality before the judge), and of deference where appropriate, combining to produce a subtle explanation of how and when the Secretary of State has to take account of his earlier decision.

To wrap up this discussion, it is apparent that there are four factors influencing when and how adjudicators feel able to change/interpret legal norms in this way. First, of course, is the existing state of the law and the presence or absence of any real lacunae in the law. Second, there is the degree to which they feel mandated to respond to the intention of Parliament on the one hand, and the purpose of the legislation on the other. Third, the significance of any potential environmental

[97] *DLA Delivery Ltd v Baroness Cumberlege of Newick* [2018] EWCA Civ 1305, [2018] Env LR 34.
[98] ibid [34].

harm, and the public interest in preventing that, will also be a powerful force shaping adjudicator approaches. Finally, the wider legal context within which each adjudicator operates, especially regarding their power vis-à-vis other adjudicators, and the expected norms of behaviour relevant to each avenue, will also limit their freedom to innovate in this respect.

VI. Power to Confer and Deny Access

The final element in respect of the power-brokering aspect of the avenues comes in the form of limitations and authorisations of access to the forum in the first place. In a sense, this is the most fundamental of all adjudicator powers. It involves denying the parties the ability to have their dispute resolved by the institutional forum. It is also important to emphasise that the conferral of standing on an individual is also a conferral of power on them. The decision as to whether or not the decision is challenged moves from the adjudicator deciding whether or not to hear the dispute, to the claimant in deciding whether to bring it. In the standing rules, therefore, a relationship is created between the parties and the adjudicator, as in the case where there is no standing, there is only a relationship between the parties.

Having the ability to challenge a decision is itself a form of power. In some avenues this power is widely distributed. In judicial review, in the context of environmental law at least, the standing rules are very wide as we discussed in the previous chapter.[99] By contrast, the ability to sue in nuisance is limited to those with proprietary interest in the relevant land.[100] As well as having significant implications for the degree to which the nuisance rules are able to achieve environmental justice,[101] the limitation on access removes power for those without such property rights, and confers a sort of double power onto those with such rights. They have the power, on the one hand, through their action in front of an adjudicator to attempt to bring a nuisance action to an end. On the other, they are able, by voluntary inaction, to allow the infliction of a third party nuisance on those in a subsidiary relationship with them in respect of the affected land, such as a residential licensee. Whilst standing is often seen as a question of access to justice, it should also be seen as a critical element in determining the locus of decision-making power. It is therefore useful to conclude this chapter with some analysis of the attitude of adjudicators in environmental law to the self-determination of the scope of their own jurisdiction as mediated through the lens of standing.

[99] ch 4.IV.

[100] *Hunter v Canary Wharf Ltd* [1997] AC 655 (HOL). See also the discussion in the previous chapter.

[101] S Porter, 'Do the Rules of Private Nuisance Breach the Principles of Environmental Justice?' (2019) 21 *Environmental Law Review* 21.

We can see situations where courts are required to determine for themselves the boundary lines between different avenues in deciding an individual case, boundary lines that are hugely influential in determining outcome. This often occurs through the process of determining standing. A good example of this is the recent decision in *Environment Agency v Tapecrown*.[102] The court was required to answer, as a preliminary issue, whether it was competent to hear a proposed appeal in relation to a criminal sanction sitting as the Court of Appeal Criminal Division, or whether the correct avenue of challenge was for the court to sit as the High Court and hear the case as judicial review.[103] This mattered in part because of the actual identity of the judges, but it also made a huge difference as to the sorts of considerations that the court could take into account in adjudicating on the correctness of the earlier decision. It depended upon the rules of standing.

In the environmental context, we are also seeing a very significant development, and that is environmentally motivated changes to standing rules in specific cases to liberalise the rules which govern when an action can be brought. This influence is shown clearly in the recent decision in *R (ClientEarth) v Secretary of State for Food, Environment and Rural Affairs*.[104] In this case, the Court drew a clear link between the rules of standing, and its own power to exercise supervision over the longer term in respect of a specific administrative failure. Per the Court:

> It seems to me that the time has come for the Court to consider exercising a more flexible supervisory jurisdiction in this case than is commonplace. Such an application was made to me when the November 2016 judgment was handed down. I refused it on that occasion, opting for a more conventional form of order. Given present circumstances, however, I would invite submissions from all parties, both in writing and orally, as to whether it would be appropriate for the Court to grant a continuing liberty to apply, so that the Claimant can bring the matter back before the court, in the present proceedings, if there is evidence that either Defendant is falling short in its compliance with the terms of the order of the Court.[105]

The Court confers on the applicant here the privilege of being able to bring an action more 'easily' than would be normal given the specific kind of administrative failure and the ongoing need for supervision. In part this was clearly motivation by the significant harm being caused by air pollution, and the continued failures of the UK government to deal satisfactorily with the issue.

[102] *R (Environment Agency) v Tapecrown* [2018] EWCA Crim 1345, [2019] 1 WLR 3394.

[103] In relation to a different question, in this case the relationship between the statutory compensation scheme in the Water Resources Act 1991 and the tort of negligence, the Court had to decide whether it had jurisdiction or whether the case was appropriately for the tribunal system. Here both the purpose and the language of the statutory scheme was taken into account by the Court. See *Hall v Environment Agency* [2017] EWHC 1309 (TCC), [2018] 1 WLR 1433.

[104] *R (ClientEarth) v Secretary of State for Food, Environment and Rural Affairs (No 3)* [2018] EWHC 398 (Admin).

[105] ibid [109].

As a result, in each of these examples, it is clear how innovation in respect of standing rules consequent upon the environmental context sits in balance against the normal processes present in the relevant avenue of complaint. Whilst the Aarhus Convention in particular may prompt shifts in these rules, as explained in chapter four,[106] that is not enough to dislodge the starting points present in the avenues.[107] In statutory appeals, what matters is the text of the statute in authorising complaint; for judicial review, to a greater or lesser extent a genuine and legitimate interest must be present; for private law, violation of rights is required; and in criminal law, only specifically authorised persons can engage with adjudicatory processes. None of these rules are dislodged by wider concerns about improving the state of the environment, in part, through access to justice.

VII. Conclusions

This chapter has emphasised that in understanding how environmental adjudication works, one of the most critical issues to determine are the power structures which have been established by the 'division of labour' in decision-making through the avenues of adjudication. These power structures are at once about identity – who has the power to decide – and about substance – what do they have the power to decide about. The purpose of this chapter has been to chart some of the fault lines in these power structures across the field of environmental adjudication, and to explain how adjudicators reason about their own power in these different contexts. Whilst the law underpinning these power structures is very often familiar and so well known to almost go without saying (especially in relation to judicial review), it is nevertheless useful to look at the landscape of environmental adjudication as a whole to see where these power boundaries are drawn across different contexts. It is part of our argument that this landscape is not a comprehensively coherent one (see chapter eight), and in order to fully comprehend and understand how this incoherence operates in practice, it is necessary to see how the power over decision-making flows around the adjudicatory landscape.

What do these findings about the networks of power built up in environmental adjudication tell us about the nature of environmental adjudication in general, and what concerns do they raise? As we explained in chapter two, environmental law is an unusual field in that it engages a very wide range of adjudicatory options (as a result of existing across and within existing legal structures, as well as developing its own bespoke rules). By charting how constitutional principles

[106] ch 4.IV.

[107] UNECE Convention on Access to Information, Public Participation in Decision-Making and Access to Justice in Environmental Matters (Aarhus, 28 June 1998) 2161 UNTS 447; 38 ILM 517 (1999), in force 30 October 2001.

shape power allocation across these fields, we begin to see the landscape of environmental adjudication not descriptively, but analytically, as a landscape formed of power structures. These structures are constructed around four primary blocks: jurisdiction, fact-finding, access to adjudicatory fora, and the power to interpret and create new rules.

We have revealed that there are two primary driving forces in the creation of this landscape. The first force at work is the tension and balance maintained and manipulated between constitutional principles in general, the avenues as power-brokers, and individual norms created within highly specific contexts. The second is the fact that power within this field is for the most part self-determined, certainly at the margins, ie where there is some doubt. Whilst the broad structures might be created by statute, the precise calibrations within each avenue are a matter for the interpretive approaches of the adjudicators themselves. The high degree of self-determination, both in the acquisition of power, and in the abandonment of that power to another actor within the system, is amply demonstrated within this chapter, and it applies across avenues, even in cases of a high degree of statutory intervention.

It is this second force, therefore, which prompts consideration of the qualification of the adjudicator and the importance of that adjudicator to pay attention to concerns about their own quality, expertise, and critically, independence. That this is a significant question raised by the analysis in this chapter is emphasised when we remember the definition of adjudication outlined in chapter two. We focused on independence as a defining characteristic of adjudication, and the fact of needing to determine one's own power brings this characteristic to the fore. Redish and Marshall explain why this is so important:

> However, neither court nor commentator has paid sufficient attention to the primacy of adjudicatory independence in the due process infrastructure. In fact, the need for adjudicatory independence grows as the modern realist scepticism about the possibility of truly neutral principles of adjudication increases. In the absence of such principles, the role of the adjudicator in assuring fairness to the litigants becomes critical. Because of the special importance of the participation of an independent adjudicator and the difficulties inherent in assuring that independence on a case-by-case basis, the independence of the adjudicator must be protected through formalized, prophylactic protections.[108]

In other words, because there is so much that is subjective to the assessment of the adjudicator, particularly in terms of the reach of their own power, it is essential that the adjudicator is independent not only of the parties, but of the structures which they are judging more generally. When we move into the next chapter, a complicated picture of independence and subjectivity in reasoning emerges, and the discussion in this chapter adds to the scrutiny which we bring

[108] MH Redish and LC Marshall, 'Adjudicatory Independence and the Values of Procedural Due Process' (1986) 95 *Yale Law Journal* 455, 457.

to this point. In a previous article, one of us has argued that it is necessary to consider, 'openly … how these constitutional controls operate together that we can build up a clear, considered and coherent approach to … decision-making power'.[109] The discussion in this chapter has attempted to do just this, but what becomes apparent, as we explain in chapter eight, is that coherence as a single unified explanation of power across the landscape is not possible. Rather, the consideration of power here reveals the truly important questions: first, what is the content of the three pillars of the adjudication process – general, avenue, specific; second, what attitude does the adjudicator take to the definition of her own power; and third, is the adjudicator independent in making that assessment? This is a more important series of questions, according to our argument here, than the question of whether the overall picture of adjudication is 'coherent'.

[109] E Lees, 'Allocation of Decision-Making Power under the Habitats Directive' (2016) 28 *Journal of Environmental Law* 191, 219.

6

Avenues as Frames of Reasoning

I. Introduction

The previous chapter explored the power structures put in place through the avenues of environmental adjudication. It examined how the balance of power within each of these avenues has been produced, and how the different legal contexts shape how adjudicators conceive of, and reason about, their own power to decide. These power structures are significant in constructing adjudicator responses to the particular challenges to which environmental litigation gives rise. Furthermore, we considered what the self-determination of the scope of decision-making power means for the purpose of adjudication. Thus, the identity of the decision-maker, and their relationship with other parties in the process, are critical to the overall shape of the adjudicatory system put in place. However, these are not the only critical elements in the development of such systems. Since adjudication as a social institution is characterised by reasoned argumentation and proof,[1] what constitutes a sufficient degree of reason, sufficient proof and legitimate argumentation are central to outcome. Partly such outcomes will be a consequence of the specific substantive rules in place. But, as we shall see, the avenues of adjudication also contribute to the ways in which different reasons are handled and expressed.

For certain kinds of adjudicator, only certain kinds of reasoned arguments will be acceptable. Some forms of reasoned argument will be especially persuasive. It is not only in terms of how adjudicators conceive the scope of their powers, and their relationship with the parties, other adjudicators and the wider administrative state, that the avenues of adjudication have an important contextualising role. They also operate so as to constrain and shape the kinds of reasoning which are said to be acceptable on the one hand, and influential or powerful on the other. The purpose of this chapter is to chart the ways in which the avenues and their defining characteristics shape the substance of such arguments.

Through this interaction, the purpose of adjudication, and the substance of the norms used to resolve the dispute, become closely aligned. A picture emerges whereby the distinction between the neutral but non-expert arbiter on the one hand, and the expert but quasi-administrative decision-maker on the other, manifests

[1] See ch 1.II.C.

in the characteristics of reasoning with different legal contexts. Two conclusions become apparent. First, the acceptability of 'a reason' is as much a question of the level of scrutiny an adjudicator will engage in as it is about the inherent quality of the argument. An argument may be relevant and correct, but that does not mean that it will determine the outcome of a dispute. This is a significant conclusion when we move to consider the coherence and purpose of adjudication in chapter eight. Second, as different reasons and techniques of reasoning are acceptable only within certain of the avenues, the avenues themselves act as framing devices for the way in which a dispute must proceed. The legal 'solution' to a problem is determined first and foremost by the route by which an action is brought. Again, this poses significant questions for the coherence of adjudication.

In section II we begin, as we did in the previous chapter, with analysis of the fundamental building blocks of our argument. We define the forms of reasoning by consideration of the types of reasons that are relevant, and the processes by which those reasons are assessed. Specifically, section II considers (a) the 'reasons' taken into account in adjudication in environmental law – public and private interest, and the environment itself; and (b) the techniques or modes of reasoning by which such reasons are processed through decision-making – scrutiny, expertise and objectivity. In section III we examine the relevance of public and private interest within the avenues. Section IV explores how 'the environment' is taken into account. Section V, moving to explore the techniques of reasoning, considers the levels of scrutiny brought to bear in resolving environmental disputes. Section VI considers how scientific information is handled within the different avenues, and in particular this section demonstrates that the judicial review paradigm of non-intervention in respect of expert analysis of technical information is not mirrored in the other avenues. Section VII analyses the relevance of subjective assessment on behalf of the adjudicator and how the boundary line between subjectivity and expertise is constructed and maintained. Finally, section VIII concludes with some preliminary suggestions about the consequences of our conclusions for the purposes of adjudication, a theme we take up again in chapter eight.

In short, the previous chapter explained the identity of decision-makers – who gets to decide – and the substantive of limits of their decision-making power – what do they get to decide about. This chapter considers what kinds of reasons can be taken into account when the decisions are made. If the analysis of the avenues as power-broker explored the formal constitutional role of different adjudicators, this chapter examines the substance of that role.

II. Forms of Reasoning

Just as the matrix of power in the previous chapter was constructed of different building blocks, so too here we find a connected web of reasons which may be relevant to the disposal of a dispute concerning environmental matters. These are (very broadly) private interest, public interest and the environment itself.

Discerning how these are constructed in any one context as part of a decision made by an adjudicator is a matter of exploring intensity of scrutiny, objectivity or subjectivity as to the prevailing values, and scientific and other expert information. The former three concerns are a matter of reasons for action, and the latter three represent questions of technique in developing reasons.

In understanding our findings across the avenues in these respects, it is important to keep in mind what we said about the environment in chapter two, ie that decision-making about environmental questions inevitably often, if not always, involves the balancing of different values, and therefore of a high degree of discretion for decision-makers. In the context of adjudication, what this chapter will demonstrate is that discretion contains 'legitimate' and 'illegitimate' elements in the different avenues, and that the balancing of the relevant values and information must be carried out using different techniques, or different combinations of techniques. We show this by examining these reasons and techniques in turn.

As a starting point, by 'legal reasoning', we mean the phenomenon by which an adjudicator processes the variety of arguments for, or against, a resolution to a dispute; discards some as irrelevant; maintains and balances others as relevant; or concludes one is determinative. In this mix will be statutory norms, case-law precedent and other considerations that prove relevant on the particular facts. In picking through these different elements, given the common-law nature of the system, previous judicial decisions are critical not only where there is no statutory provision in play, but also as a guide to how provisions should be interpreted and applied. How such precedent is treated is obviously significant. As Rigoni analyses, there are a number of different ways in which precedent is addressed:

> It can strengthen a judge's belief that the case should be decided one way. That is, a judge may (i) think that, ignoring past decisions, the plaintiff should prevail and (ii) ultimately decide for the plaintiff after this conviction is strengthened by reviewing past decisions. It can also determine how a judge decides a case that she would not otherwise know how to decide. For example, a judge may have no idea whether she should decide the case for one party rather than the other until she consults precedent. Additionally, precedent can constrain the reasons for an outcome in addition to the outcome itself. For example, a judge can (i) think that, ignoring past decisions, a case should be decided for one party on the basis of certain reasons and (ii) ultimately decide for that party but give different reasons because of the way a past case or cases were decided. Finally, precedent can constrain a judge to reach a decision when she would otherwise rule to the contrary. For example, a judge can (i) think that, in absence of precedent, a case should be decided for one party and (ii) decide the case for the other party because of the way in which a previous case or cases were decided.[2]

In considering how adjudicators reason, the role of precedent is therefore first and foremost. However, what is clear, and what we attempt to bring out in this chapter, is that often precedent does not constrain the actual outcome in many cases in this area of high levels of discretion. Rather, since both the rules of precedent, and the

[2] A Rigoni, 'Common-Law Judicial Reasoning and Analogy' (2014) 20 *Legal Theory* 133, 134.

relevance of those rules in any particular case are self-determined (as discussed in chapter four), precedent tends to be most important in making reasons or techniques of reasoning critical or inappropriate to the resolution of a dispute. We do not ignore the force of precedent here, or indeed that of statute. Rather, we examine where precedent has taken different adjudicators in terms of their approach to reasoning. Our inquiry is *not* into the substantive environmental rules developed, but into the norms of adjudication which thereby emerge.

Furthermore, we also recognise that the driving forces behind systems of precedent, ie consistency and equality, are not the only powerful forces at play in environmental adjudication. It is important to emphasise that '[r]easoning also involves our capacities for thought and judgment, and concerns the justifications we offer for our choices'.[3] We therefore highlight the importance of the study of reasons within the adjudicatory process, echoing the emphasis of Chapman:

> [A] legal decision is meant to be more than just an administrative decision about some particular case. Rather, the judgment of an appellate court is typically stated in general terms, and its authority is intended to extend beyond the confines of its own particular facts to other like cases. This more extended claim to authority will be significantly affected by the quality of the reasons provided in support.[4]

These reasons become elements of the generalisable rules which are so central to the outcome of adjudication. Let us now define these categories of reason.

A. Reasons

Figure 6.1 Matrix of Decision-making considerations

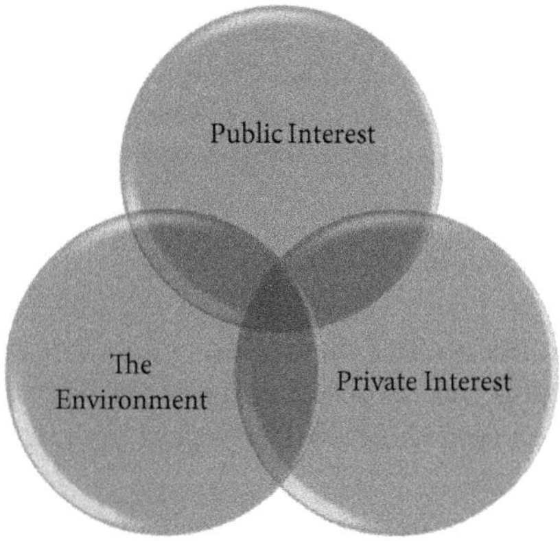

Figure 6.1 represents the matrix of decision-making considerations which are taken into account in resolving disputes in an environmental context.

[3] B Chapman, 'The Rational and the Reasonable: Social Choice Theory and Adjudication' (1994) 61 *University of Chicago Law Review* 41, 42.
[4] ibid 43.

i. Public and Private Interest

We commence our discussion with exploration of public and private interests. It might be said that consideration of environmental factors should fall within this discussion. However, as we show 'environmental considerations' as a category of reason bring their own significance within the structures of environmental adjudication beyond merely that of the public (or indeed, private) interest as a whole. Thus, we discuss them separately below. Furthermore, as Figure 6.1 demonstrates, there is a degree of overlap between these categories. That does not prevent us distinguishing them to an extent. A distinction between public and private interest is merely a starting point in thinking about the avenues as reasoning limiting, rather than a claim that such a distinction can exist in binary form in practice.

By private interest, we mean an individualised motivation for seeking to resolve a dispute in a particular direction, where that motivation is grounded in the personal preference, wealth or rights of the individuals concerned. We can contrast this with public interest. The action need not be altruistic in the sense that there is no private benefit to the resolution of a dispute in a particular direction, but the benefited parties must extend beyond the instant disputants. Public and private interests, clearly, by these definitions, exist on a spectrum. But which forms of consideration are emphasised in any one avenue gives a clear insight into the role of adjudication.

Before we explore these considerations in detail, as they play out in the decisions of the relevant adjudicators, it is important to acknowledge that public and private interest, as well as existing on a spectrum, are also closely intertwined. Depending upon one's perspective, the private and the public become interchangeable. A starting point here is Sunstein's argument:

> Regulated entities are themselves the beneficiaries of statutory limits on agency power – and of the common law insofar as those sources of law protect them from public or private incursions into their legally created spheres. The beneficiaries are the objects of regulation insofar as positive law authorizes such intrusions and affords them less protection from private conduct than they would like.[5]

The distinction between public and private presupposes where rights have been conferred by the state on private individuals in the first place. The fact of regulation creates zones of liberty and prohibited action in the same way as private rights. Private rights alter our understanding of regulation, and vice versa. The distinction between the two is therefore contingent upon the content of the law as it stands, and is not absolute.

Furthermore, there are essentially three forms of private interest in effective maintenance of the public interest. First, there is a general consideration, especially in relation to public goods, that a private individual may seek to defend the

[5] CR Sunstein, 'Standing and the Privatization of Public Law' (1988) *Columbia Law Review* 1446, 1447.

quality of air, the cleanliness of water and the accessibility of natural landscape *in general*, but as a member of the public collective they are an individual beneficiary of any successful outcome.

Second, a person may have a private interest in the resolution of a dispute in a particular way – because, for example, any administrative failure would result in the destruction of a landscape feature critical to their favourite leisure activity. This private interest (which is not rights-based) only emerges as a point of concern because of the failure of the administration to properly comply with its own legislative requirements. The public interest lies in the maintenance of legality within the administrative state. If that legality is maintained, then the claimant happens to be affected privately although there is no impact on their rights and obligations. If there is no public interest failure in the form of illegality, then a private setback to interests will also not come into being. The private benefit provides motivation for action but may not be legally relevant. In almost all cases of administrative action, any failure to comply with legal requirements is likely, in some more or less predictable or known ways, to affect the private interests of individuals. In that sense there will always be private interest in upholding public standards of good governance, but that does not necessarily mean that the case is one involving private interest concerns. Much, in such cases, will depend upon the identity of the claimant and the proximity between themselves and the administrative act.

Finally, there is an attenuated private interest in the maintenance of legality in the administrative state arising from the precedent values of rules. Where an individual is not directly concerned that public authority decide questions of planning permission in a particular way, they are nevertheless desirous that this planning authority act in a lawful way and be accountable as a means of protecting themselves against arbitrariness or illegality in future decisions. In this we see a link with Honoré's explanation of the legitimacy of legal obligation in the maintenance of group structures.[6] As part and parcel of the legal community both protected and constrained by the planning regime in a particular area, each individual has a legitimate interest in the maintenance of that order for the protection of the interests of the group as a whole. There is a private interest in ensuring accountability in public decision-making, but that does not mean that a challenge is done on the basis of private interest. As a result, when we explore the public and private interest distinction in this section, again we do so cognisant of the blurring between the two concepts and we do not claim that the two can be entirely separated.

It is also important to note that the distinction is itself an invention of politics. As Horwitz explains, the distinction between the two is as much a creation of the law as it is a driver behind its development. He explains the 19th-century origins (in America) of the distinction, and the goal behind a desire to 'insulate' a set of private concerns behind the wall of private law

[6] T Honoré, 'Groups, Laws and Obedience' in *Making Law Bind* (Oxford, Oxford University Press, 1987).

> Above all was the effort of orthodox judges and jurists to create a legal science that would sharply separate law from politics. By creating a neutral and apolitical system of legal doctrine and legal reasoning free from what was thought to be the dangerous and unstable redistributive tendencies of democratic politics, legal thinkers hoped to temper the problem of 'tyranny of the majority'.[7]

This is not the place to engage with a lengthy discussion of the 'hidden politics' of framing questions as being about private rather than public interests, but keeping this in mind is useful as we begin to explore the kinds of reasoning employed in the different avenues, and in particular how private interests are conceived and expressed in these contexts.

Finally, it is important to emphasise that there is a very significant distinction here between public and private interests, on the one hand, and public and private law on the other. Public law engages both forms of interest, as does private law. The idea that there are 'specifically private law reasons, something which systematically releases us from the tyranny of seeking out extra-legal reasons for private law decisions'[8] in a field as political as environmental law, is false. Any decision, whether public or private law, will, to a greater or lesser extent, engage with both kinds of interest. The question is how these are explained, what weight they carry and where they have influence in the decision-making processes characterising adjudication. There is a symbiosis, however. As Sunstein explains:

> Once public-law plaintiffs are authorized to appear in court, they do not argue that the government has breached a duty owed to them – at least not in the common-law sense – but instead that the government has behaved unlawfully.[9]

The adjudicator of *legality* of action carries out a different role than does the adjudicator of breach of rights. As we see in the next chapter, which role is being prioritised also has a significant impact upon the remedies awarded. Focus on legality or rights-infringements as priority considerations shapes the power of the adjudicator to decide (through standing rules – see chapter four), but it also has a profound influence on the kinds of consideration which are relevant for the court, and which form the right 'kind' of reasons to be taken into account. Private law, in prioritising certain forms of reasoning, thereby engages with public and private interests in a different way than does public law.

ii. The Environment Itself

The third type of reason we explore here is discussion of 'the environment itself'. When we talk about the environment itself, it is possible to reason about this in two different ways. The first is to say that we really mean that aspect of both public

[7] MJ Horwitz, 'The History of the Public/Private Distinction' (1982) 130 *University of Pennsylvania Law Review* 1423, 1424.

[8] J Gardner, 'The Purity and Priority of Private Law' (1996) 46 *University of Toronto Law Journal* 459, 462.

[9] Sunstein, 'Standing and the Privatization of Public Law', 1446.

and private interest which is categorised by a connection with the natural world for its own sake, or for instrumental values such as recreation and biodiversity services. On this conception, environmental interests cross-cut within both public and private interests. The second way is to reason from the perspective that the environment *itself* has interests or possibly on some conceptions rights which are protectable in and of themselves.[10] This later approach does not represent the prevailing wisdom of the English and Welsh legal system.

However, when we think about the environment as a factor in decision-making, there is a tension between cases where protection of the environment sits on one hand, and public and private interests sit on the other (eg job creation, housing supply, upholding of private rights, and the like), and cases where 'the environment' forms part of either one or the other factors, eg planning permission for housing construction versus the maintenance of a protected habitat, and private interests in maintaining the character of an area. In many cases the environment will sit on both sides of the equation. In exploring how the environment is understood in adjudicatory decision-making, therefore, it is essential to recognise the multifaceted roles which such arguments may play. Given the nature of our inquiry in this work, and the different forms such arguments may therefore take, there is merit to be found in a separate consideration of 'the environment', as distinct from the public or private interest more generally.

B. Processes

Figure 6.2 Process in reasoning

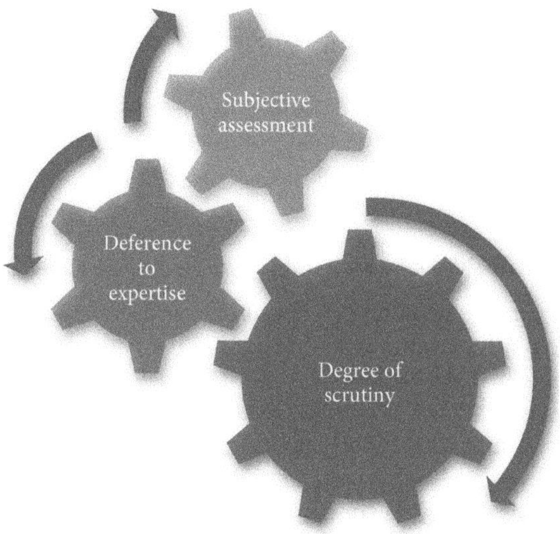

[10] See the scholarship around CD Stone, 'Should Trees Have Standing? Toward Legal Rights for Natural Objects' (1972) 45 *Southern California Law Review* 450.

These processes represent the means by which the balance between reasons is established. Such processes emerge both in the interpretation and development of generalisable norms, and in the application of law to the facts in an instant case. As with reasons, they are not entirely distinguishable. The degree to which an adjudicator is able to bring a high degree of scrutiny to a decision is relevant to the degree to which they will defer to the advice or decision of an expert body (Figure 6.2). However, there is still merit in considering them separately. A decision-maker may be entirely non-deferential to a public authority, but defer in respect of the scientific merits to the scientific adviser. There is therefore an important distinction between these two concepts. Finally, in this field where the balancing of values is so significant, we must also be able to consider whether that balance by an adjudicator is assessed subjectively taking account of their own reasons and their own expertise, or whether it is done objectively on the basis of an external set of criteria. Let us explain these concepts further.

i. Scrutiny

By scrutiny, we mean here the substantive level of analysis that will be brought to bear by the adjudicator in relation to the original decision. In particular, we examine whether the adjudicator considers themselves to be assessing the 'reasonableness', the legality or the correctness of a decision. In some cases, the precise scope of adjudicator power, as we discussed in the previous chapter, is unclear and will need to be self-determined. In part, this determination is a consequence of the kinds of reason which can be relied upon by claimants in challenging a decision, and in part it is a question of the techniques and processes which will be employed by an adjudicator in reaching their decision. The level of scrutiny is but one aspect of this process. Whilst it is clear that scrutiny is relevant in a public law context, it is not irrelevant in criminal law, where sentencing in particular is subject to subsequent analysis, and is occasionally relevant in private law, particularly where questions as to the likelihood of an intention materialising and the like form part of the outcome.

ii. Deference to Expertise

Related, but different to the question of scrutiny *in general*, is the question of reliance on expertise. Whilst some cases concerning the question of scrutiny involve hands-off decision-making *because* the original decision-maker is an expert, very often the decision-maker will instead be reliant upon expert advice. The degree to which adjudicators are prepared to analyse and unpick such expertise is very often determinative of outcome. Whilst our focus is on scientific expertise, there are of course other relevant forms of expertise, including aesthetic judgement in respect of planning decisions, and experience in a criminal law context (eg decisions of magistrates' courts).

iii. Subjective Assessment

Finally, we also consider the degree to which subjective reasoning is legitimate in any context, looking at ideas of independence, impartiality, objectivity and neutrality. The notion of subjectivity is explained in more detail below, but it is important to note here that we do not mean subjective in a pejorative sense, as would be expected perhaps in a legal context where subjectivity is discouraged. Rather, we mean to connote by this word the situation where an adjudicator is required, on the basis of a more or less unguided discretion, to rely on their own judgement, expertise and experience. They must come to an answer relying in part on their own pre-existing understanding of the law and the wider context of the particular decision, rather than asking them to come afresh to a decision without taking account of that wider knowledge. It will be shown that subjectivity in this sense is encouraged in decision-making as it is essentially the corollary of expertise in decision-making in a field dominated by discretionary action and the need to balance competing values and interests. Waits refers to subjectivity in this sense as the 'judicial hunch',[11] which is the way in which judges reach a decision where there is no clearly determined standard to apply. She argues, citing Summers, that:

> If the existence of the judicial hunch is obvious, then the reader will hopefully forgive an even more obvious observation: all legal decisions, whether arrived at by hunch or otherwise, involve value judgments. 'The law is not a mere formal receptacle. It includes substantive content. Insofar as law is consciously made and applied, its content is necessarily determined by values.'[12]

Taken together, these techniques explain how adjudicators reason about whether an argument brought before them is acceptable, and therefore how ultimately to decide between the parties in question. Considering how these reasons for action, and the techniques for processing them interact, in different contexts in environmental law, gives a significant degree of insight into the operation of our adjudication systems.

III. Public and Private Interest

We commence this discussion by emphasising the symbiosis between public and private *law* distinction, and the relevance of public and private *interests*. It is inevitable that public interest will be taken into account in planning cases,

[11] K Waits, 'Values, Intuitions, and Opinion Writing: The Judicial Process and State Court Jurisdiction' [1983] *University of Illinois Law Review* 917, 925.

[12] ibid, citing RS Summers, 'Pragmatic Instrumentalism in Twentieth Century American Legal Thought – A Synthesis and Critique of our Dominant General Theory About Law and its Use' (1981) 66 *Cornell Law Review* 861, 904 n 125.

environmental licensing and the like. In such cases, however, the combination of a hands-off attitude for adjudicators, and the presence of a scientific assessment of environmental factors (so that at least part of the public interest is captured in expert opinions), as well as a high level of reliance on policy, means that discussion of such public interest is funnelled down certain routes. The content of the likely disputes in each of these avenues frames the ways in which public or private interests might be relevant.

In analysing these issues in this section we first consider private interests (section III.A), and then consider the relevance of public interest (section III.B). Our analysis will reveal that adjudicators are grappling with two competing ideas: on the one hand there is a certain inevitability to a predominance of private *motivation* for the bringing of cases, giving many cases which proceed to formal adjudication a strong private interest dimension. On the other hand, especially in the public law field, the substantive norms are often structured so as to capture public interests. How the private interests of a claimant are integrated into this public interest analysis shows the framing effects that the route of challenge brings.

A. Private Interests

Let us commence our discussion of this framing effect with private interests. The Planning Inspectorate and other planning law decision-makers regularly emphasise that the relative consequences for private individuals arising from a planning decisions are not relevant.[13] The increase or decrease in the value of land (in some cases very dramatic changes) that a planning decision might result in for a private landowner is a 'prohibited' consideration in respect of planning decisions. By contrast, in relation to nuisance claims, subject to the discussion about remedies emerging from *Coventry v Lawrence*[14] which we consider in the subsequent chapter,[15] public interest is not relevant to the question of liability in nuisance. However beneficial an activity is, this will not alter the fact of its being a nuisance.[16]

The irrelevance of such private interest considerations in the planning process is demonstrated by the reasoning of the Planning Inspector in *Airwave Solutions*:

> It is not for the planning system to protect the private interests of one person against the activities of another. PPG8 indicates that the material question is not whether owners of nearby property might suffer financial or other loss, but whether the installation would have a detrimental effect on the locality generally, and on amenities that ought to be protected in the public interest. In this case I have concluded that the loss of amenity

[13] *Stringer v Minister of Housing and Local Government* [1970] 1 WLR 1281.
[14] *Coventry (t/a RDC Promotions) v Lawrence* [2014] UKSC 13, [2014] AC 822.
[15] ch 7.II.C.
[16] *Coventry (t/a RDC Promotions) v Lawrence* [2014] UKSC 13, [2014] AC 822.

> would be slight and confined to a small area, and that the optimum environmental and network solution has been found. Consequently I do not believe that there is a wider public interest that merits protection.[17]

This statement provides an almost perfect contrast with the reasoning of the Court of Appeal in *Network Rail v Williams* where the very definition of an actionable interference between the parties was the effect of the action of one on the private property value of the other.[18] In neither case was there a clear pre-existing norm which dictated what the outcome should be: both involved balancing the interests of two groups of persons, but in the private law avenue private value was a determining (or at the very least legitimate) concern in a way that in planning law it is explicitly irrelevant.

The statement that the planning system should not prioritise the interests of one person over another is regularly repeated, but it should also be noticed that the merits-reasoning power of the Planning Inspectorate can also allow it to take more account of some individuals than others, even if this expressed in terms of the public interest as a whole. Thus, in cases involving particularly severe effects on health (and especially on the health of children), Planning Inspectors have shown that they will indeed prioritise the needs of one individual over another.[19] This again emphasises the link between the public and private. In this case because the impact upon one family would be so severe (and as it is related to health and not wealth), it was said that the individual concern was so strong as to morph into a public interest concern.

Finally, in relation to criminal law, as we might expect, private interests play a very limited role, with the exception, of course, of the private interest in the maintenance of liberty, given the social control purposes of criminal law provisions (see chapter four). The degree to which this is true is demonstrated most obviously by the approach taken by the courts to the Sentencing Guidelines[20] (we discuss sentencing in more detail in chapter seven). The public interest in deterring the commitment of such offences is demonstrated amply by the discussion of the Court of Appeal in *Thames Water*:[21]

> This was a breach of environmental regulations committed by a very large organisation as a result of corporate recklessness. The size of the organisation meant that the figures provided within the table applicable to a large company were of little relevance. The previous history of the organisation was little short of lamentable. To bring home to the directors and shareholders the need to protect the environment required a very substantial fine. In those circumstances a fine measured in millions of pounds was entirely proportionate.[22]

[17] *Airwave Solutions Ltd v Dartmoor National Park Authority* [2010] PAD 34, [87].
[18] *Network Rail Infrastructure Ltd v Williams*, [2018] EWCA Civ 1514, [2019] QB 601.
[19] *Grange Wind Farm v North Lincolnshire Council* [2010] PAD 31.
[20] Sentencing Council, 'Environmental Offences: Definitive Guideline' (London, HMSO, 2014).
[21] *R v Thames Water Utilities Ltd*, 2019 EWCA Crim 1344.
[22] ibid.

By contrast, the private interest of the shareholders and directors of the company was seen as unimportant. However, this will not always be the case. The tenor of the comments in *Thames Water* can be usefully compared with the decision in *National Grid Gas* relating to contaminated land, where the interests of shareholders were very relevant in determining liability for clean-up costs under the Environmental Protection Act 1990, Part IIA, in cases involving statutory successors to utility companies.[23] The House of Lords reached the conclusion that it would be inappropriate to interpret the provisions in such a way as to render a successor company a 'polluter' for the purposes of the regime, on the grounds that they had not in fact caused or knowingly permitted the substance in question to be in, on or under the ground, not existing at the time.[24] This approach of limiting the liability of successors in title was confirmed in *Powys CC v Price*,[25] where a successor local authority was not liable under the regime.[26] In both of these cases, it could be said that the private interest of the rights and obligations of the successor companies was elevated above the public interest in ensuring clean-up of contaminated land.[27] However, there is also a degree to which these cases could be characterised as involving competing private interests, as residual liability in such cases lies theoretically on the owner or occupier of contaminated land[28] (albeit in practice that it rests either on developers through the planning system, or on local authorities).[29]

B. Public Interest

Moving on to public interests, the most nuanced consideration of the meaning and relevance of public interest, is to be found in the jurisprudence of the FTT in relation to the EIR.[30] Here, thanks to the exceptions in regulation 12, the Tribunal is regularly required to deal with a complex mixture of public and private considerations and to weigh these in a public interest balancing test. For example, the FTT must determine whether an administrative authority is justified in non-disclosure of information on the basis that the request of the applicant is

[23] The liability in this situation takes the form of a responsibility to pay such costs, which is 'backed up' by criminal liability in cases of failure to pay. Given the possibility of the invocation of such a criminal penalty, this situation sits between criminal and public law. *R (National Grid Gas Plc (formerly Transco Plc)) v Environment Agency* [2007] UKHL 30, [2007] 1 WLR 1780.

[24] Ibid [33]–[35].

[25] *Powys CC v Price* [2017] EWCA Civ 1133, [2018] 1 WLR 1717.

[26] ibid [46].

[27] See E Lees, 'Liability for Contaminated Land: *Powys County Council v Price*' (2018) 20 *Environmental Law Review* 39.

[28] Environmental Protection Act 1990, s 78F.

[29] S Vaughan, 'The Contaminated Land Regime: Still Suitable for Use?' [2010] *Journal of Planning and Environmental Law* 142.

[30] Environmental Information Regulations 2004, SI 2004/3391.

'manifestly unreasonable'.[31] This unreasonableness test, although not defined in the legislation itself, has been equated to the vexatious test under the Freedom of Information Act 2000. The FTT has therefore reasoned by reference to the decision in *Dransfield* (see the Court of Appeal in *Craven*[32]).[33] This case, although not establishing a definitive test for vexatious requests, nevertheless explains four criteria which will usually be relevant to a determination that a request is vexatious (and therefore by analogy, manifestly unreasonable). These criteria are: '(1) the burden (on the public authority and its staff); (2) the motive (of the requester); (3) the value or serious purpose (of the request) and (4) any harassment or distress (of and to staff)'.[34]

Account is taken, on the one hand, of motive, and on the other, of purpose, objectively ascertained. However, even if the request is shown to be manifestly unreasonable, ie it is not for proper motive, and it does not serve a valid objective purpose, the FTT is still required to assess whether *on balance* public interest in non-disclosure (for the reason that the request is unreasonable) outweighs the public interest in disclosure both generally – ie transparency and accountability in decision-making – and specifically in the context of the particular circumstances of the case.[35]

It is notable that the majority of decisions made under this jurisdiction relate to environmental issues only in so far as they relate to the lived environment of the claimant. It is inevitable, given the time and effort involved, that many of these cases will be motivated by private interest. The degree to which this is true is perhaps surprising nevertheless. Indeed, in engaging in the public interest balancing approach which the regulations require, in cases where a public authority seeks to withhold information on the grounds, for example, that it represents personal data or where the claimant's request has been found to be manifestly unreasonable, it is rare that the tribunal mentions the environmental context at all. Much more common is consideration of the importance of openness and transparency in general. This may be the case even though the public interest in the actual document sought by the claimant (often planning-related information) appears not to hold interest for the public at large. A clear example of this is the decision in *Kushner v Information Commissioner*, which is unremarkable but for the fact that it is a typical example of the sorts of questions the FTT is addressing in this jurisdiction.[36] In this case, a private landowner was seeking information concerning action that his neighbour, a bicycle shop, was required to take in respect of a statutory nuisance. The nuisance occurred through damp issues in the shop premises which were affecting the claimant's property. The FTT was required to assess

[31] ibid, regulation 12(4)(b).
[32] *Craven v Information Commissioner* [2014] EWCA Civ 850.
[33] *Dransfield v Information Commissioner* [2015] EWCA Civ 454, [2015] 1 WLR 5316.
[34] ibid [19].
[35] Environmental Information Regulations 2004, SI 2004/3391, regulation 12(1)(b).
[36] *John Kuschnir v Information Commissioner* [2012] UKFTT EA_2011_0273 (GRC).

what the public interest might be in disclosing this information to the claimant, and relied on the general importance of transparency, as well as the listed nature of the claimant's property.[37] The public interest is expressed in very general terms, in contrast to the highly specified private motivation which was encouraging the claimant to act.

The most striking element of the FTT's jurisdiction in giving a window into the tensions that exist regarding the purpose of adjudication in general and the degree to which claimants are clearly attempting to use this avenue of adjudication to enforce or protect some environmental (narrowly or broadly drawn) feature of their locality, rather than in any meaningful sense in a pursuit of information. The claimant is attempting to use adjudication on the question of disclosure of information as a proxy for determination of the legality of a prior decision. For example, in *Fortun v Information Commissioner*, the court was asked to consider whether the council ought to be required to disclose information to the claimant regarding its policy in inspecting local authority land for contamination, in line with the provisions in the Environmental Protection Act 1990.[38] In discussing the information request, the FTT emphasised that the real purpose of the claimant here was to seek evidence that the council was not in fact complying with its statutory duties. Similarly, in *Edmonds v Information Commissioner*, the court emphasises the limitations on its owner powers in this respect:[39]

> The scope of this appeal is limited by the powers of the Respondent Information Commissioner and by the Tribunal's own powers. The role of the Respondent is not to consider the lawfulness or otherwise of an EIA, it is to consider whether information which is held by a public body should be published. The Tribunal's role is to consider the lawfulness of the Respondent's decision in the light of the evidence.[40]

This desire to prompt substantive assessment of authority action, rather than a genuine desire for information, is a clear thread which runs through the FTT decisions. This is perhaps unsurprising, but as the FTT concludes in one of the many *Latimer* decisions, 'Mr Latimer [the applicant] is seeking to use EIR to provide a solution to an environmental problem as he understands it. That is a burden too great for EIR to carry.'[41]

It is also interesting to note when and how courts reframe private law disputes to acknowledge a public interest element, and when it is seen purely as a dispute resolution situation as between the parties to the case. We can see this dimension in the case-law in the judgment of Etherton LJ in *Network Rail v Williams*,[42] where he also considers *Blue Circle Industries*.[43] Both of these cases involved,

[37] ibid [14].
[38] *John Fortun v Information Commissioner* [2015] UKFTT 2015_0087 (GRC).
[39] *Brian Edmonds v Information Commissioner* [2016] UKFTT 2016_0195 (GRC).
[40] ibid [10].
[41] *Latimer v Information Commissioner* [2018] UKFTT 2017_0195 (GRC), [13].
[42] *Network Rail Infrastructure Ltd v Williams*, [2018] EWCA Civ 1514, [2019] QB 601.
[43] *Blue Circle Industries v Ministry of Defence* [1999] Ch 289 (HC).

effectively, noxious or harmful emanations from the land of one private individual onto the land of another. They are both effectively pollution cases, albeit that the knotweed case involves the spread of a living rather than a chemical substance. Thus:

> The facts were that land owned by the plaintiffs, which joined the land of the Atomic Weapons Establishment ('the AWE'), was contaminated, following a storm, by radioactive material containing plutonium from an overflowing pond on the AWE's land. It was contended by the defendants that the plaintiffs' land had not been physically damaged by the radioactive properties of the plutonium. … [However, the] plaintiffs' land was less valuable because the estate was unsalable until the contaminated soil had been removed and less useful because the level of contamination was such that the topsoil of the marsh had to be excavated and removed from the site because the level of radioactivity exceeded that which was allowed by the regulations. In short, the cause of action arose because the amenity or utility of the plaintiffs' land was impaired by contamination from the plutonium.[44]

Both of these situations involve some kind of environmental effect – be that pollution with radioactive material, or the introduction of an invasive weed. However, the dispute is not labelled as being 'about' the environment. Rather, the framing of the dispute in private interest terms of the value of land allowed liability for the relevant activity or omission under the rules of nuisance. However, in *Coventry v Lawrence*,[45] we see an alternative characterisation, whereby the fact of existing environmental legislation is taken into account as part of the matrix of determining what is and what is not acceptable within the boundaries of the principle of give and take. Per Lord Carnwath:

> After more than 60 years of modern planning and environmental controls, it is not unreasonable to start from the presumption that the established pattern of uses generally represents society's view of the appropriate balance of uses in a particular area, taking account both of the social needs of the area and of the maintenance of an acceptable environment for its occupants. The common law of nuisance is there to provide a residual control to ensure that new or intensified activities do not need lead to conditions which, within that pattern, go beyond what a normal person should be expected to put up with.[46]

In this case, the existing regulatory controls were said to represent the public interest, with the residual concerns being a matter for private interest.

Drawing this discussion to a close, it is clear that the web of reasons which make up both public and private interests will be relevant in almost all cases, in different ways. In providing a funnel through which these different arguments must be processed, the different avenues of adjudication affect how these concerns must be expressed to and by adjudicators in reaching their decisions. In judicial

[44] ibid [117].
[45] *Coventry (t/a RDC Promotions) v Lawrence* [2014] UKSC 13, [2014] AC 822.
[46] ibid [183].

review and statutory appeals, and in a different way, criminal law, private interests are legitimate reasons for actions only when expressed in such a way that the private interest, in effect, becomes part of wider public goals. Whilst this is relatively straightforward to do in many cases, it is the fact of having to do it which changes the character of reasoning. The reverse is true in private law, where public interest concerns being outwith the 'traditional' province of private law reasoning morph into contextualising factors shaping principles such as that of reasonableness and give and take in nuisance. In short, the avenues do not necessarily change the fundamental substance of an argument, but they change its flavour and mode of presentation.

IV. The Environment

When considering questions of environmental adjudication, and the substantive limits on the kinds of reasons taken into account in the different avenues, it may be thought that the degree to which decision-makers are able, and do, take account of environmental harm as a standalone consideration would be hugely significant. Of course, in some cases a specific legislative rule will mandate that such is a valid consideration. There will, however, be many situations where there is no explicit instruction that environmental harm be taken into account but where, on the facts, such consideration appears to be relevant. This section explores both where environmental considerations are relevant and where adjudicators emphasise their irrelevance to the specific question at hand. The ability of a claimant to rely on environmental considerations within their complaint varies significantly, not only from avenue to avenue, but within avenues, posing challenges for coherence, as we explain in chapter eight.

Commencing our discussion with statutory appeals, it is notable that a large proportion of the Planning Appeals Decisions to which we refer involve applications relating to wind turbines.[47] In part, this is a consequence of the relatively high level of interest, complexity and significance associated with wind turbine decisions such that these decisions are routinely published and commented on. Partly, however, it is also a consequence of the fact that in relation to wind turbine cases three key issues emerge which make the discussion in such cases particularly pertinent for our project. First, they engage heavily with subjective considerations of visual impact. This means that the Inspector is required to make this assessment, and their approach to their own task in this regard is instructive. Second, the cases often involve analysis of scientific information, be that about the noise levels produced, or in relation to biodiversity and ecological impacts. It is in these cases therefore that we are able to see how the Inspector as adjudicator approaches their

[47] See E Fisher, 'Law and Energy Transitions: Wind Turbines and Planning Law in the UK' (2018) 38 *OJLS* 528.

task of reviewing the available scientific evidence. Finally, and most significantly, wind turbine cases are, quintessentially, cases where we could say 'the environment' is pitted against 'the environment'.

The long term and world-wide goal of carbon emissions reduction is generally contrasted with the (often but not always) more localised arguments concerning visual impact, landscape preservation, amenity and recreation of open countryside, and effects on protected species and sites. In assessing the effects on the environment in such cases, therefore, the adjudicator is required to assess the wider importance of wind farms in general, versus the specific environmental effects of the wind farm existing at a particular site. The comments of the Inspector in *Enertrag v South Norfolk District Council* are particularly instructive in this regard:

> Conversely, however, I do not accept the appellant company's argument that the need to address climate change overrides any requirement to turn more than three of the turbines off at such times … there would be little point in addressing climate change if the effect of doing so in itself damages biodiversity – in medical parlance, the cure would be no more beneficial to that particular interest than the illness.[48]

Similarly, we can see clearly how the environmental pressures involved in particularly planning decision-making changes how the court approaches its task as a reviewing body in judicial review situations. Thus, the means by which the court assesses agency motivation and the quality of agency reasons is demonstrably affected by the environmental nature of a case, albeit unevenly and in potentially unpredictable ways. It is also important to note that some of this adjustment to the environmental context is consciously motivated by outside legal sources, including soft law sources and international treaties. Other of the adjustments appear not to be motivated by a clash of environmental *law* and judicial review principles, but rather a clash of environmental concerns with the pre-existing public law. Both of these forms of influence are demonstrated in the recent Supreme Court decision in *Dover DC v Campaign to Protect Rural England (Kent)* (*CPRE Kent*).[49]

This case involved a decision by a Kent planning authority to allow a large housing development in a designated Area of Outstanding Natural Beauty (AONB). The controversy in the case was a matter not so much of the grant of permission per se, but rather that in granting the permission the authority had ignored their own Planning Officers' advice to restrict the number of houses in the development below the level proposed by the developer. In ignoring this advice, the result was that the damage to the AONB would be more significant. The environmental concerns expressed by the planning officer were not obviously accounted for in the decision. Nor were the reasons for departing from this advice clearly demonstrated in the authority's notice. This resulted in a number of issues

[48] *Enertrag v South Norfolk DC* [2010] PAD 13, [63].

[49] *Dover DC v Campaign to Protect Rural England (Kent)* [2017] UKSC 79, [2018] 1 WLR 108. This case is also considered in ch 3.III.E.

emerging. First, the objectors to the development claimed that the council was obligated to provide reasons for the decision reached. Second, there was an argument that where a case involved an environmental dispute, those reasons would be scrutinised particularly closely. The Supreme Court held clearly that reasons were required notwithstanding that reasons for grants of planning permission will not always be required.

This was (a) a result of pressure for clear reasons emerging from the Aarhus Convention and (b) from a more general recognition of the importance of protecting designated sites of national significance. The first reason was a binding legal reason emerging, convolutedly, through EU law (as opposed to through the non-binding effect of the international treaty). The second reason, which was clearly persuasive in the Court's mind, was a softer influence which resulted not from a legal rule, but from judicial recognition that environmental decision-making and the importance of the environment justified a departure from the normal principles of judicial review in a planning context. We can see this web of reasoning in the judgment of Lord Carnwath JSC where he analyses the pre-existing authorities:

> In the planning context, the Court of Appeal has held that a local planning authority generally is under no common law duty to give reasons for the grant of planning permission. … Although this general principle was reaffirmed … the court held that a duty did arise in the particular circumstances of that case: where the development would have a 'significant and lasting impact on the local community', and involved a substantial departure from Green Belt and development plan policies, and where the committee had disagreed with its officers' recommendations. Of the last point, Elias LJ (giving the leading judgment, with which Patten LJ agreed) said, at para 61:
>
> 'The significance of that fact is not simply that it will often leave the reasoning obscure. In addition, the fact that the committee is disagreeing with a careful and clear recommendation from a highly experienced officer on a matter of such potential significance to very many people suggests that some explanation is required … the dictates of good administration and the need for transparency are particularly strong here, and they reinforce the justification for imposing the common law duty.'
>
> His conclusion was reinforced [note – reinforced but not necessarily prompted primarily] by reference to the United Kingdom's obligations under the Aarhus Convention.[50]

Taking this further, Lord Carnwath emphasised that the combination of public interest, seriousness for the environment and departure from expert advice, was 'found in the present case, and, in my view, would if necessary have justified the imposition of a common law duty to provide reasons for the decision'.[51] In other words, his Lordship was of the view that the very fact of the environmental harm, and the concomitant departure from the advice in this respect, would be enough to change the general application of judicial review principles in this sort

[50] *Dover DC v Campaign to Protect Rural England (Kent)* [2017] UKSC 79, [2018] 1 WLR 108, [115].
[51] ibid [116].

of situation, even without surrounding legal context in the form of the Aarhus Convention.[52]

There are also cases relating to EIR where the claimant's interest in finding the information, and the FTT's attitude to its task, is clearly shaped by the environmental significance of the question at hand. Some notable examples of this include a series of cases where claimants were seeking information from central government regarding policy on climate change.[53] The effect on adjudicator attitude of cases involving genuine environmental complaints, however, can be most clearly seen in the series of cases brought by a Mr Latimer against the IC. These related to coastal protection and sewage on the Northumberland coast.[54] There are a number of these decisions, and, generally, where a claimant is engaging in repeated requests for information on related or the same topic from a local authority, the IC, and in turn the FTT, will very likely conclude that the requests for information are manifestly unreasonable. Despite the forthright tone of Mr Latimer's communications, his genuine desire to protect the natural environment, rather than private interest, appears to have meant that the FTT accorded him a degree of latitude in his dealings with the local authority. The conclusion that his requests had become manifestly unreasonable appears to have been made more reluctantly than in many cases involving 'forthright' claimants.

However, it is also apparent that the degree to which 'the environment' itself will be taken into account is not only variable, but also that it will not be a hugely significant consideration in the face of precise legal rules, and a variety of other competing concerns, unless specifically required by statute. A good example of the limits of 'the environment' as a factor affecting decision-making (and specifically statutory and other interpretation) is to be found in *Mott*.[55] In this case, the Supreme Court reasoned that:

> [Counsel] is right to emphasise the special importance to be attached to the protection of the environment. However, this does not detract from them need to draw a 'fair balance', nor from the potential relevance of compensation in that context.[56]

In the context of human rights, the fact that the environment was a factor advanced in favour of limitation of individual rights, whilst relevant, was not determinative of the issue. It certainly did not justify (in this case) expropriation of property without appropriate compensation. This conclusion was reached notwithstanding

[52] See also J Bell, 'Kent and Oakley: A Re-examination of the Common Law Duty to Give Reasons for Grants of Planning Permission and Beyond' (2017) 22 *Judicial Review* 105.

[53] See eg *Lucas Amin v Information Commissioner* [2014] UKFTT 2013_0103 (GRC) and *Lucas Amin v Information Commissioner* [2016] UKFTT 2015_0103 (GRC).

[54] *Robert Latimer v Information Commissioner* [2009] UKIT EA_2009_0018; *Robert Latimer v Information Commissioner* [2013] UKFTT EA_2013_0101 (GRC); *Robert Latimer v Information Commissioner* [2014] UKFTT EA_2013_0252 (GRC); *Robert Latimer v Information Commissioner* [2018] UKFTT 2017_0195 (GRC).

[55] *R (Mott) v Environment Agency* [2018] UKSC 10, [2018] 1 WLR 1022.

[56] ibid [37].

the fact that the flexibility of the statutory licensing system in question is the very method chosen to protect the environment. Not only was the environment only one (relatively unpersuasive) element of the fair balance, it was also deemed necessary to subjugate the flexibility of environmental licensing to individual human rights. The argument here is not that this was the wrong conclusion per se, but rather to emphasise that in the final reckoning, 'the environment' was a very weak factor in the court's decision, notwithstanding the fact that the legislation in question was specifically designed to serve environmental purposes.[57]

The significance of environmental concerns in environmental law would, one might think, be obvious. In practical terms, as this section has demonstrated however, that is not always the case. This results from the fact that environmental law, as we explained in chapter four, is parasitic upon other legal disciplines for its structures of adjudication. Once one is within these structures, it is difficult, if not impossible, to bring arguments from without the traditional province of those forms. Given the relative youth of many environmental law provisions, it is not surprising, therefore, that the kinds of amorphous, uncertain and wide-ranging environmental arguments which may be relevant do not fit easily into these existing avenues. But it is also clear that where there is a significant degree of potential environmental harm, adjudicators can innovate so as to take them into account. Both the common law and statutory provisions can be moulded to accommodate protection of the environment.

V. Level of Scrutiny

If we move now into considering the techniques of reasoning that are employed, we can see how adjudicators examine the influence of the reasons we have discussed above. To link this to the previous chapter, it is useful to recognise that there is a parallel here between the fact of being able to scrutinise a decision (jurisdictional power), and the level of scrutiny an adjudicator will bring. The two issues are not perfectly divisible: the distinction between legitimacy of argument, and the scope of jurisdictional reach, is not clear-cut.

In the judicial review avenue, as we might expect, we see a highly deferential attitude to decision-making 'earlier in the chain'. This is the case both with original administrative planning authorities, and, perhaps more interestingly, in cases involving the decision of the adjudicator in the form of the Planning Inspector. Particularly, the level of scrutiny applied to arguments as articulated by a decision-maker is notably low in cases involving decision letters in relation to planning. This is a well-established rule. At all levels, planning 'decisions' (whether from a planning authority, or an Inspector) are read generously, and without the scrutiny of 'legal' documents. In *Kenyon* this mantra was repeated,

[57] See also ch 7.III.

and indeed extended, but the high authority of the general principle is apparent from this quotation:

> It is well-established that planning decision letters should be read fairly and in good faith, and as a whole, in a straightforward manner, without excessive legalism or criticism (see *Clarke Homes v Secretary of State for the Environment (1993) 66 P & CR 263*, per Lord Bingham at 271; *South Somerset District Council v Secretary of State for the Environment (1993) 66 P & CR 83*, per Lord Hoffmann LJ at 84).[58]

In this case, this principle was extended to cover screening assessments for the purposes of habitat protection. The connotations of 'nit-picking' here are particularly telling, and tap into a general attitude in the planning sphere that an over-legalisation of policies has rendered the system somewhat unwieldy. 'In my judgment, the Claimant's submissions that the Defendant failed properly to consider pollution and air quality and, failed adequately to assess cumulative effect, were based on an unduly forensic and nit-picking reading of the assessments.'[59]

Furthermore, this suggests that the substantive limit to the degree of scrutiny applied by an adjudicator to an original decision is narrow, both in purely domestic cases, and in cases involving European law. Not only is the constitutional underpinning of the division between administrative authorities and the courts relevant here, but also important is a recognition of the fact that ultimately the majority of planning decisions will involve the balancing of values and interests, and that this is not something which can ever be reduced to a mechanical assessment. As a result, the system will always need to rely on the prevailing judgement of one actor. Clearly, a decision has been made by the courts that in judicial review of planning decisions, whatever the legal context, the weight of judgement rests with administrative authorities and the bespoke adjudication system in the form of the Planning Inspector.

This does not mean that the lack of scrutiny always feels appropriate. Although in theoretical terms, the lack of scrutiny is well known, it can nevertheless be somewhat shocking when one is confronted with it. For example, in the recent decision in *Norman v Secretary of State for Housing, Communities and Local Government*, the court reasoned as follows:

> An inspector's decision letter should not be laboriously dissected in an effort to find fault. Decisions are to be read benevolently and on the basis that they are written principally for parties who know what the issues between them are and what evidence and argument has been deployed on these issues. The Court must be astute to ensure that challenges are not used as a cloak for a rerun of the arguments on the planning merits. An adverse inference that a decision maker misunderstood something will not readily be drawn and should only be drawn where all other known facts and circumstances point overwhelmingly to a different conclusion.[60]

[58] *R (Kenyon) v Secretary of State for Communities and Local Government* [2018] EWHC 3485, [34].
[59] ibid [34].
[60] *Norman v Secretary of State for Housing, Communities and Local Government*, [2018] EWHC 2910 (Admin), [2019] Env LR 14, [40].

In this articulation of the low levels of scrutiny present in planning cases, the symbiotic relationship between power allocation and reasoning is apparent. The courts' vigilance to ensure that the arguments being brought by the parties are not 'secretly' about planning merits, but rather are about legality, results in the balance of decision-making power being very heavily weighted in the original decision-maker's favour. This is twinned with a desire to be 'benevolent' towards the original decision-maker, and the concern this raises is that there is a blurring of the distinction between the *kinds of reason* which are legitimate in challenging planning decisions, and the *techniques of reasoning* which ought to be used in response to those arguments.

A further example of the concerns that this low level of scrutiny can engender is to be found in *Baci*,[61] a case involving a decision about environmental permitting. The court was required to analyse whether the decision made by the EA was vitiated by an admitted, and in the circumstances one would think significant, error in the scientific evidence presented to them by the applicant for a licence.[62] The applicant had, in their report, explained that there would be no possibility of a discharge of heavy metals into the surrounding environment following their operation because they would be able to filter such metallic residue out of water discharged from their plant. This was based on the argument that heavy metals do not dissolve in water, whereas, in fact, they do. Thus they could not be filtered out. There was no doubt that this was a mistake in the scientific report. The question was whether this affected the EA's decision. In this regard, the court reasoned as follows:

> On reviewing the evidence, summarised above, I am satisfied that the Defendant did not make the same mistake as Covanta. It is elementary science that heavy metals dissolve in water. The Defendant is the regulator, with wide experience of [energy recovery facilities], and its officers have scientific expertise. I find it implausible that the Defendant would make this mistake.[63]

In other words, whilst the court did not have explicit evidence that the EA had not made this mistake (there was some indicative evidence that they had not in the terms of their report), the scientific expertise of the EA was taken by the court to be a reason to assume that the applicant's mistake could not have affected the EA's decision. This seems a rather extreme response to the principle that levels of scrutiny of decision-making should not be too high. The rules relating to the intensity of the adjudicator gaze can be seen to go beyond the levels of power that the adjudicator has in relation to the original decision-maker, to actually affect the substance of an outcome even where there is a lack of evidence to justify the benevolence shown to the original decision-maker. What we see, therefore, is a merging, in both statutory appeals and judicial review cases, of

[61] *R (Baci Bedfordshire Ltd) v Environment Agency* [2018] EWHC 2962 (Admin), [2019] Env LR 15.
[62] ibid.
[63] ibid [52].

scrutiny of *legality* and scrutiny in general. Adjudicators are reluctant to engage in the latter, but that does not mean that they should avoid the former. It is here that the prevailing 'wisdom' of these avenues, of the hands-off attitude of the courts, is so significant.

Refusing to go through a decision letter or policy drafted for planning decision-makers with 'a fine-tooth comb', and refusing to look at it at all, are on a spectrum. The degree of scrutiny is about the substance of reasoning that takes place within the avenues, but it is also critically about the balance of decision-making power in this context. If we examine this discussion from the perspective of quality of reasons and the kinds of arguments that can be made, it boils down to an acceptance in some contexts that there is no possibility of a right/wrong assessment, but rather that there are a range of legitimate responses to a question. Reasoning about right or wrong responses is to lead the adjudicator down a blind alley.

But, as we would expect, this level of scrutiny is not uniform across the environmental law landscape. In many areas the degree of scrutiny brought to bear on decisions is much more intense, although surprisingly this cannot always be said about the criminal law field. Whilst there is the proper amount of attention paid to issues such as the committing of an offence, in sentencing cases it must be remembered that a reviewing court, taking the attitude of an appellate jurisdiction, will only interfere with a sentencing decision in cases where it is shown to be unreasonable, or out of compliance with the sentencing guidelines.[64]

VI. Handling and Analysis of Scientific Information

One more specific area where we can examine the process of reasoning is in relation to scientific information and its handling through the adjudication process. In almost all environmental case-law, some form of scientific information will be necessary to judge the effects a particular action is having or might have on the environment. Yet in some of the avenues, we see a marked reluctance for adjudicators to make a direct analysis of the quality of the scientific information being provided to them. In others, there is a much more open attitude to this kind of analysis. This is not simply a question of jurisdictional power. It refers instead to the kinds of reasoned argument which are acceptable within an avenue, or which are more likely to be accepted within that avenue. The prevailing wisdom on where scientific information is integrated into legal decision-making about the environment is focused on lessons learned from the judicial review/statutory appeals in a planning context. Yet, as we shall see, this 'accepting and hands-off' attitude is not mirrored elsewhere. Three themes emerge: first, there are cases where the adjudicators not only review expert evidence, but in fact also engage

[64] See ch 7.II.D.

with and critique expert methodology; second, such engagement appears to be considerably less likely where the expert in question is either NE or the EA; and third, there will also be cases where although the expert evidence itself is not under scrutiny, agency use of the expert evidence will be a matter for adjudicator review.

A. Engagement with Methodology

In many environmental cases, a hands-off approach to scientific examination is in evidence. For example, in the Court of Appeal in *Mott*,[65] Beatson LJ considered how a court should handle an assessment by an administrative decision-maker of scientific information. He criticised the judge at first instance, concluding that in reviewing such assessment 'he fell into error and strayed beyond what is proper for a reviewing judge dealing with complex scientific material'.[66] The court's attitude to whether and how it handled the scientific information in this particular case was influenced not by the nature of that science, or its environmental importance, but by the fact of the case being judicial review. This also ties into the point made above regarding *Mott* and the emphasis paid in that case to the irrelevance of the environment as a consideration in that case.[67]

The point made by the Court of Appeal (and supported by the Supreme Court),[68] however, was *not* that courts should not handle science – cases involving medical negligence, patent applications and the like are all demonstrative of the fact that courts are perfectly happy to handle complex scientific information. The point is that they do not do so where an administrative authority has already assessed that information and they are being asked to review, not remake the decision. This treatment of scientific information – which is present in many cases – is not therefore a question of the judicial role per se but rather the judicial role in respect of judicial review. As we shall see below, even in judicial review cases, the *use* of technical information is often the subject of analysis.

Critically, we cannot transform this 'tendency' to keep hands of scientific information into an absolute rule. Such an approach is certainly not present in the other avenues of adjudication. That this is not an absolute rule was emphasised in *Wealden DC v Secretary of State for Communities and Local Government*, where the Jay J reasoned that:

> I appreciate that this is a specialist area and that the court must avoid delving into the minutiae of expert opinion evidence which is beyond its competence. The court should be doubly slow to criticise expert opinion where there is no contrary evidence being

[65] *R (Mott) v Environment Agency* [2016] EWCA Civ 564, [2016] 1 WLR 4338.
[66] ibid [67].
[67] See also ch 7.III.
[68] *R (Mott) v Environment Agency* [2018] UKSC 10, [2018] 1 WLR 1022.

> advanced by WDC. Even so, these self-denying ordinances, although salutary, are by no means absolute.[69]

Furthermore, as this section will show, in many cases not only will the adjudicator review the use of expert opinions, it will engage directly with the methodology of those opinions. Advocating for a hands-off approach is, on this view, a conclusion consequent upon the role of the adjudicator as understood broadly within the avenue of adjudication, not a determinant of that role. There will be cases where the ways in which the science has been handled, or the content of that scientific information, have encouraged the court to take a closer look in the same way that the de novo adjudicators clearly feel able to do. In such cases, as we shall see, the factor pushing the courts to engage in a more enhanced scrutiny can be the degree of environmental harm which might thereby result. This is encouraged not only by the levels of environmental harm that are possible, but also by the wider environmental-legal context, with EU rules relating to the precautionary principle having a particularly influential role in encouraging courts to be more intense in their scrutiny of scientific information.

Indeed, if we commence with analysis in *Warren v Natural England*,[70] a case concerned with the Regulatory Enforcement and Sanctions Act 2008 sanctions,[71] the FTT was diligent in analysing competing expert evidence, in challenging methodologies, and assessing the comparative weight to be given to scientific conclusions. In this case, the judge addressed the evidence of NE, and of the competing expert views, and directly engaged with the methodology of both. It is difficult to imagine a more hands-on approach to scientific evidence. Judge McKenna here reasoned:

> In reviewing the weight of evidence, I also found it unhelpful that Natural England's witnesses frequently did not address themselves in their witness statements to the statutory threshold for serving a Stop Notice. Their assessments of the risk of harm were often put into colloquial terms. … I was concerned that Ms Hay appeared to be applying a reverse burden of proof at paragraph [54] above.
>
> I am grateful to Dr Alonso for addressing so directly the statutory test in her evidence repeated at paragraphs [60] to [62] above. She very fairly acknowledged that there is a paucity of scientific studies directly concerned with the risk factors she had considered and that it had been necessary for her to reach her conclusions by extrapolating from studies which were designed to investigate different issues. Nevertheless, I found her opinion as the only heathland specialist to give evidence in this case cogent and compelling as to a significant risk of serious harm arising from the changes to the habitat brought about by disturbance and soil enrichment. She was able to supplement her evidence of the theoretical risk in these respects with first-hand evidence. … She also gave first-hand evidence of vehicle disturbance. I take into account the importance

[69] *Wealden DC v Secretary of State for Communities and Local Government* [2017] EWHC 351 (Admin), [2017] Env LR 31.

[70] *Warren v Natural England* [2018] UKFTT NV_2018_0006 (GRC).

[71] Regulatory Enforcement and Sanctions Act 2008, Part 3.

> that she attributed to preserving the heathland, both for its intrinsic value as a primary reason for the notification of the site and also as a habitat for the species she identified. I also take into account here Mr Lakin's evidence about the importance of heathland as a habitat for the Nightjar and Woodlark populations. I note Dr Alonso's evidence was that the degradation of heathland may take time to become apparent and I am grateful to Mr Kokelaar for referring me to Case C-282/15 *Queisser Pharma GmbH & Co KG v Bundesrepublik Deutschland*, in which the ECJ approved the taking of protective measures in accordance with the precautionary principle without having to wait until the reality and seriousness of those risks were fully demonstrated, so long as the assessment of the risk was not based on purely hypothetical considerations. I consider that Dr Alonso's evidence of the risk of greening is consistent with this approach.[72]

There is clear and detailed discussion of the degree of 'peer corroboration' of expert opinion, the means by which an expert opinion is expressed, and the different kinds of evidence (theoretical, first hand, etc).

However, in considering the appeal in *Warren*, the Upper Tribunal condemns the analysis of the scientific evidence although not, notably, the fact of having undertaken such an assessment. In respect of the FTT's conclusion that the employment status of the NE witnesses meant that they could not be considered 'expert', the Upper Tribunal said this:

> The first error is that the First-tier Tribunal incorrectly said at paragraph 43 that none of Natural England's witnesses had the status of an expert witness because they were employed by Natural England. In *Forager* the Upper Tribunal rejected a similar submission, saying that it 'confuse[d] the concepts of "independent" and "expert"' …
>
> The First-tier Tribunal acknowledged the witnesses' professional standing and/or knowledge of the SSSI and said that it would 'admit their opinion evidence and … give such weight to it as I consider appropriate in the circumstances'. Unfortunately, apart from Dr Alonso, the First-tier Tribunal did not then explain how the witnesses' expertise and standing was factored into the assessment of their evidence. One is left with a suspicion that the tribunal's erroneous view of their status influenced its approach to their evidence and led the tribunal to afford less weight to their evidence than it would otherwise have done.[73]

In other words, this analysis by the Upper Tribunal represents a review of the FTT's own opinions regarding the quality of the scientific evidence (rather than a review of the NE's use of such evidence). We see here an appellate jurisdiction carrying out a scrutineering analysis of the FTT's scientific approach. However, the Upper Tribunal itself also considered the quality of the scientific information provided by the witnesses at first instance:

> [T]he witnesses' phraseology of suspicion, concern, or possible harm for which the First-tier Tribunal criticised them was consistent with a precautionary approach of finding a likely significant effect if it could not be excluded on the basis of objective evidence. The witnesses' opinions were not merely speculative. They were backed up

[72] *Warren v Natural England* [2018] UKFTT NV_2018_0006 (GRC), [95]–[96].
[73] *Natural England v Warren* [2019] UKUT 300 (AAC), [103]–[104].

> both by their own observations and expertise, and also by such evidence as was available. For example, Mr Lakin set out and summarised the conclusions found in literature as to the effects of shooting, release of birds and other activities. He acknowledged, as did the literature, the gaps in current evidence and the need for more work to be done, but he explained how he was able to extrapolate his opinion as to risks from the available evidence and his conclusions were thoroughly referenced to scientific literature. This is but one example. Natural England's response to Mr Warren's closing submissions in the First-tier Tribunal summarised (at paragraph 35) the considerable body of detailed evidence, based on available scientific evidence and evidence from the site including of existing harm, as to how the identified risks would take effect and their impacts. Against this body of evidence, the witnesses' phraseology was not inappropriate.[74]

The reference to the scientific literature here is significant.

A similar attitude, especially in respect of the importance of peer consensus, is to be found in the discussion of the Planning Inspector in *Airwave Solutions v Dartmoor National Park Authority* in respect of acceptable noise limits. Here, the Inspector reasoned that:

> I have taken account of the recently published scientific material and the claims therein that adverse health effects have been observed, but I do not believe it is reasonable to draw meaningful conclusions from a small number of studies without knowledge of the wider spectrum of latest research. Much greater weight should be placed, in my view, on the regular peer reviews mentioned above.[75]

Furthermore, the Inspector explicitly took account of the fact that the precautionary principle was already accounted for in the government guidance and so he did not 'double count' precaution in this respect.[76] Whether one agrees or disagrees with this approach, it is clear that a good deal of attention is being paid to the nature of the scientific consensus relied upon, and what this means for policy-making off the back of such guidance.[77] In *Derbyshire Wind Energy Ltd* too the Planning Inspector felt comfortable in criticising an expert report on the basis of the methodology employed:

> The appellant's ornithological surveys followed the thrust of the guidance in Scottish Natural Heritage's (SNH's) Survey Methods for Use in Assessing the Impacts of Onshore Windfarms on Bird Communities (November 2005). Nevertheless, to my mind, some of the survey work fell short of best practice. For example, no surveys were carried out in April, the month that is generally considered to be the most important for recording species. In addition, only 8.5 hours of nightjar surveys were carried out, instead of the recommended 25 hours.[78]

It is clear from this example that not all adjudicators are 'self-denying'.

[74] *Natural England v Warren* [2019] UKUT 300 (AAC), [106].
[75] *Airwave Solutions v Dartmoor National Park Authority* [2010] PAD 34.
[76] ibid [77]–[79].
[77] ibid [77].
[78] *Derbyshire Wind Energy Ltd* [2010] PAD 32, [67].

B. Deference to Natural England and the Environment Agency

However, in a lot of the cases above, the comparative expertise of the Planning Inspectors themselves (when pitted against a generalist court), or the experience of judges in the FTT, is providing them not only with the intellectual tools to be sufficiently familiar with such methodologies and reasoning to engage directly with them, but also the legitimacy in so doing. This argument reaches its apogee in *Enertrag v South Norfolk DC*[79] where the Planning Inspector had been so critical of the original environmental statement's methodology that he required an additional survey to be carried out by NE. In calling for this new scientific guidance, he 'advised that Natural England is the Government's main source of technical advice on ecological matters and that my findings on the "bats issue" would be led by its advice'.[80] This is particularly interesting as the Inspector was fully prepared to re-evaluate the applicant's own scientific advice for its merits and shortcomings, but indicated that he would be deferential to NE in its assessment. The degree to which this 'relative expertise' is therefore malleable according to the identity of the scientific advisor is significant. A similar approach to the advice of NE specifically is to be found in *Grand Union Marine & Leisure Services v Solihull MBC*.[81] In these cases we therefore see the emergence of our second theme, that there is a tendency to be *more* deferential to NE's and the EA's opinions than to other experts.

This general approach to handling science in judicial review actions emerges from the perceived relationship between the courts and the administrative decision-maker and the place which scientific information holds in the processes of the latter. Thus, the validity of scientific information as understood by such administrative bodies is unlikely to come under the gaze of the court (*Warren*,[82] discussed earlier, is an exception, although the UT redressed the balance in favour of NE[83]). The general principle is expressed clearly in *Spurrier*:

> For our part, we consider *Mott* is a helpful reminder of well-established good law: the court should accord an enhanced margin of appreciation to decisions involving or based upon 'scientific, technical and predictive assessments' by those with appropriate expertise. The degree of that margin will of course depend on the circumstances: but, where a decision is highly dependent upon the assessment of a wide variety of complex technical matters by those who are expert in such matters and/or who are assigned to the task of assessment (ultimately by Parliament), the margin of appreciation will be substantial. That will be a potentially important consideration when we examine some of the grounds of challenge, which do relate to matters of technical judgment and

[79] *Enertrag v South Norfolk DC*, [2010] PAD 13.
[80] ibid [59].
[81] *Grand Union Marine & Leisure Services v Solihull MBC* [2011] PAD 39.
[82] *Warren v Natural England* [2018] UKFTT NV_2018_0006 (GRC).
[83] *Natural England v Warren* [2019] UKUT 300 (AAC).

> expertise, modelling and predictive assessments, some of which were made by independent expert bodies or by the Secretary of State assigned to make such assessments on the basis of expert evidence.[84]

The key principle here is the assignment of decision-making power by Parliament in the light of expertise. We considered the relevance of parliamentary conferral of power in the previous chapter.[85] Its effects on techniques of reasoning is clear here too. This more limited scope of review in respect of competing scientific evidence is also evidenced in *R (RSPB) v Natural England*.[86]

In *R (Friends of the Earth Ltd) v Environment Agency*, the court emphasised that where the standard is a *Wednesbury* irrationality standard, there will be a 'high hurdle when challenging the decision of the expert regulator in a complex technical field'.[87] This is not only a question of expertise, it is also a question of allocation of power. A similar argument is present in *King v Environment Agency*, where the Court held that:

> Where a delicate balancing of interests is required, where Parliament has charged the Environment Agency with supervising flood risk management in England, and where the agency has considerable expertise, the court is in no position to second guess its expert judgment and cost/benefit analyses.[88]

This deference also applies in cases involving the Health and Safety Executive, as *R (Dennett) v Lancashire CC* demonstrates, where the court refused to provide its own risk assessment where an expert regulator had already done so:

> Essentially, the claimant contends that the only reasonable conclusion is that the fracking operations present a high risk. However, there is no evidence before this court to support this contention. It is not for this court to substitute its own risk assessment for the risk assessment based on robust specialist technical expertise. There is no basis for the contention that the assessment of medium risk is irrational.
>
> I am satisfied that the assessment of the risk as 'medium' was a conclusion that could properly be reached on the available evidence. The assessment was based on the expert evidence of HSE and the product of a lengthy and detailed regulatory scrutiny, which has continued up to the present time.[89]

Whilst it is clear that adjudicators will not always take the word of 'expert' regulators, it is apparent that very often they will. This is significant where the 'expert' and the administrative decision-making body are one and the same thing. It is potentially more problematic where the deference given is deference to the original decision-maker themselves because of their own expertise, where the challenge

[84] *R (Spurrier) v Secretary of State for Transport* [2019] EWHC 1070 (Admin), [2019] JPL 1163, [179].

[85] See ch 5.III.A.

[86] *R (RSPB) v Natural England* [2019] EWHC 585, [2020] Env LR 2.

[87] *R (Friends of the Earth Ltd) v Environment Agency* [2019] EWHC 25 (Admin), [2019] Env LR 19, [44].

[88] *King v Environment Agency* [2018] EWHC 65 (QB), [2018] Env LR 19.

[89] *R (Dennett) v Lancashire CC* [2018] EWHC 2721 (Admin), [16]–[17].

by the parties is to the quality of the exercise of that expertise. Despite this tension, in judicial review cases the courts are very clear that a hands-off approach, which is generally acceptable in judicial review, is even more important where dealing with review of an expert decision in a technical field. The only strong counteracting considerations to such, as *Mott v Environment Agency*[90] shows, is where individual rights and obligations are challenged by any decision, in which case the courts will 'reassert' a higher degree of scrutiny.

The reason for the court's hands-off attitude to scientific information is, however, as much a question of how science affects policy-making as it is about how adjudicators view science. Fisher et al explain such a lack of intrusion, particularly with the view of scientific regulatory agencies (eg NE): 'By granting courts authority to review science-based regulatory decisions, there is a risk they will unravel layers of careful scientific work as a result of their combined ignorance and judicial second-guessing.'[91] Again, we see the critical perceived importance of expertise as well as the focus on the allocation of decision-making powers as considered in the previous chapter. 'Courts are not to second-guess agency fact-finding',[92] is a powerful rule constructed of a number of arguments, of which expertise and legitimacy form the most important bloc.

As we have seen in respect of the other avenues of adjudication, however, it is not *generally* the case that independent adjudicators are 'supposed' to be hands off when it comes to the assessment of scientific information upon which a decision has been based. Rather, it is only in judicial review that we see this paradigm emerging, to the point where courts are reluctant even to engage in the hearing of expert information except where they need it in order to understand the fault lines of the dispute at hand. This, as discussed elsewhere, creates a very interesting dynamic between the administrative decision-maker (who may not be in a position to challenge the advice given to them by expert bodies), the expert body themselves (who become in effect the determining voice in any decision), and the adjudicator, who is deferential both to the expert themselves,[93] and then in judicial review cases also to the administrative authority on the basis of hands-off review. The levels of scrutiny that this model represents are therefore doubly 'hands off'.

C. Reviewing Use of Expert Opinion

Finally, there are cases where although the adjudicator will not review the expert evidence itself, it will review the use of that evidence by a decision-making

[90] *R (Mott) v Environment Agency* [2018] UKSC 10, [2018] 1 WLR 1022.

[91] E Fisher et al, 'Rethinking Judicial Review of Expert Agencies' (2015) 93 *Texas Law Review* 1681, 1682.

[92] ibid 1684.

[93] Lees, 'Allocation of Decision-Making Power under the Habitats Directive'.

authority. In most cases, this review will be relatively hands off. As an example, in *R (Mynnyd y Gwynt Ltd) v Secretary of State for Business Energy and Industrial Strategy*,[94] the court emphasised that a decision-maker was legitimate in seeking only clarity from the evidence before them, rather than levels of proof perhaps unattainable in the context.[95] The court would allow decision-makers to seek more information where that was required on the basis of an administrative assessment only. The Court was supportive of the approach of the Secretary of State in ascertaining for himself whether more information was needed, rather than requiring a judicial pronouncement to that effect. Similarly, in *Preston New Road Action Group v Secretary of State for Communities and Local Government*,[96] the Court supported administrative authorities in themselves assessing the weight of the evidence before them. The 'reviewing' rather than 'remaking' function of adjudication is emphasised.

However, in other cases, a more intense look is given to the use of expert evidence, particularly in respect of lower courts. *Davies v Campfield*[97] is instructive in this regard. In this case, the first-instance judge had assessed the factual situation and made findings of facts about the extent of past flooding. He had then reviewed the expert reports, and had preferred the one which predicted that which the past evidence demonstrated. The defendants claimed that this was the wrong way of assessing expert evidence, and that he should have looked at the strength of the theory. The court rejected this and emphasised the importance of real-world fact-finding in the approach to expert evidence:

> Not only was the judge entitled to take this approach, in my judgment it was a preferable approach to take as a matter of principle. When there is direct evidence about what the degree of flooding actually was at the material times, to start with the rival theories and then use a preference for one theory over another to resolve a dispute about the primary facts risked coming to the wrong conclusion. The theories should be fitted to the primary facts, not the primary facts fitted to the theory.[98]

The court does not review the evidence itself, but it does review the use to which that evidence was put, albeit here by a lower court rather than an administrative decision-maker. Such administrators are not immune from this analysis though. In the unusual case of *R (Shimbles) v City of Bradford MDC*,[99] the court was required to consider reliance by the local authority on the opinion of NE, where NE itself was utilising a private contractor's expert report. In so relying, NE had a 'change of view' midway through the decision-making process. The judge, in assessing this

[94] *R (Mynnyd y Gwynt Ltd) v Secretary of State for Business Energy and Industrial Strategy* [2018] EWCA Civ 231, [2018] Env LR 22.
[95] ibid [29].
[96] *Preston New Road Action Group v Secretary of State for Communities and Local Government* [2018] EWCA Civ 9, [2018] Env LR 18.
[97] *Davies v Campfield* [2017] EWHC 2746 (Ch).
[98] ibid [31].
[99] *R (Shimbles) v City of Bradford MDC* [2018] EWHC 195 (Admin), [2018] Env LR 25.

situation, concluded that: 'I do not think there was anything wrong or irrational in Natural England accepting the reasoning and conclusions in that report or in statements derived from it.'[100] It is telling that this was not based on deference to the expert evidence itself, but rather was evidence of support of NE's use of that evidence. This case, therefore, whilst supportive of the administrative authorities, does nevertheless show that on occasion a court will interrogate how expert evidence is handled by such authorities.

What this demonstrates is that the approach to handling of expert evidence is not a one-dimensional one. There are a multiplicity of ways in which such evidence can filter into decision-making by adjudicators, of which 'ignore entirely' and 'follow blindly' are but two. In between these sits analysis and critique of methodology; review of use of evidence if not the evidence itself; and a flexible deference depending upon the context of the decision and the identity of the decision-maker and their own comparative expertise.

In recent cases, we have also seen development regarding understandings of scientific certainty. In the Court of Appeal judgment in *Langton* (concerning the badger cull), the Court reasoned:

> By its very nature, scientific knowledge is a developing concept. Contrary to popular thinking, scientific knowledge cannot always deliver certainty. Experts may not know that a specific experiment will achieve an identified result; but based on their experience and expert knowledge they are properly able to conclude that an experiment is logically justified on the information available. In the circumstances of this case, what was proposed was an adaptive process which would be monitored. The monitoring and the results would be used to evaluate the effectiveness of the activity which would add to existing knowledge of the effect of supplementary culling as a means of controlling the spread of disease. There is nothing in section 10 which states that the procedure is lawful only if the outcome is certain. Its purpose is to seek to achieve a particular end, the prevention of the spread of disease. The dichotomy raised by the appellant between scientific certainly and scientific opinion is a false one.[101]

This recognition of the inability of an adjudicator (or a scientific advisor) to generate the kinds of certainty which many hope for is significant, and it highlights the importance of judgement, a topic to which we now turn.

VII. Objectivity, Impartiality and Neutrality

The final technique we explore is that of subjective and impartial assessment. We noted in chapter two that an essential characteristic of adjudication as we define it is adjudicator independence.[102] This independence manifests itself

[100] ibid [123].
[101] *R (Langton) v Secretary of State for Environment, Food and Rural Affairs* [2019] EWCA Civ 1562, [69].
[102] See ch 2.II.E.

and is tested, for the most part, on the basis of structural factors. That is, where an adjudicator is structurally independent from the original decision-making parties, or in the case of private law, from the parties to the dispute, then the relevant independence is achieved. However, this independence can go deeper, and if pushed far enough, becomes neutrality. Neutrality is not a necessary element for an adjudicator to be worthy of the name. For example, we could imagine a situation where an adjudicator was specifically tasked with upholding consistency across the planning system. They would not therefore be neutral *as between the parties* because they would have the specifically assigned role of upholding consistency which would mean that they did not approach the dispute between the parties from a neutral standpoint. This is of course true of any pre-existing norm – fidelity to that norm would undermine neutrality. It does not undermine independence.

But there is a middle ground here, and that is where we call upon the subjective assessment of an adjudicator regarding matters over which there may be more or less agreement, or more or less consternation. One thinks here of taste-based criteria, or subjective assessment of degrees of harmfulness, significance and impact, or a discretionary evaluation of competing concerns and interest with no legal guidance as to how these relative criteria should be weighed. Any such subjectivity is controversial because of our prevailing understanding of what the role of the adjudicator is. As Brudney and Ditslear explain: 'The tension between judges as value-promoting policymakers and judges as principled, impartial actors implicates a core aspiration of our legal culture: that judicial techniques of reasoning are or ought to be both reasonably predictable and outcome-neutral.'[103] And yet, it is not possible to create an 'outcome-neutral system'. The discussion above regarding the political nature of the public/private distinction demonstrates this.[104] It is even more apparent when the values at play in environmental law are brought to the fore.

Indeed, it is necessary to engage with a subjective balancing of values in environmental adjudication. These labels feel very pejorative, but in fact a degree of subjectivity is sought (a) because very often we are seeking to answer subjective questions, it is just that we need someone independent to bring their independent subjective assessment to the question; and (b) because in expertise lies subjective considerations. We do not define subjective as an irrational application of the relevant norms. Rather, these decisions are subjective in the sense that they require the decision-maker to look to their own personal experience, expertise and assessment, in order to reach a conclusion as to whether a particular legislative or common law test is met. We see considerations of these types playing a role in all the avenues. The acceptability and legitimacy of taking such 'personal' value

[103] JJ Brudney and C Ditslear, 'Canons of Construction and the Elusive Quest for Neutral Reasoning' (2005) 58 *Vanderbilt Law Review* 1, 4.
[104] See ch 6.III.

preferences into account varies according to the expected adjudicator role which is the paradigm within each avenue.

This tension was addressed head on by the Planning Inspector in *Airwave Solutions*, who reasoned that:

> Some disquiet was expressed that, as an inspector acting for the Secretary of State and required to have regard to Government policy, I am not in a position to undertake an impartial assessment of this case. I ascertained at the inquiry that the criticism was not aimed at me as an individual, but at the system that exists to deal with telecommunications appeals. The principle of the independence and impartiality of an inspector has been established in the courts, where it has been held that the right to challenge a particular decision by recourse to the High Court provides a sufficient safeguard, even in cases where another Government department or agency is involved. For the same reason there is no merit to the contention that there is a breach of Art 6 of the European Convention on Human Rights, the right to a fair hearing.[105]

The Inspector here addresses the differing forms of independence which define their role: impartiality, independence, neutrality, objectivity. There is an acceptance in this that a local authority decision-maker, whilst independent in respect of individuals within their region, is not a neutral decision-maker themselves given their close democratic connection with the local area. By contrast, although the decision-making jurisdiction, power and content resting with the Planning Inspectors is the same, there is not the same degree of closeness. Thus, Planning Inspectors are both independent and impartial, but that does not mean that they are unable to take advantage of their familiarity with and fidelity to promulgated policy. Furthermore, review of planning decisions quickly demonstrates that there can be disagreements between the Inspectorate and the Secretary of State personally, which also reveals the complexity between the Planning Inspectors and the more explicitly political Ministry.[106]

However, there must be a limit to what sorts of subjective arguments will overstep the requirement of independence, and therefore skew or adjust the role and purpose of adjudication. The planning appeals process is designed to engage Inspectors precisely because their own professional expertise allows them insight into the effect that a development may have, particularly visually and in landscape preservation terms. However, the degree to which such adjudicators feel comfortable in making manifestly subjective aesthetic judgements varies. For example, in relation to wind turbines, the question of whether wind turbines are attractive or not, is, as the reports recognise, an entirely subjective one. This has given rise to the concept of 'valency' within the planning parlance. Inspectors are regularly asked to conclude that since people have such differing views on the visual impact of wind farms, it is not possible to reach a legitimate conclusion on the question of pure aesthetic value. The Inspectorate has rejected this approach.[107] Instead Inspectors

[105] *Airwave Solutions v Dartmoor National Park Authority* [2010] PAD 34, [82].
[106] An example of such disagreement is *Doran v Rochford DC* [2011] PAD 22.
[107] *E.ON v East Riding of Yorkshire* [2010] PAD 17, [18].

emphasise that they are able to assess each individual development on its merits and that part of their task is to engage their own aesthetic judgement. However, as the Inspector in *E.ON v East Riding of Yorkshire* explained: '[I]t is incumbent upon me to address the landscape impact of this specific proposal in an objective manner. I could not reasonably base my conclusion in terms of landscape impact on a predilection.'[108] Whim is in this sense different from the engagement of personal expertise and judgement on competing values. But despite the Inspector's assertion that the assessment must be purely objective, it is clear that this is not the case if by objective is meant without the engagement of personal judgement (indeed, such would not even be possible).

The departure into the subjective and personal is not necessarily explicit, however. Thus, in *Enertrag*, the Inspector described the local landscape in these terms:

> These range from relatively unobstructed panoramas of 'big Norfolk skies', to more intimate sylvan glimpses of the immediate environs including, for example, scarecrows guarding a winter field of winter barley, a church tower nestling among trees, or the edge of a small settlement.[109]

Even without reading the rest of this judgment, it would be relatively easy know what the Inspector concluded into this case.

This objectivity is related to independence in another direction as well. We noted in chapter four that in cases involving planning appeals there is often closeness between adjudication and administration, and this closeness was emphasised too in the decision in *Airwave Systems*.[110] Where there is a remaking of any decision on the basis of a de novo fact-finding jurisdiction, there is a 'primary' decision which is being challenged (and in cases of planning it is necessary that this decision was a rejection of a planning permissions, or the only possible route is that of judicial review). The initial decision forms a background against which the adjudication will take place.[111] Adjudicator decisions are not therefore made from a blank starting point, but where the decision is made afresh entirely, as in the Planning Inspectorate, or in the IC/ FTT, there is a degree to which the adjudicator is not adjudicating, but rather is stepping into the shoes of the primary decision-maker. As a result, the goal of impartiality between two parties morphs by virtue of the requirement that the adjudicator not only decides who wins, but also makes an administrative decision themselves.

Adjudication in statutory appeals can be very close in 'task' to that in private law, where there is no pre-existing determination of outcome which is being challenged. The adjudicator must adjudge the merits of the case afresh. In discussing

[108] ibid.
[109] *Enertrag v South Norfolk DC* [2010] PAD 13, [12].
[110] *Airwave Solutions v Dartmoor National Park Authority* [2010] PAD 34.
[111] See the argument regarding the primacy of the initial decision in the judicial review process in ch 4.IV.

Weinrib's approach to encapsulating the 'purity' of private law, Gardner explains the nature of private law adjudication (as distinct from engagement of public and private interest):

> Private law adjudication is certainly characterized, in part, by its motivational non-transparency. Judges are heavily restricted, in private law and public law alike, in the reasons that they may rely upon in arriving at their decisions. The success and value of their work qua judges … depends crucially upon it.[112]

This 'motivational non-transparency' is, on this account, an essential element of appropriate private law reasoning. Where does subjectivity enter into this picture? The fact that ostensibly private law adjudication does not involve the balancing of competing instrumental or intrinsic 'values', but rather the assessment of the content of legal rights, skews how judges reason in this area to obscure the engagement of values. However, even in private law we can see the effect of value judgements being made. This is most apparent in nuisance cases, where the driving goal is said to be the establishment of good neighbourliness through a principle of give and take to ensure reasonableness on both sides. Such a standard is not, however one expresses it, capable of assessment in the abstract. Rather, a judge must engage their own skills and expertise to explore whether the interference 'goes too far'. Thus, whilst 'judges are bound to ignore many of the further reasons which would, apart from their judicial role, be relevant to their decision-making',[113] they will inevitably engage with a degree of subjectivity in conducting this sort of balancing act.

In concluding this section it is useful to return to the argument we developed at the end of the previous chapter, that of the importance of independence in the context of decision-making processes which allow an adjudicator to self-determine the scope of their power. Where, as we demonstrated, there are no fixed objective principles at play, the need for an independent adjudicator becomes all the more pressing. When we think about objectivity, we think about it not only in the context of, for example, specialist judiciary specifically tasked with protection of the environment and what that means for the objectivity of their process in balancing the public, the private and the environmental, but also about neutrality in values. If we seek the latter we run into an inevitable problem which is that it is precisely because there is a balancing exercise to be carried out in such a context between the environmental and the public and private that we want experienced adjudicators in the first place. We do not seek their neutrality, we seek their expertise in balancing these considerations and indeed in making subjective assessments *given* their independence. The role is in this sense paradoxical.

[112] Gardner, 'The Purity and Priority of Private Law' 462.
[113] ibid 464.

VIII. Conclusions

This chapter has explored the substance of the reasons which can be considered in the different avenues, and how these forms of consideration affect the overall processes of adjudication in relation to environmental matters. Three conclusions have become clear. First, in respect of the kinds of argument considered legitimate in any avenue, the degree to which an adjudicator will look beyond the parameters of the instant dispute into the effects of the dispute on the 'wider world' is critical. This affects the degree to which public interest concerns are taken into account in purely private disputes, but also shapes the adjudicatory response to arguments about environmental harm in general. Second, the seriousness with which an adjudicator will take arguments about flaws in an original decision – both in terms of the scientific evidence which underpins that decision, and more generally in respect of the level of scrutiny they are prepared to bring to that original decision – has a challenging and morphing effect on the substance of decisions about the environment. Some arguments are simply illegitimate in the adjudicatory forum in question – but the patterns of what can and cannot be considered are not the same across the different avenues, skewing how discussion about the environment is conducted in these divergent contexts. Finally, the requirement that an adjudicator be 'independent' from the parties in the instant case is an essential element of adjudication, but this is not the end of the question of neutrality. The level of objectivity, deference, closeness and consequences of the decision in terms of administration, all mean that in substance as well as in form the boundary line between adjudicator and administrative state can often be very fine, especially in a context where we demand the rehearing and replaying of subjectively-balanced environmental values. At first glance we may think that such 'subjective preferences' forming part of our adjudicatory systems is a problem. In fact, as this chapter has shown, in many of the avenues this has been deliberately built in. It is the flipside of expertise, and therefore can in many contexts be embraced.

Drawing these threads together with the previous chapter we see a nuanced picture emerging of how environmental adjudication works. We have, in the first place, formal limitations on power, both in terms of the scope of jurisdiction, and in the ability to hear a case brought by a particular individual in terms of standing, motivation and affordability. On top of this sits the power structures that exist between the parties themselves and the adjudicator. This power is constructed of formal decision-making power, but also of informal or more subtle powers to interpret norms, create new ones, and significantly to shape the narrative of how a case develops through powers (or absence of powers) to make findings of fact and to re-review evidence.

In this we start to see the shift from the formal to the substantive, and this chapter has taken that discussion further to consider how reasons and reasoning are constrained and shaped within the different avenues of adjudication and within different fora. Thus, we have seen that once we move beyond the paradigm of judicial review the scope of adjudicator scrutiny over scientific information, over the genuine content of public interest and private rights, and of the values which build up the corpus of environmental law becomes much greater, both explicitly, and in more subtle ways. The picture thereby constructed is a rich analysis of how the processes and systems of environmental adjudication are shaped and formed through the decisions of individual adjudicators; through the formal conferrals of jurisdiction that underpin them; and of inherent understandings of the constitutional set-up which establishes the relationships between parties, administration, expert and adjudicator. It is perhaps telling that in drawing together the threads of reason and argumentation, we return to the question of power, as this is clearly *the* significant element of environmental decision-making.

The primary argument of the previous chapter was that in the context of the avenues of environmental decision-making, the prevailing characteristic is that power is self-determined. In this chapter, it is clear that the prevailing characteristic in terms of reasons and techniques of reasoning is that the adjudicatory role is a paradox: at once we need neutral arbiters between potentially inconsistent and irresolvable reasons for action, and we need an experienced hand independently making this balancing exercise for themselves without deference to an alternative decision-making forum in all cases. On the other hand, we also ask for judges to prioritise one of these considerations, whilst also asking them to provide a degree of deference to the original decision-maker and not bring their own personal assessment of the relative weights between the different considerations to the table. A single judge, and single judgment, or even a body of case-law, cannot possibly achieve all of these goals at once. When, in chapter eight, we consider incoherence in the system, therefore, at the heart of that incoherence lies the fact that the role of the adjudicator is, to a greater or lesser extent in the different avenues, a paradox of neutrality and independence; expertise and subjectivity; deference and intervention. This paradox is amply demonstrated when we consider existing decisions through the lenses of the reasons and techniques of reasoning employed when reaching a decision on the relative winners and losers in any environmental law dispute. In the final chapter of this part, we now turn to examine what the results of these structures of power and reason are for the parties, and what this means for the system as a whole.

7

Avenues as Remedy Determining

I. Introduction

We turn now to the final aspect of adjudication identified in chapter two. Adjudication is dispute resolution. An adjudicator cannot simply hear a dispute, and then shrug their shoulders and tell the parties to sort it out themselves. Rather, it is necessary, having determined the norms applicable, and the facts as found, that a remedy or resolution is reached. As chapter four explained, that does not mean that the primary purpose of adjudication as a social institution will always be the resolution of a dispute. Rather, by definition, there must be a live case which needs resolving and winner/loser status will be assigned. However, in terms of real-world consequences, the remedy conferred by the court will be at least as important as the answer as to who is 'right' in any dispute. The effect that the avenues have on remedies (and as we shall see, this impact is powerful) is hugely important in determining how the law works in practice. Thus, the final consequence of the avenues of adjudication is that they are remedy determining.

This chapter will consider the effects that the avenues have in respect of remedies. In section II we consider the different forms of remedy available through the avenues. Section III examines how environmental considerations are relevant to determinations of remedies, and the variation that exists in this through the avenues. Here too we consider costs adjudication as part and parcel of the final 'remedial' determination. In section IV, the 'remedy' of doing nothing and its significance in environmental adjudication is examined. It will be shown that it is in the remedial approach that the consequences of the fact of environmental effects are most clearly seen in the adjudication process.

In many ways, the remedies element of adjudication gives the most unambiguous window into the variety of purposes of adjudication. As a result, in section V, we tie together the discussion from chapter four to conclude our analysis of the avenues. We argue that whilst the power-broker function and the reason-shaping function both produce complex and subtle webs of considerations to be taken into account, the remedy aspect is more concrete. One can trace a direct link between the avenue and its function, and the remedies that are available within it. We consider this the culmination of 'the dispute pyramid, which traces potential pathways from "perceived injurious experiences" to remedies, via grievances, claims, disputes, and remedial institutions like lawyers and courts',[1] and conclude that in the practice of multidimensional environmental law, analysis of remedies reveals much about the fundamental operation of this social institution.

II. Forms of Remedy

Before we analyse the different remedies available in these fora, it is important as a first step to clarify what is meant by remedy. We are using the term loosely to mean that outcome of the adjudicatory determination for both parties where (in some way or another) the adjudicator concludes that the factual situation which existed prior to their resolution of the dispute involved a legal error, wrong or harm. We therefore examine remitting decisions, as well as the more usual forms of remedies such as the provision of damages awards or injunctions. In this chapter we also cover the remaking of decisions directly by the adjudicator. This latter is more controversial as in a sense it is not a remedy for a legal wrong, but the expulsion of that wrong from the legal position; nevertheless it represents a legal response to the adjudicator decision and results in concrete action emerging from the legal determination. We include costs awards within the scope of our gaze, as they represent a consequence of the legal determination, and there will often be adjudication on the costs position as well as the substantive law applicable. Finally, we consider sentencing as a concrete outcome in criminal law cases.

A. Statutory Appeals

The landscape of remedies in environmental law is a diverse one. Perhaps unsurprisingly, we see the greatest variation of remedies available in the statutory appeals avenue. This is partly as a result of the variety of decision-makers who have been given adjudicatory powers under the statutory provisions;[2] and partly a consequence of the range of forms that such adjudication takes. As we explain in chapter five, in many cases involving statutory appeals, the adjudicator will simply substitute their own decision for that of the original decision-maker.[3] In others they are authorised to amend decision notices emerging from primary decision-makers; to award damages or some other form of compensation; or to remit decisions to the original decision-maker.

Many of the comments here regarding remedy in the context of statutory appeals are very closely linked to those made in chapter five regarding the power

[1] WLF Felstiner et al., 'The Emergence and Transformation of Disputes: Naming, Blaming, Claiming' (1980–81) 15 *Law and Society Review* 631.

[2] See the discussion in ch 4.III.A.

[3] See ch 5.III.

structures created through and by the avenues of adjudication. This is because the power to remake a decision conferred on adjudicators such as the FTT in cases involving the IC results as much in the conferral of power on the FTT and away from the IC as it does a shaping of remedial outcome. However, it is nevertheless useful to consider this jurisdiction from the perspective of remedies. It is especially important to draw a contrast between the remedial approach of statutory adjudicators (such as the IC and the FTT) and that of the courts *both* in statutory appeals (such as in planning cases under section 288 Town and Country Planning Act 1990 (TCPA 1990)) and in judicial review.

If we first consider the powers of the FTT, both in terms of information regulation decisions and environmental sanctions, and of the Planning Inspectorate in planning appeal decisions, the close relationship between institutional power and remedy is apparent. In respect of both of these bodies, there is a good deal of remedial discretion, as well as a far-reaching power in terms of amends to be made. It is in the existence of this discretion that we see the importance of remedy. The jurisdiction of the FTT is clearly one of remaking, not remitting decisions. 'Remade' decision notices are apparent in a number of the FTT's cases, but the notice in *Bruton v Information Commissioner* is instructive in this regard.[4] Here, the original notice of the IC was completely abandoned and an entirely new approach taken to reflect the different conclusion reached by the FTT on the question as to whether the Duchy of Cornwall was a public body susceptible to information requests under the regulations. Although this decision was later overturned on the facts in the Upper Tribunal,[5] this was on the legal question of the definition of public authority for the purposes of the Environmental Information Regulations,[6] not on the question of the power of the FTT to make the radical change to the decision notice.

Perhaps the most significant element of such discretion is the ability to remake decisions so as to transform the adjudicator from adjudicator into a primary decision-maker. The consequence of the legal wrong in this sense will be a power transfer. Where there is a fixed remedial outcome, the significance of the decision becomes only the assessment of the substantive merits. The remedy would be an unavoidable consequence of the substance. But in statutory appeals, remedial options tend to be wide.

Indeed, in statutory appeals, as we explained above, in the majority of cases the adjudicator will simply substitute their own decision for that of the original decision-maker. However, in judicial review cases (see below), and in some statutory appeals, the route is more appropriately for the quashing of a decision, and a remitting of the case to the original decision-maker so that they can reach a new decision, or the same decision but based upon different reasons. Primarily this relates to section 288 planning appeals. In such cases the powers of the High Court

[4] *Michael Bruton v Information Commissioner* [2011] UKFTT EA_2010_0182 (GRC).
[5] *The A-G for the Prince of Wales v the IC and Mr Michael Bruton* [2016] UKUT 154 (AAC).
[6] The Environmental Information Regulations 2004, SI 2004/3391, regulation 2(2).

are constrained by statute to temporary suspensions of planning permissions (or similar), and quashing in cases where there is shown to be an illegality in the decision made. Thus, the statutory provisions, in section 288(5)(b), stipulate that the High Court

> if satisfied that any such order or action is not within the powers of this Act, or that the interests of the applicant have been substantially prejudiced by a failure to comply with any of the relevant requirements in relation to it, may quash that order or action.

Notwithstanding the wording of the section, the courts have exercised discretion not to quash decisions even where the complaint does not relate to 'relevant requirements' if it appears that no substantial prejudice has been caused. The ability or otherwise of a court to refuse to quash a planning decision where there is no prejudice is discussed in the 'remedy of doing nothing' section below.[7]

B. Judicial Review

In judicial review cases, as with planning appeals under section 288, the route is more appropriately for the quashing of a decision, and a remitting of the case to the original decision-maker so that they can reach a new decision, or the same decision but based upon different reasons. However, as we examine in section IV below, in some situations, despite the presence of a legal 'wrong', the courts will conclude that the appropriate remedy is to do nothing given that the legal error was not material in the outcome. This is a reflection of the constitutional role played by judicial review of administrative action and we discuss it in more detail shortly. In this sense, whilst there is discretion in judicial review, in the form of the analysis as to whether the court is able to quash by reviewing the criteria in section 31(2A) Senior Courts Act 1981 (SCA 1981) (see later), the substance and the remedy are intimately connected.

C. Private Law

The different forms of private law shape the remedy available, be that an injunction, specific performance or, most commonly, damages. The substantive outcomes both shape and are shaped by the remedial preferences in these avenues. Until recently,[8] the judicial preference for the grant of injunctions in cases involving nuisance was having a substantive impact on the possibility of liability (especially in cases where there had been a positive planning decision). The shift to damages affects the issue of liability, not only the remedy. In contract law, there is a preference for damages except in cases where contractual performance relates to a

[7] See s III.C below.
[8] *Coventry (t/a RDC Promotions) v Lawrence* [2014] UKSC 13, [2014] AC 822, [120]–[125].

'unique' act (eg contracts for the transfer of interests in land) where specific performance may be preferred. This again has substantive effects as it results in the need to value that which has been lost, and the approach to valuation in environmental cases is far from straightforward.

More so than in the other avenues, when dealing with private law, it is not possible entirely to disaggregate the effect of remedies and the reasons discussed in the previous chapter. In respect of public law generally – both statutory appeals and judicial review – the test for the quality of decision-making is almost always legality. Adjudicators will assess whether the decision was within the legal purview of its maker. The consequence of adjudication will almost always relate to a *decision* reached by a public authority, ahead of the materialisation of any actual effect from that decision.[9] In private law, adjudication more often will follow the consequences of the decision. Remedies in private law do not therefore have to be, and often cannot be, predictive (for the most part). As such, the reasons that are relied upon for liability in private law tend to include the actual emergence of a demonstrable harm. The parameters for remedies are set by the fact of the harm actually having taken place. An essential element of the condition for liability at all will then determine the form of remedy.

Furthermore, this makes private law closer to criminal law than might first appear. The evaluation of both substance and remedy in private law are critical in determining what the purpose of those rules is in the legal system as a whole. One way of thinking of this problem is, as Sebok discusses, to analyse the role of remedy in private law as signifying either deterrent effects (as in criminal law); as redressing wrongs that have been committed so as to maximise overall welfare; or as a means of protecting certain kinds of interests within the private law system.

> One could argue, as modern law and economics scholars do, that the redressive function of private law and the sanction function of criminal law should have the same purpose: to deter inefficient conduct ex ante and thereby maximize social welfare. Or one could argue, in the tradition of progressive and critical legal scholarship, that the redressive remedies of private law are coextensive with the sanctions imposed through public law, in that both public and private law ultimately serve to promote and preserve the interests of a subset of society (usually capital).[10]

The consequences of these forms of remedies in private law, therefore, reveal much about where the valuation of environmental interests sits within the legal system as a whole. Since remedy is tied to harm, how that harm is conceived of and explained tells us what is of value. But the discretion in such forms of valuation is not entirely at the behest of an adjudicator. Rather, in many cases there will

[9] See ch 4.II.IV.

[10] AJ Sebok, 'What Does it Mean to Say that a Remedy Punishes' (2003) 78 *Chicago-Kent Law Review* 3, citing RA Posner, *Economic Analysis of Law*, 1st edn (Boston, MA, Little Brown, 1973) 358–59. See D Kennedy, 'Form and Substance in Private Law Adjudication' (1976) 89 *Harvard Law Review* 1685.

be claimant discretion in terms of what remedy to seek. For example, a claimant may seek specific performance of a contract given the uniqueness of the situation from their perspective. The court will have discretion to grant such or not, but in cases where it is not sought, the fact that specific performance is not given tells us nothing about judicial attitude to the content of the contract.

D. Criminal Law

As Sebok's analysis above emphasised,[11] there is a perhaps unexpected degree of confluence between private and criminal law when we think about the purpose of adjudication through the lens of remedies (at least if one subscribes to a broadly 'deterrent'-focused paradigm). In criminal law, however, the remedies are obviously very different. Questions about sentencing and the consequences following a successful defendant appeal are all determined by the principles of this avenue as a whole. In criminal cases the prevailing approach is affected by the role of adjudication as supporter of social coercion,[12] rather than the resolution of disputes per se.

The consequence is that governmental policy (in the form of the Sentencing Guidelines)[13] is much more relevant to the question of remedy in criminal law than it is to other contexts where an attempt is being made to directly counteract or make up for the specific legal wrong, error or harm. In criminal law, whilst the sentencing guidelines are drafted so as to vary according to the nature of the act committed, they are not tied directly in scale and form to the harm. Unusually too the 'remedy' in criminal law takes account of the identity of the defendant.

This very brief and generalised discussion of different remedial preferences in the avenues points to an important element of our argument: that remedies are part of the 'culture' of avenues, but that, as we shall see, that cultural influence is susceptible to outside effects. Galanter emphasises the 'cultural' element of remedy preference:

> We recognize that remedies are cultural constructs: it is not a natural given that an injury is adequately erased or cancelled or balanced by revenge, payment, condemnation, or apology. What satisfies our sense of an appropriate and adequate remedy clearly depends on the cultural presuppositions that we bring to the question.[14]

Indeed, when we think about remedies, culture becomes so much more apparent here than it does when we think about reasons. Reason, and at the very least a minimum degree of rationality, are not entirely constructed by the legal system. However, preference for a particular remedial approach – damages or specific

[11] Sebok, 'What Does it Mean to Say that a Remedy Punishes'.
[12] See discussion in ch 4.V.
[13] Sentencing Council, 'Environmental Offences: Definitive Guideline' (London, HMSO, 2014).
[14] M Galanter, 'The Dialectic of Injury and Remedy' (2010) 44 *Loyola of Los Angeles Law Review* 1, 2.

performance, for example – shows no inherent hierarchy. There is merely choice based on the effects of the different remedies, and their perceived justification in the context. As an indicator of the prevailing culture of any avenue, therefore, remedial preference is an excellent starting point.

If we consider the different avenues of adjudication, it is worthwhile to note that those with remaking power tend (a) to be lower in the adjudication chain in terms of the precedent value of their decisions, and in the number of appeals that would result in a decision being before such an adjudicator; and (b) to involve specialist or non-traditional judicial fora. For example, the FTT and the Planning Inspectorate both have a remaking jurisdiction. They are not carrying out review at all, but are making a fresh decision. It is hugely significant, as we have seen in the previous chapters, that these adjudicators are precisely those with a high degree of framing power in respect of fact-finding and evidence review, and who also impose a very high level of scrutiny on earlier decisions. They are providing the highest intensity of scrutiny, and are the most responsive in being able to ensure that no further legal errors occur.

If we contrast this with the courts in judicial review, it is clear that the scope of their power is limited. The degree to which they will take a genuine hard look at administrative decision-making can be questioned, at least in cases involving a high level of expertise or technical information. Their response will be very limited in cases where an error is found. And yet, when we look at the power structures between adjudicators, and the ability to innovate new norms, and interpret existing ones, it is in the higher courts that we see these powers most strongly.

Discussion of remedies therefore shows us that a division has been created between adjudicatory fora whose focus is very clearly on the instant dispute, and its resolution to the highest possible degree of legality, and the focus on the wider ramifications and systemic consequences a decision has for the public as a whole. It is therefore perhaps concerning, or should at least give us pause for thought, that as we demonstrated in the previous chapter, the degree to which environmental considerations and the public interest more generally are taken into account at the higher court level is limited. If we are going to rely upon a system that creates significant powers for instant dispute resolution for some fora, with limited systemic power, on the one hand, and fora that have high levels of systemic power but a low level of impact on individual situations, on the other, then we might want to give the power to consider environmental consequences generally to the latter.

III. Environmental Considerations and Remedies

Let us now examine how these general remarks play out more specifically in the environmental context by looking at statutory appeals, judicial review, private law (specifically tort law) and criminal law (considering sentencing); and how the generalised remedial approach in these areas has been moulded, if at all, by the perceived importance of environmental considerations at play. The final subsection (section III.C below) considers the role of costs as part of the 'final determination' of the outcome in any case, recognising, for example, that even in cases where no 'remedy' is awarded, there is likely to be a costs award such that the outcome does still matter for the parties from a financial perspective, even if the legal wrong is not 'righted' by the remedial approach taken.

We examine how the different avenues channel the relevance of environmental considerations when assessing remedy. Whilst substantive rules may not have been amended in the light of particularly serious environmental considerations (see chapter six), in respect of remedies, environmental harm is driving innovation. Whilst criticisms of the legal paradigms driving our legal system on the basis that they have not appropriately responded to the pressures on the environment created by climate change, for example, are justified, in the field of remedies we see the greatest, or at least the first, acceptance of such pressures. Whilst straightforward claims for damage to the environment might not yet be recognised by a private law action to that effect, in the ways in which valuation exercises are carried out, discretion is directed, and sentencing and costs are analysed, we do see such a response to environmental pressures. Conversely, in cases where environmental issues appear to be straightforward, the 'cultural' preference of the avenues returns to the fore. Thus, in *Champion v North Norfolk*,[15] the fact that '[t]his was not a case where the environmental issues were of particular complexity or novelty'[16] affected the court's exercise of its remedial discretion. However, such recognition of the importance of taking account of environmental factors in reaching a conclusion as to remedies is certainly not absolute, nor wholesale. In many cases decisions which have very significant environmental consequences are made with little reflection of that fact in the approach to remedies.

Indeed, it is apparent from *Mott v Environment Agency* that environmental concerns are far from determinative, and may have no influence at all, in reaching a remedial conclusion.[17] The conclusion regarding deprivation of rights in breach of Article 1 of the first protocol to the European Convention on Human Rights in the Supreme Court decision in this case has the potential to seriously undermine the effectiveness of the environmental licensing system, given the limitations it imposes on EA flexibility in altering such permits. Fears immediately emerged after the case regarding the ongoing viability of the licensing system given the inflexibility engendered by the granting of effective proprietary status to the content of an environmental licence. But the true extent of this limitation, and its impacts on EA funding, would only be apparent following consideration of the appropriate remedy. The High Court in the remedy hearing made the following

[15] *R (Champion) v North Norfolk DC* [2015] UKSC 52, [2015] 1 WLR 3710.
[16] ibid [60].
[17] *R (Mott) v Environment Agency* [2018] UKSC 10, [2018] 1 WLR 1022.

assessment in discussing their ability to restrict the remedy given the importance of the state interest in the case:

> It [the EA] seeks to pursue, in a modified form, the argument that in matters involving the protection of the environment, striking a 'fair balance' between the interests of the state and the Convention rights of citizens cannot require compensation to be paid to citizens affected by executive action. That argument was made and was unsuccessful at all levels. It was summarised by Lord Carnwath at paras 29–30 of his judgment, and clearly rejected; see paras 33–36. If the action taken amounts to expropriation, or something closely akin to it (as I found in this case) it does not seem to me that there can be any principled basis for awarding less than the actual loss incurred, which would be in effect to require the citizen to shoulder some of the cost of the state's unlawful action against him. The required 'fair balance' is struck by the court determining whether state action taken without in fact offering compensation to the citizen is disproportionate, and not by the court, if it decides that question in favour of the citizen, awarding him some amount less (on an arbitrary basis) than the amount of his actual loss. No authority was cited for any such course, nor any example of a case in which assessed financial loss had not been awarded in full.[18]

As such, the Court, in explicitly rejecting the argument that the environmental protection concerns at play would not be counted in assessing remedy, rejected the idea that state resources in this context should affect their liability as against the holder of a licence who finds that licence modified substantially, causing them loss. In addition to the practical consequences of reaching such a conclusion, this sits at odds, as we shall see, with the more flexible approach to liability apparent in criminal law.

However, the approach of the Supreme Court in *Coventry v Lawrence* shows how the heavily regulated environmental context (if not the goal of environmental protection) can prompt a revolution in respect of remedies. In this case, the Court recognised that planning permissions (and by extension, we might surmise, environmental licensing), whilst irrelevant to the question of liability in tort, could be relevant to the question of remedy. In particular, the fact of administrative control was seen as sufficient to prompt a move away from the preference for injunction in nuisance cases. Whilst there was disagreement amongst their Lordships as to how far this shift takes the law, the majority certainly felt that there should not be a presumption in favour of an injunction in cases where the use was the subject of a planning permission.[19] Per Lord Carnwath:

> First, I would not regard the grant of planning permission for a particular use as in itself giving rise to a presumption against the grant of an injunction. As I have said, the circumstances in which permissions may be granted differ so much as to make it

[18] *Mott v Environment Agency* [2019] EWHC 1892, [2020] Env LR 6. This hearing followed the decision of the Supreme Court that Mott had been unlawfully deprived of his human rights (specifically his possessions as protected by Art 1 of the first protocol to the European Convention on Human Rights), and was concerned with the valuation of his right.

[19] *Shelfer v City of London Electric Lighting Co* [1895] 1 Ch 287; *Coventry (t/a RDC Promotions) v Lawrence* [2014] UKSC 13, [2014] AC 822, [120]–[125].

> unwise to lay down any general propositions. I would accept however that the nature of, and background to, a relevant planning permission may be an important factor in the court's assessment.[20]

The flexibility shown in this case in respect of remedies demonstrates the consequences that remedies can have with regards to the substance of the rules. The shift away from a presumption in favour of injunctions through the sidelining of the *Shelfer*[21] test creates a system of nuisance where not only are the rights of the aggrieved party effectively undermined by the possibility that the nuisance will continue, but this comes about *not* by the existence of a countervailing, more powerful private right, but by the invocation of the public interest. The change of remedy here is demonstrative of a fundamental change of philosophy.[22]

However, the proper functioning of both the private law of tort, balancing respective rights and uses between neighbours, and of the planning permission/licensing system, requires a harmonious interaction between the two. This cannot be achieved in absolute terms purely through reliance on the substance of the standard of behaviour permitted by nuisance. Planning authorities are not concerned to prevent the creation of actionable nuisances (and nor might they be able to predict them). A degree of harmony can be created through courts being willing to vary their remedial approach in order to strike an appropriate balance. Support for this flexibility can be derived also from comments of the Court of Appeal in *Barr v Biffa Waste*.[23] Indeed, it is hard to disagree with Lee's assessment that: 'The continued strength of private nuisance in a regulatory state depends on a more flexible approach to remedies.'[24]

However, more fundamentally, what this discussion highlights is that remedies indicate what is perceived to be of value. As a result, it becomes very important in understanding the dimensions of environmental adjudication, and particularly the operation of the avenues, to determine the patterns that emerge in remedial choice as indicative of a prioritisation of values. As Galanter explains:

> So injury and remedy are not fixed and determinate, but moving and changing. Is this change random, or is there a pattern? Is there some force driving the moving frontier? These questions take us back to naming and blaming – to changing perceptions of injury and changing attributions of responsibility for causing injury and providing remedy. In the long run, new ways of envisioning and understanding troubles and remedies are the hidden fount and engine of our expanding sense of injustice.[25]

The ways in which remedies shift to take account of environmental protection issues results not only in changes or at least reflection on the substance of liability

[20] *Coventry (t/a RDC Promotions) v Lawrence* [2014] UKSC 13, [2014] AC 822, [246].

[21] *Shelfer v City of London Electric Lighting Co* [1895] 1 Ch 287; *Coventry (t/a RDC Promotions) v Lawrence* [2014] UKSC 13, [2014] AC 822, [120]–[125].

[22] M Dixon, 'The Sound of Silence' [2014] Conv 79.

[23] *Barr v Biffa Waste Services Ltd* [2012] EWCA Civ 312, [2013] QB 455, [75] onwards.

[24] M Lee, 'Tort Law and Regulation' [2011] *Journal of Planning Law* 986.

[25] Galanter, 'The Dialectic of Injury and Remedy' 4.

rules, but also shows changing adjudicator attitudes as to what is of value in the environment.

That environmental considerations and the value of environmental protection can significantly shape conclusions in respect of remedies, or even as to assessments of the existence of a remediable harm, is demonstrated in the statements of Neuberger LJ in *R (Trailer & Marina (Leven) Ltd) v Secretary of the State for the Environment*.[26] In this case, his Lordship was required to assess whether there should be redress for landowners in the loss of liberties to use their land in a particular way consequent upon notification of that land as a Site of Special Scientific Interest (SSSI). He reasoned that:

> Compensating land owners for agreeing not to carry out damaging operations [would be] inappropriate, because resources should be devoted to the encouragement of conservation … this repeated the Government's preliminary suggestions, and, in particular, repeated that it was not prepared to pay out public money simply to dissuade operations which could destroy or damage SSSIs, on the basis that such money should be devoted to ensuring that conservation objectives were achieved.[27]

In this reflection that remedies are not 'consequence free' in terms of diverting resources away from beneficial outcomes, the Court recognises the value of environmental protection.

Another way in which environmental considerations can be seen to affect remedial approaches relates to the possibility of obtaining interim injunctions in respect of planning. Generally speaking, courts will err against providing such remedies on the basis that without a clear determination as to an illegality in the act of a private party, well-established constitutional principles demand that liberty be the presumption.[28] However, in *South Downs v Daroubaix*,[29] the court was required to weigh up the clearly important private interest of the individual in having a suitable home, and the public interest of maintaining an AONB in the granting of an interim injunction to prevent development.

> If an interim injunction is refused but a final injunction is one that it transpires ultimately should have been granted then the public interest in the proper planning of the Area of Outstanding Natural Beauty in the National Park is likely to be frustrated, at least for some period, and that may lead to other unauthorised developments on other plots on the field magnifying the damage to the character and appearance of the area. If an ex parte injunction is not granted now then the objective of protecting the character and appearance of the area from further unlawful development may be frustrated and further proceedings may have to be taken to remove any mobile home and further unlawful development.

[26] *R (Trailer & Marina (Leven) Ltd) v Secretary of the State for the Environment* [2004] EWCA Civ 1580, [2005] 1 WLR 1267.

[27] ibid [61].

[28] *Entick v Carrington* 95 ER 807, (1765) 2 Wils KB 275.

[29] *South Downs National Park Authority v Daroubaix* [2018] EWHC 1903 (QB).

> If, on the other hand, an interim injunction is granted but a final injunction is ultimately refused for some reason then the Defendants will have been restrained in the interim from doing something that is plainly unlawful. It is true that they may not have more satisfactory accommodation than their tent in which to continue to live. What consequences that may have on them and what other options they may have are not matters on which I have any information. However, they can present information about such matters on the return day for any ex parte injunction which I may now grant. The time for which they will be restrained from acting unlawfully before they could be heard is thus limited.[30]

The tensions between values, and the fragility of the environment, are both reflected in the considerations of the court here.

In both *Trailer and Marina* and *Daroubaix*, there is a divergence from the approach of both the Supreme Court and the High Court in the context of human rights violations emerging from changes to environmental licences in *Mott*. In all cases (emerging through statutory appeals, judicial review and tort), the question as to when private rights relating to the use of land by their owners are legitimately constrained on the basis of environmental protection is pitted against the freedom of such owners of make good economic use of their land. However, in *Mott* we see the consequences of regulatory interventions granting permissions being withdrawn, rather than reliance by landowners on their residual freedoms emerging merely from the existence of private rights. The differences in remedial approach and in valuation of what is lost in these two cases not only point to the consequences of focusing on practical outcome rather than expressions of the substance of a particular rule, but also highlight the different focuses engendered by the principles of the avenues through which these questions emerge.

The consequences the environment has from a remedial innovation perspective cannot be seen more clearly, however, than in the recent decisions in the *ClientEarth* litigation.[31] In *Clientearth No. 3*, given the repeated failures of the Government to comply with the requirements of the Air Quality Directive, Garnham J raised the possibility of alternative remedial approaches in public law being used to ensure compliance with the law:

> It seems to me that the time has come for the Court to consider exercising a more flexible supervisory jurisdiction in this case than is commonplace. Such an application was made to me when the November 2016 judgment was handed down. I refused it on that occasion, opting for a more conventional form of order. Given present circumstances, however, I would invite submissions from all parties, both in writing and orally, as to whether it would be appropriate for the Court to grant a continuing liberty to apply, so that the Claimant can bring the matter back before the court, in the present proceedings, if there is evidence that either Defendant is falling short in its compliance with the terms of the order of the Court.[32]

[30] ibid [18]–[19].
[31] *R (ClientEarth) v Secretary of State for Food, Environment and Rural Affairs (No. 3)* [2018] EWHC 315 (Admin), [2018] Env LR 21.
[32] ibid [109].

This 'remedy' of ability to reapply to allow for judicial supervision is not only innovative in public law as a remedy, but also has a substantial impact on both procedural and standing rules. That it was in part the environment context which prompted this change of approach by the courts, given that the normal rule was that courts would not oversee the process, is made clear by the court which explicitly highlights that this was not a 'routine' judicial review challenge.[33] On the other hand, in deciding the relief given, and the timeline for compliance by the Department for Environment, Food and Rural Affairs (DEFRA), the Court took account of the resources and ability of DEFRA to comply, albeit only to a limited extent.[34] Taken together, the level of remedial innovation, and the effect that this has on the substance of the operation of the law, is clear.

Similarly, in respect of tort, in *Bristol City Council v MB Estate Ltd*[35] the Court upheld the Council's decision to prosecute under anti-social behaviour legislation in cases involving the spread of Japanese knotweed. In addition to a fine, the Court also mandated that the landowner create a plan for appropriate treatment and eradication steps. This mandate of behaviour is not a 'typical' remedy and certainly is not a usual step in a criminal action. But it is evidence of how traditional remedies may not be best suited to dealing with the complex ongoing issues to which environmental harm gives rise. Since protection of the environment requires not only cessation of damaging activities, but also ongoing proactive and responsible management, a remedial approach that looks only to the redressing of harms done will not be capable of achieving the desired goal. When we turn the lens onto the purpose of adjudication in such cases, we can see that it morphs from assigning rights or wrong in terms of past behaviour, to a form of administration controlling ongoing acts.

A. Sentencing

The power of environmental considerations to change legal attitudes is shown nowhere more clearly, however, than in respect of sentencing in criminal law and in costs. We commence with the former. A good example of this is *Thames Water*.[36] In this case, a combination of the Sentencing Guidelines and the increasingly clear judicial recognition of the importance of strong deterrent effects on environmental cases is shown by the Court's comments.

> The object of the sentence is to bring home the appropriate message to the directors and shareholders of the company: Sellafield paragraph 6 and step 6 of the Guideline. Sentences imposed hitherto in a large number of cases have not been adequate to

[33] ibid [12]. See *R (P) v Essex CC* [2004] EWHC 2027.
[34] ibid [4] and [6].
[35] *Bristol City Council v MB Estate Ltd*, unreported.
[36] *R v Thames Water Utilities Ltd* [2015] EWCA Crim 960, [2015] 1 WLR 4411.

> achieve that object. This Court has on two occasions observed that it would not have interfered with fines 'very substantially greater' or 'significantly greater' than six figure fines imposed for environmental offences.[37]

The Court was praised for its innovation[38] but there was already a growing pressure within the court system for such large fines to be imposed, especially in cases of statutory water companies and their well-documented failures to properly monitor sewage leaks. Perhaps most notable is the attention paid in these cases to the identity of the defendant. In environmental crime, defendants are not equal before the law (and maybe that is perfectly justified, but that does not mean that it is not notable). This can be seen further in the two cases of *Thames Water* (2019)[39] and *Day*.[40]

The former case, as is obvious from the defendant, involved breach of environmental licensing by a statutory water undertaker. The question for the Court of Appeal was whether the identity (and specifically resources) of the defendant were relevant to sentencing (as was made plain in the Sentencing Guidelines[41] and as mandated by section 164(3) Criminal Justice Act 2003) and if so, how it should be taken into account.

> This was a breach of environmental regulations committed by a very large organisation as a result of corporate recklessness. The size of the organisation meant that the figures provided within the table applicable to a large company were of little relevance. The previous history of the organisation was little short of lamentable. To bring home to the directors and shareholders the need to protect the environment required a very substantial fine. In those circumstances a fine measured in millions of pounds was entirely proportionate. A fine after a trial of £3 million was appropriate. As we have indicated we consider that the credit given by the judge may have been generous. Certainly the resulting fine of £2 million was not manifestly excessive or wrong in principle.[42]

This does not just apply to companies as is apparent from *R (Natural England) v Day*:

> It was the judge's duty to impose a fine that would not only punish the appellant for what he had done for commercial gain but which would also deter others and protect the public. As the judge rightly identified, the protection of the environment and particularly protection of SSSIs are of great importance. SSSIs represent the common heritage of mankind; they are not subject to the commercial interests of a person who holds the land for the time being. It is also important to take account of the obvious fact that Natural England has significant difficulties in monitoring SSSIs; deterrence

[37] ibid [38].

[38] See J Thornton, 'Sentencing for Environmental Crime' (2016) 28 *Journal of Environmental Law* 370.

[39] *Thames Water v R* [2019] EWCA Crim 1344.

[40] *R (Natural England) v Day* [2014] EWCA Crim 2683, [2015] Env LR 15.

[41] Sentencing Council, 'Environmental Offences: Definitive Guideline' (London, HMSO, 2014).

[42] *Thames Water v R* [2019] EWCA Crim 1344, [30].

is of considerable importance. The fine therefore had to be of such a size that it would achieve each of these objectives.[43]

This case involved a very wealthy landowner cutting down trees on an SSSI without the relevant consent. In assessing the scale of the fine, the Court took account of the landowner's identity and assets. This is based both on the deterrent effect and on the value of environmental protection.

Perhaps even more significant has been the willingness, in making assessments about the identity and resources of a defendant, to pierce the corporate veil. Even in notable environmental disasters, this has proved a remarkably durable principle, and not just for English and Welsh courts. Its inviolability stands in contrast to the malleability of many legal principles. In *R v Ineos Chlorvinyls Ltd*,[44] however, the resources of a parent company were central to the Court of Appeal's conclusion. In this case, the Court took account of the size and liquidity of the parent company in applying the Sentencing Guidelines.

> We note however that the turnover of this company upon which the guideline fines are based is vastly larger than the indicative figure given in the baseline for 'a large' organisation. True it is that it has had some losses in recent years on the face of the accounts. However, as the guideline indicates the court is entitled to take into account, as did the judge here, the resources of any linked organisation available to the particular offender. Further, director's remuneration, although it was significant, even though not at the top range of comparable industries. We note the point taken in that regard in the papers.[45]

The Court emphasises that the Sentencing Guidelines explicitly permit this, but that does not make the move any the less innovative.

On the reverse side, we also see the environmental context being used as part of a discussion of appropriately low sentencing. This is most apparent in *R (Basto)*.[46] This case was concerned with sentencing for climate change protests at Heathrow. The cost of the protest, which shut the runway for a number of hours, was unknown, but its scale was enormous, affecting the flights of 92,000 passengers. The question was the appropriate approach to sentencing given the nature of climate change protests and the importance of the issue, as well as the protesters' 'genuine' commitment to this cause. The Court's comments in this regard are very instructive, and so it is worth their lengthy citation here. They give insight not only into how the environment shapes sentencing, but more widely the purpose of criminal law prohibitions and adjudication generally.

> I have to have regard to the purposes of sentencing as set out in the Criminal Justice Act 2003: punishment, the reduction of crime, reform and rehabilitation, the protection of the public from harm and reparation. In the present case reform and rehabilitation

[43] *R (Natural England) v Day* [2014] EWCA Crim 2683, [2015] Env LR 15, [43].
[44] *R v Ineos Chlorvinyls Ltd* [2016] EWCA Crim 607, [2017] Env LR 7.
[45] ibid [20].
[46] *R v Basto (Robert Anthony)*, unreported, [2016] 2 WLUK 630.

> doesn't really arise. I am unlikely to pass a sentence which will alter your beliefs or your pride in what you did. I can not pass a sentence which will come anywhere near effective reparation making amends for the losses you caused. I am therefore concerned to protect the public from similar harm, the reduction of crime and appropriate punishment.
>
> The fact that you are principled and hold strong views about what is in the best interests of the public does not mean you are entitled to break the law. It does not mean that criminal offences will go unpunished or that the courts should ignore the impact of your activities on others.
>
> There are no sentencing guidelines for aggravated trespass. The maximum sentence is 3 months imprisonment. I am required to look at culpability and harm. Your culpability is high. It is true that you had regard to safety and called the police to alert them to your presence for reasons of safety, but these offences were carefully orchestrated, timed for a date which was convenient to you, and designed to cause the maximum possible disruption to flights on that day. You timed the protest for 3.45 am shortly before the first planes were due to land. It was no thanks to any of you that you were removed as quickly as you were. Although it has been suggested on your behalf that the planned nature of the offence is a mitigating feature because it made the action less likely to lead to harm, I am afraid that I can not accept this as a sensible argument.
>
> The level of harm was also high in the context of this type of offence. 92,000 victims. There is no question that when looking at the offence of aggravated trespass it is difficult to imagine a more serious offence. I can not accept Mr Summers assertion that it would be more serious if you were there to plot criminal offences or carry out activities. If that were the case then other charges would follow and different sentencing guidelines would apply.[47]

The fact that this was a climate change protest did not change the approach to sentencing in that it did not indicate that leniency was warranted. However, when considering whether to suspend the protestors' sentences, the Court returned to the value of that which, albeit unlawfully, they were seeking to protect. The judge reasoned as follows: 'Giving you all credit for your genuinely held beliefs and the fact that you acted according to your conscience … I am prepared to suspend the sentence.'[48] In other words, both the genuinely held belief of the defendants and, perhaps more importantly, the fact that the Court clearly considered those beliefs to be *legitimate* ones shaped the approach to sentencing. It is difficult to imagine a trespass causing disruption to 92,000 people resulting in a relatively generous sentence in many other contexts.

Finally, we can also see the influence of the perceived importance of environmental protection influencing the interaction between criminal and private law concerns. In *Ratten v NRB Wales*,[49] the Court was required to assess whether or not it should issue a stay of prosecution in relation to alleged environmental offences against a company which was in the process of liquidation. The Court concluded

[47] ibid [30]–[33].

[48] ibid.

[49] *Ratten v NRB Wales* (also known as *Re Paperback Collection and Recycling Ltd*) [2019] EWHC 2904 (Ch).

that it did not have jurisdiction to issue such a stay. However, in case it was later held that it did have such jurisdiction, the Court was clear that it would not have exercised its discretion to do so in this case. The reason for the Court's reluctance to bring an end to any such prosecution was the significance of ensuring the integrity of the environmental offences regime. The importance of this outweighed the interests of the creditors which would be protected by insulating them against the effects of any fine. The Court reasoned:

> Conversely, in my judgment, there are compelling public interest grounds to allow the Criminal Proceedings to continue. These substantially outweigh the attendant disadvantage to the creditors.
>
> Firstly, the alleged offences are of a serious nature. … It is in the public interest for such offences to be prosecuted and to be seen to be prosecuted. It is true that the Company's directors, Mr Gordon Anderson and Ms Terry Anderson, are also being prosecuted. However, in itself, that is no good reason for the Company to avoid prosecution.
>
> Secondly … it is an important part of NRW's case that the Company's unlawful activities significantly undermine the regulatory regime.
>
> Thirdly, NRW has brought the prosecution under an open policy published in the Environmental Permitting (England and Wales) Regulations 2016. When deciding to prosecute the Company, it took into account inter alia the seriousness of the offences, the actual or potential harm to the victims and the impact on the community. It also considered whether prosecution was proportionate.
>
> Fourthly, in the event that the Company is convicted, the officers of the Company could be precluded from holding an environmental permit in the future.[50]

These four reasons taken together were sufficient to indicate to the Court that it should not issue a stay. To reiterate, the consequence of this is that the interests of the creditors, which could be seriously affected by the successful prosecution of the liquidated company, were seen as being significantly less important than the public interest in seeking prosecution given the importance of environmental offences being prosecuted.

To summarise, in respect of sentencing, four trends are identifiable, and all show the effect that the perceived value (and changing perceptions in that respect) of the environment has in respect of remedies. First, the scale of punishment is increasing, especially in cases involving deliberate, reckless or negligent acts. Second, the identity of the defendant is critical, and this applies both to private individuals and to companies. Third, unusually, the courts have shown a willingness to pierce the corporate veil in assessing size and resources of a defendant by taking account of those of a parent company. Finally, the importance and legitimacy of environmental concerns are demonstrated both in the lenient sentencing of climate change protests in *Basto*, and in the refusal to stay proceedings in *Ratten*. Of course, not all cases show these trends. The relatively harsh approach to sentencing for

[50] ibid [34]–[38].

protests in the context of fracking at some levels of the judicial hierarchy clearly shows this.[51] Nevertheless, the increasing centrality of the environment and its value as a consideration in such cases is confirmed by the overturning of these 'manifestly excessive' sentences on appeal.[52]

B. Costs

Part and parcel of this discussion of remedies is a cost determination. Whilst it may not appear at first glance that the question of costs is a question of remedies per se, it is nevertheless very important for the parties who will be awarded costs, and what proportion of their actual expenditure will be recovered from the opposite side. Furthermore, since costs, for the most part, will follow the result, it can fairly accurately be said that costs awards are part of the outcome of the resolution of a dispute. Certainly, until it is known who is the winner, and the substance of the dispute is decided (particularly in reference to questions such as a manifestly unreasonable nature of any claim, vexatious litigation, etc), then it is not possible to know who is going to bear the burden of the costs. Of course, in the environmental context the costs position has been radically altered by the provisions of the Aarhus Convention and associated rules. In the judicial review context, there are special costs protections rules in place for Aarhus claims. A similar position applies in relation to statutory appeals.

Detailed consideration of the precise operation of these costs rules is not necessary here (they are explored in chapter four). Our argument is not that these rules do in fact create costs regimes which make access to justice in environmental matters straightforward, but merely to emphasise two things. First, costs rules are a significant element of a system of adjudication, and in taking the approach that we have (primarily, costs follow results, but with limitations on costs in environmental cases) we emphasise that the cost of obtaining a resolution to a dispute is one which ought to be borne by the person who loses the cases. This is so even where the merits may be very finely balanced; where there was no way in advance of parties either predicting the outcome or settling; and even where the person who loses the case has no choice but to engage in litigation. The idea of costs following the result is generally premised upon the notion that the person who is legally 'in the right' should not have to bear the cost of demonstrating their rectitude. This has an obvious appeal, but the flip side, that a person who happens to be on the wrong side of a legal rule which they might have been entirely unable to predict has to pay for their opponent's ability to prove them wrong, seems less intuitively correct.

[51] See the discussion of the first instance judgment in *R v Roberts (Richard)* [2018] EWCA Crim 2739, [2019] 1 WLR 2577.

[52] *R v Roberts (Richard)* [2018] EWCA Crim 2739, [2019] 1 WLR 2577, [2]. See J Hawkins, 'Fracking and the Scope for Public Dissent' (2019) 21 *Environmental Law Review* 128.

In cases where the 'loser' is a public authority, or otherwise receives public funding in the form of legal aid, the fact that they are bound to pay the cost of uncertainty – uncertainty which is high in the field of environmental law – seems justified. In cases where an unfunded private party, who does not chose to engage in litigation, loses a dispute where the rule that they fall foul of is not one which they could have known about in advance, has to pay for the privilege of losing out, the merits of a 'follows the results' costs rule seem less clear. In such cases, the private party has to pay for the consequence of a lack of clarity in the law, a law that was obviously not of their creation. In the context of environmental disputes where this lack of clarity is well documented, the costs position can be difficult to justify.

Second, in making the exceptions that are made to costs rules, especially in judicial review, in relation to environmental law (based upon the Aarhus Convention), the system demonstrates that there is a public interest in allowing environmental litigation. When we twin the costs considerations with the other issues raised in this chapter, the priorities within the system and the prevailing role of adjudication become less clear.

However, it must be noted at this point that the Aarhus rules do not necessarily cover the entirety of the ground covered in this book, and indeed in some of the other avenues, eg in criminal law, the cost of defence counsel will not be automatically recoverable in cases of a non-guilty verdict. Rather such costs can only be recovered if the judge is of the view that the case should never have been brought in the first place.[53] In the environmental context this is very unlikely, given the EA's prosecution policy (which means that in essence all but the very worst offences will not result in formal prosecution) and as a result of the fact that there are alternative sanctions which can be applied or entered into which make prosecution relatively unappealing for the EA. Similarly, Aarhus has, for the most part, not affected the ways in which costs are handled in purely private law actions, such as a nuisance action, where essentially reasonable costs follow the result (although actual incurred costs are often not recoverable – rather at the outset of proceedings a costs budget may be established so that the position of the parties is relatively known in advance).

This issue was discussed at length in *Austin v Miller Argent*,[54] where it was made clear that the simple fact of a claim engaging environmental issues was not enough to bring the claim within the province of the Convention such as to make either party suitable for protection in relation to their costs. Thus, the court reasoned that:

> It seems to us that there are two requirements which have to be met before a particular claim can fall within the scope of the provision. First, the nature of the complaint must have a close link with the particular environmental matters regulated by the Convention, even although the action in private nuisance does not directly raise them.

[53] Legal Aid, Sentencing and Punishment of Offenders Act 2012, schedule 7.
[54] *Austin v Miller Argent* [2014] EWCA Civ 1012, [2015] 1 WLR 62.

> Second, the claim must, if successful, confer significant public environmental benefits. In our judgment, if on the particular facts the court were to conclude that the purpose of the claim was principally to protect private property interests and any public benefit was limited and incidental, it ought not to attract the procedural costs protections afforded by Article 9.4.[55]

Furthermore, the Court emphasised that its analysis of how costs protections should work in private law is in part influenced by a desire to ensure the effectiveness of the Aarhus Convention, and in particular, by the desire to uphold 'environmental standards'.

> The question is whether the particular claimant bringing a specific private nuisance claim can demonstrate that the proceedings are prohibitively expensive. That submission cannot be met by a generalised statement that there are other cheaper procedures available. We would accept, however, that the existence of alternative and potentially cheaper procedure, provided that it affords a realistic, practical and effective remedy, is a relevant factor to consider when a court is exercising its discretion whether to grant a PCO or not. But where it is clear that the public authority is either unwilling or unable to take the necessary action, the only option may be a private action. It is then in our view unrealistic to say that the authority's lack of action can itself be challenged by way of judicial review. That is hardly an effective way of securing the environmental standards which the Convention is designed to achieve.[56]

A direct link is drawn between environmental protection and costs rules in private law, underlining the power of the influence of such considerations on the cultures of remedies, costs and sentencing.

Furthermore, this latter paragraph emphasises the links between power, reasons and remedies. It demonstrates that in exercising its discretion in respect of remedies, a court will recognise the importance of the environmental questions at stake, even where the litigation is not specifically a public interest issue. The unwillingness of a public authority to act in respect of public harm is taken into account in assessing whether a claimant should be responsible for a level of costs beyond that which they would have to endure in a public law claim. This is interesting because this is all premised upon the claimant *losing* their challenge, and therefore arguments about upholding the public interest are about upholding the public interest notwithstanding the fact that in the ultimate analysis it is concluded that the public interest (as defined by the legal rules) was not in fact harmed in the first place, otherwise the claimant would have won.

C. Absence of Remedy

Thus far, we have explored the forms of remedy available to adjudicators within the different avenues. The differences are stark. In private law, damages or

[55] ibid [22].
[56] ibid [24].

injunctions directly related to harm, predicted or occurring, will be the primary approach. In public law, the decision will be remitted to the public authority, with little by way of comfort for the individual complaining that an unlawful decision has been made (with the important exception, as *Mott* demonstrates, of where that illegality consists of a breach of their individual rights).[57] In both of these cases, the identity of the 'defendant' is irrelevant to the scale and form of the remedy. Instead the focus is on the nature and consequences of the wrong. Whilst this latter consideration is also relevant in criminal law, so too are the resources, identity and culpability of the defendant. But in all cases, there exists the possibility that although an adjudicator finds the presence of a legal wrong (and, by definition here we are considering situations where there has been the threat, potential, risk or actual occurrence of harm to the environment), no remedy will be granted. This is particularly prominent in public law where, as we have already mentioned, there is a statutory conferral of a power (and in some cases, duty) on adjudicators to simply allow the unlawful decision to continue unaffected by the conclusion of its illegality. This section considers this remedy of 'doing nothing' and how it plays out in the context of environmental law.

We commence with discussion of judicial review. Following the Criminal Justice and Courts Act 2015, the Senior Courts Act 1981 (SCA 1981) was amended to include a new section 31(2A). This states that

> (2A) The High Court –
>
> (a) must refuse to grant relief on an application for judicial review, and
> (b) may not make an award under subsection (4) on such an application,
>
> if it appears to the court to be highly likely that the outcome for the applicant would not have been substantially different if the conduct complained of had not occurred.

This is not merely a discretion to refuse relief, but a mandatory consideration (except, as provided for by section 31(2B) in cases of exceptional public interest). This means that there is a narrow discretion vesting in the court to quash a decision anyway notwithstanding the lack of effect, to reflect the importance of procedures, for example, in any particular context.

The considerations that ought to be taken into account when considering the duty not to quash were discussed in *Dover v CPRE Kent*.[58] We have already examined this case in the context of exploring the multidimensional practice of environmental adjudication in chapters three and six. However, briefly to summarise, in this case, the Council had granted planning permission for the construction of a significant housing development in an AONB. The Council's own Planning Officer had recommended the grant of permission but for a smaller number of houses on the basis that this would minimise the impact on the AONB.

[57] *R (Mott) v Environment Agency* [2016] EWCA Civ 564, [2016] 1 WLR 4338.
[58] *Dover DC v Campaign to Protect Rural England (Kent)* [2017] UKSC 79, [2018] 1 WLR 108.

In granting permission, the Council had not given reasons for its departure from the advice of its own officer. The Supreme Court concluded that reasons were required for such a departure (the decision was covered by the EIA Directive).[59] The decision as communicated was unlawful. The problem for the objectors was that the Council was clearly minded to grant the permission, as it did. The provision of reasons for why it had not followed the advice of its own Officer was unlikely to change its mind (given that the Officer's own report had not achieved this).

On its face, this looked like a case where the quashing and remitting of the decision would likely result in no difference in eventual outcome, albeit that the outcome would have the benefit of reasons. However, the Supreme Court decided that the duty in section 31(2A) did not apply here. It reasoned that the Council's failure to explain its reasons produced doubt as to whether it had properly considered those matters it was mandated to consider.

> These points were not merely incidental, but were fundamental to the officers' support for the amended scheme. The committee's failure to address such points raises a 'substantial doubt' … as to whether they had properly understood the key issues or reached 'a rational conclusion on them on relevant grounds'. This is a case where the defect in reasons goes to the heart of the justification for the permission, and undermines its validity. The only appropriate remedy is to quash the permission.[60]

One might reasonably surmise from this that the conclusion that a difference might have been made was not entirely realistic. Rather, the Court was desirous to be reassured by the Council that the latter had made all necessary analyses to reach the right decision in the case. Remitting the decision would guarantee that the right considerations had been taken into account. The outcome might not be different were the permission to change, but the outcome in terms of the considerations that had been taken into account would be potentially substantial. In this, we see the fundamental ambiguity in section 31(2A), because a difference in 'outcome' depends critically on how one assesses the 'outcome'.

Nevertheless, the remedy of doing nothing is regularly exercised in the context of judicial review, given specific statutory authorisation to refuse to quash decisions, even if vitiated by a legal flaw, if there is no prospect of the decision changing. On the one hand this is a recognition of the pointlessness of wasting resources and time 'remaking' a decision. On the other, it does emphasise the instrumental quality of many of the legal rules. Whilst the rules are there to ensure procedural rectitude on the grounds that this is more likely to produce high-quality decision-making, in cases where those procedures are not followed, that can be excused if the actual decision would not change (but not if the actual decision would be better). The remedy of 'nothing' can be seen in *Goring-on-Thames v South*

[59] Directive 2011/92/EU of the European Parliament and of the Council of 13 December 2011 on the assessment of the effects of certain public and private projects on the environment, as amended.

[60] *Dover DC v Campaign to Protect Rural England (Kent)* [2017] UKSC 79, [2018] 1 WLR 108, [68].

Oxfordshire DC.[61] The court here also considers *Walton v Scottish Ministers*.[62] Similar arguments are present in *Birchall Gardens*.[63]

The Court in *PS v Greenwich LBC* gives a useful summary of the duty in section 31(2A), its relationship with the court's previous discretion to provide no remedy, and how this should be understood in the context of potential environmental harm.

> The court has always had a discretion in deciding whether notwithstanding any unlawfulness in a decision relief should be granted. But that has been exercised, submits Ms Wigley, on a narrower basis than 'highly likely', namely would the decision necessarily have been the same. Section 31(2A) makes mandatory what was discretionary but does not remove the power to exercise discretion in a particular case. The submission seems to depend on arguing that the wording of s 31(2A) in using the past tense looks back to the time of the decision and does not include any future material and means the situation before the amendments were made resulting in s 31(2A). There is certainly scope for arguing that s 3 should be narrowly construed, but in that case there is no need to consider those details. It is clear to me that outcome for the claimant would have been no different since, if he succeeded, the 2012 permission would go ahead and the same emissions from the ships would occur. Thus whether under s 31(2A) or in the exercise of my discretion I would have refused relief.[64]

The fact that it is possible for the courts to conclude that no remedy is an appropriate outcome in cases involving judicial review tells us a lot about the purpose of adjudication. In chapter five we considered the power structures created by the possibility of judicial oversight of legality. Where the appropriate response to a lack of legality is effectively to sanction that going forward so that an unlawful decision remains 'in currency', however, the place that rule of law and procedural proprietary take in the face of limited resources, time and in acknowledgement of the discretion accorded to primary decision-makers in many areas of environmental law is made clear. In this, we can return to the consideration that we emphasised in the introduction to this work: environmental law happens in administrative offices, not in court rooms, and the remedy of doing nothing is an explicit acknowledgement of this.

The residual discretion to which the court in *PS* refers[65] is one that has been exercised in planning law cases. The statutory basis for challenges to planning permissions (as opposed to appeals against the refusal to grant planning permission) is in section 288 Town and Country Planning Act 1990. This section provides that courts have a discretion (not a duty) not to quash where the illegality consists in a failure to take account of relevant requirements (arising under a range of

[61] *R (Goring-on-Thames Parish Council) v South Oxfordshire DC* [2018] EWCA Civ 860, [2018] 1 WLR 5161.

[62] *Walton v Scottish Ministers* [2012] UKSC 44, [2013] JPL 323.

[63] *R (Birchall Gardens LLP) v Hertfordshire CC* [2016] EWHC 2794 (Admin), [2017] Env LR 17.

[64] *PS v Greenwich LBC* [2016] EWHC 1967, [2017] JPL 165, [27].

[65] ibid.

statutory provisions) and no substantial prejudice is caused. It makes no mention of such a discretion where the failure consists of a breach of the principles of *Wednesbury* reasonableness. Nevertheless, in *Simplex GE Holdings*,[66] the Court held that in planning cases too the courts retain such a residual discretion not to quash. In cases where the error was a 'significant factor' in the decision made, then the decision should be quashed. Where it was not a significant factor, and a different outcome would not be reached, then there is a flexibility for the courts to provide no remedy.

In the other two avenues – private and criminal law – whilst there is always the possibility that no remedy (in the form of damages, injunction, specific performance, etc, or no custodial sentence, fine or other penalty) will be awarded, it should be noted that this is generally not because there is harm (a legal wrong) which the court concluded should go 'unrectified', but rather because there is *no longer* any harm. In private law there are cases where no damages will be awarded precisely because the harm has not caused any relevant loss, not because the court concludes that the loss, although legally relevant, should not in this case be recovered. The 'harm' emerging from the illegality does not therefore remain unchallenged. Furthermore, in all of these cases it must be remembered, as discussed above, that a conclusion on the merits will have implication for costs, even if no additional remedy is given, and in that sense the 'remedy' of doing nothing does not mean that the outcome does not involve real-world financial consequences for both parties.

IV. Conclusions

In drawing together the threads of this chapter, we return, naturally, from this discussion of the remedy of doing nothing to the question of purpose. The purpose of adjudication is not the same in all the avenues. This defining characteristic of the culture of the avenues is most clearly reflected in the approach to remedies that dominates in each. Thus, in private law, where the purpose of adjudication is to indicate rights, to protect capital and to allow for the use of contractual and other means as a predictable and binding form of promise-keeping, the remedies reflect what is lost when those rights are breached, capital risked and promises broken. Where no remedy is given, it is because the breach of rights has caused no loss. In environmental law, the challenge for this avenue becomes its ability to value that which has been lost when it is not easily expressed – indeed, may be inexpressible – in financial terms.

By contrast, in public law, the purpose is more accurately seen as the upholding of certain minimum standards of legality in public life. In statutory appeals, the primary responsibility for upholding this legality is shared – both original

[66] *Simplex GE (Holdings) Ltd v Secretary of State for the Environment* (1989) 57 P & CR 306 (CA).

decision-makers and subsequent adjudicators are often tasked with creating decisions which themselves substantively comply with the rules at hand. In planning challenges in court and in judicial review, the adjudicator is tasked simply with assessing whether a decision complies with these standards of legality, not with the more substantive task of rendering a decision that does so comply. This makes the ability to refuse to quash a decision appear even more significant.

If the purpose of adjudication is simply and only to uphold standards of legality, then a conclusion that those standards have been breached but that no new decision needs to be taken is a stark acceptance of the value placed upon compliance with those legal standards. Nevertheless, if we consider this from the perspective of environmental protection, particularly given the approach of the Supreme Court in *Dover v CPRE Kent*,[67] the decision to provide no remedy is unlikely to produce substantive harm to the environment (except where the decision-maker had decided to cause such harm anyway). In all of these avenues, however, it is clear that the environmental context is certainly pushing and shaping the remedial approach.

Whilst remedies may seem to be the 'afterthought' in an adjudication process, as this chapter has demonstrated, the range of remedies available to adjudicators within the different avenues we have considered produce the final part of the 'jigsaw' (to mix metaphors) of the landscape tapestry of environmental adjudication. Consideration of remedies in this chapter has demonstrated two key elements of how these systems operate. First, the remedy available, and in the willingness in some cases to provide 'no' remedy, is a salutary reminder that for the parties themselves, the remedy is what matters. Norm construction and relationship-shaping discussions are all fine and well, but where, as they might do, they result in no change in the legal outcome for the parties themselves or for the environmental outcomes, the significance of these institutional structures becomes more theoretical than real in an instant case. Second, it is important to emphasise that far from being the inevitable conclusion of the development of a series of rules, the remedies provided are also shaping the substance of the rules.

Remedialism in adjudication is generally frowned upon. The approach whereby the substance of a decision is driven by the available remedies and the desire to produce a particular outcome 'at the end of the day' is seen by many as being an illegitimate exercise of judicial power specifically, and perhaps adjudicatory power more generally. However, as this chapter has shown, it is not a necessary leap from that scepticism about remedialism to fail to take account of the enormous significance of the remedies which exist for the systems of adjudication we have in place. It is for this reason that the remedial power of each avenue of adjudication is represented in our general description of the avenues in chapter four.

[67] *Dover DC v Campaign to Protect Rural England (Kent)* [2017] UKSC 79, [2018] 1 WLR 108.

If, as we argued in chapter two, the essence of adjudication is resolution of disputes, then this chapter has discussed how the nature of that resolution varies according to the context within which it takes place. This is largely a matter of remedies, but it is important not to take too narrow a view on what remedies are in this context.

8

The Bricolage of Environmental Adjudication

I. Introduction

In the preceding chapters we have identified the main avenues of environmental adjudication and explored the ways in which these avenues shape the power relations, the reasoning and the provisions for remedies in adjudication. The picture that emerges from this analysis is clear: environmental adjudication is a multifaceted social process in which adjudicators perform a variety of roles across a spectrum of avenues. Ultimately this results in a process in which context becomes highly determinative. The wide variety in environmental adjudication that we have uncovered is nevertheless important on a number of levels. First, the fact that adjudication takes place across a range of avenues in which adjudicators perform fundamentally different functions has implications for our understanding of environmental adjudication and therefore of environmental law more generally. This point is important for environmental law scholars as well as anyone engaged in adjudication. Second, the variety we have identified in the preceding chapters becomes important when we subsequently come to consider what role we ideally prefer adjudicators to play in environmental adjudication. This latter point is of course a big question, but once we have laid bare the realities of environmental adjudication, it is relevant to consider whether this has any implications for our normative assumptions about environmental adjudication. However, a central argument of this book is that, purely as a matter of description and epistemology, in order to put forward answers to the question of what role we ideally see environmental adjudication playing in environmental law, we need to properly understand what environmental adjudication looks like. Up to this point, we have focused our energy on answering this initial question, in this chapter we turn our attention to what the consequences of our discoveries are.

The central argument of this chapter is that environmental adjudication in England and Wales is best conceptualised as a bricolage. By bricolage we mean that environmental adjudication is a patchwork made up of different constitutive parts without any purposeful coordination, given force through institutions and avenues that are already deeply embedded in the legal culture. Importantly, the bricolage of adjudication is not designed specifically with environmental adjudication in mind but is made up of institutions, avenues and structures that have been developed and matured in other legal fields. This results in a social practice that is neither uniform nor unified. An important point to make in this context is that the argument that environmental adjudication is a bricolage is not the same as saying that the law is necessarily indeterminate or that there is an absence of judicial doctrine in environmental law. As the analysis in the preceding chapters shows, there clearly is. Nor does it necessarily follow from our claim of bricolage that the law is wildly inconsistent.[1] We use the term bricolage here as a description of what environmental adjudication looks like. Nevertheless, conceptualising environmental adjudication as a bricolage has implications for ongoing disciplinary discussions among environmental law scholars and the perceived prevalence of incoherence in the law. As discussed later, focusing on adjudication as a bricolage made up of several distinctive avenues of adjudication provides a descriptively accurate account of the diversity encountered in environmental adjudication whilst also allowing for the development of a certain degree of coherence, albeit on a local level. This chapter expands on this argument by considering the relationship between this bricolage and questions of incoherence, in section II. Section III considers the consequences of this conclusion for our understanding of what constitutes good adjudication, before section IV concludes.

II. Bricolage and Incoherence

Much has been written about the perceived lack of coherence in environmental law as both a legal field and a scholarly discipline.[2] Recent scholarship asserts that 'incoherence is a functional and perhaps productive reaction to the extreme difficulties environmental law confronts'[3] and that 'environmental law … has so single guiding logic, no overarching doctrinal framework'.[4] As a result, whilst many other legal fields are subject to similar critiques and claims, incoherence seems particularly prevalent in the discussion of environmental law.[5] Having said that, environmental law scholars seem increasingly willing to embrace the idea that incoherence is a disciplinary feature of the law. In this chapter we consider the role of incoherence not in environmental law as such but in the context of environmental adjudication. We argue that what may at first look like incoherence

[1] For a discussion, see eg K Kress 'Legal Indeterminacy' (1989) 77 *California Law Review* 283.

[2] eg E Fisher et al, 'Maturity and Methodology: Starting a Debate about Environmental Law Scholarship' (2009) 21 *Journal of Environmental Law* 213; TS Aagaard, 'Environmental Law as a Legal Field: An Inquiry in Legal Taxonomy' (2010) 95 *Cornell Law Review* 221; and OW Pedersen 'Modest Pragmatic Lessons for a Diverse and Incoherent Environmental Law' (2013) 33 *OJLS* 103.

[3] Aagaard, 'Environmental Law as a Legal Field' 278.

[4] Fisher et al, 'Maturity and Methodology' 219.

[5] eg FH Easterbrook, 'Cyberspace and the Law of the Horse' [1996] *University of Chicago Legal Forum* 207 and P Craig 'English Administrative Law History: Perception and Reality' (2019) Oxford Legal Studies Research Paper No 48/2019 on https://papers.ssrn.com/sol3/papers.cfm?abstract_id=3404029 on private law.

is instead better explained as a patchwork, or bricolage.[6] We argue that once we approach environmental adjudication as taking place across different avenues, an altogether more coherent picture emerges. First, however, we will need to scrutinise the relationship between environmental adjudication and incoherence in more detail.

As noted earlier, a central feature of environmental adjudication is that adjudication takes place without what Warnock calls a masterplan.[7] This lack of a masterplan is particularly pronounced in the context of adjudication in England and Wales.[8] In fact, in environmental adjudication, the main factor behind any perceived incoherence is institutional. As identified in chapter four, the standout feature of environmental adjudication is that it takes place across a range of different avenues. These avenues shape the power yielded by adjudicators when it comes to the important role of fact-finding, interpretation and creation of norms, as well as when it comes to determining the importance on a claimant's case and whether the claimant has access to the adjudicator. Similarly, as demonstrated in chapter six, the various avenues of adjudication constrain the forms of reasoning available to claimants and regulate the balance between the relevant interests at play. To this institutional picture, we can add disciplinary factors contributing to a sense of incoherence such as the fact that underlying legal norms found in the law come from a range of different jurisdictions (domestic, EU law and international law) and the fact that environmental law relies heavily on non-legal ideals grounded in policy and principle.[9] On the face of it, it seems entirely reasonable to conclude that a certain level of incoherence is at play in environmental adjudication.

This claim becomes even stronger when we bear in mind the historical development of environmental law and environmental adjudication in England and Wales. Historically grounded in private law adjudication of nuisance, present-day environmental law is a paradigmatic example of incremental statutory developments gradually put in place against a background of the rise of the administrative state.[10] Moreover, and notwithstanding its historical foundations, environmental law remains inherently and normatively contested because answers to basic questions of what types of risks to regulate and how best to do so are often subject

[6] In making this point we do not intend to use the term bricolage to describe a method of scholarship or a process of adjudication as the term is sometimes applied in the context of common law scholarship and adjudication. See eg W Lucy, 'Private Law: Between Visionaries and Bricoleurs' in P Cane and J Gardner (eds), *Relating to Responsibility: Essays in Honour of Tony Honore on his 80th Birthday* (Oxford, Hart Publishing, 2001) 188.

[7] C Warnock, 'Reconceptualising Specialist Environment Courts and Tribunals' (2017) 37 *Legal Studies* 391.

[8] See also C Warnock and OW Pedersen, 'Environmental Adjudication: Mapping the Spectrum and Identifying the Fulcrum' [2017] *PL* 643.

[9] Fisher et al, 'Maturity and Methodology' 225.

[10] S Coyle and K Morrow, *The Philosophical Foundations of Environmental Law: Property Rights and Nature* (Oxford, Hart Publishing, 2004) and S Bell et al, *Environmental Law*, 9th edn (Oxford, Oxford University Press, 2017) ch 2.

to debate.[11] Against this background, the development of environmental law and environmental adjudication is, to use Raz's phrase, the result of rough and tumble politics, reflecting the vagaries of pragmatic compromises and changing political fortunes.[12] Where this is the case, the law is likely to be at least untidy.[13]

The perceived presence of an untidy legal system becomes particularly important if we consider the inclination of lawyers to, as Aagaard puts it, classify the law into fields to make sense and patterns of otherwise disparate connections.[14] In other words, when encountering what we perceive as a lack of tidiness, lawyers respond by trying to minimise this disorder through rethinking and reconceptualising structures of law. This inclination is important on two levels. First, it suggests that central to any understanding of legal coherence is the role of the individual engaged in an analysis of the law. That is, the argument that a body of law is incoherent is arguably as much a reflection of the cognitive inclinations of the individual (the lawyer) towards favouring a legal regime that possess properties of order, clarity and coherence as it is a reflection of the law itself.[15] Cue Balkin: '[C]oherence is more than a property of law; it is the result of a particular way of thinking about the law.'[16]

In this projection of preferences from the subject (lawyer) to the object (the law), purpose comes to play a central role. Where we as lawyers are inclined to classify laws into fields and disciplines to make sense of them, a central feature often becomes the core purpose and function of a discipline or field.[17] But here environmental lawyers necessarily run into trouble as it is not clear that the discipline of environmental law (and by extension environmental adjudication) has a core singular purpose. With specific reference to adjudication, our analysis in the previous chapters reveals that each of the different avenues of adjudication carries with it different purposes and assumptions about what the roles of the adjudicator and parties are.[18] Across the avenues of environmental adjudication, no central, no core purpose stands out. As a result, in order to understand environmental adjudication, we have two choices. First, we can break down the object of analysis into smaller pieces to the point at which order is more forthcoming, to the point at which we are able to identify enough of a core substance and purpose that it yields some level of coherence. That is what we have done in the previous chapters by breaking environmental adjudication into a series of distinct avenues.

Alternatively, we can come to accept that the picture of environmental adjudication is so untidy and disorderly it necessarily entails the acceptance that there

[11] Pedersen, 'Modest Pragmatic Lessons for a Diverse and Incoherent Environmental Law'.
[12] J Raz, 'The Relevance of Coherence' (1992) 72 *Boston University Law review* 273, 294.
[13] ibid 310.
[14] Aagaard, 'Environmental Law as a Legal Field'.
[15] See in general JM Balkin, 'Understanding Legal Understanding: The Legal Subject and the Problem of Legal Coherence' (1993) 103 *Yale Law Journal* 105.
[16] ibid 106.
[17] ibid 112.
[18] See ch 4.

is a high degree of incoherence, with whatever implications this might have for environmental law as a legal field. If so, we can come to understand environmental adjudication (and environmental law) as having more than one purpose.[19] Our response to this conundrum is to argue that environmental adjudication on a general level takes the form of a bricolage, which represents a system of different avenues, each with their own purposes, structures and rules. Viewed as a whole, the bricolage is untidy and lacking in structure and order. But viewed more closely through the lens of separate avenues, a certain level of order is restored. When encountering what might look untidy and disorganised, one is necessarily inclined to focus on smaller points of analysis to gain some level of understanding.

When environmental adjudication is understood as taking place across a series of different avenues, rather than as a whole, we encounter not an incoherent system but instead a bricolage made up of different and distinctive parts. This is because once we appreciate that adjudication in the confines of statutory appeal stands apart from adjudication in the context of private law and judicial review, with each avenue containing different structures of powers, responsibilities and ultimately adjudicatory purposes, we can come to see each avenue as being consistent and coherent from within the confines of itself. Once environmental adjudication is 'broken down' to the level of the different avenues, adjudication becomes locally coherent insofar as adjudication within a particular avenue takes place subject to the constraints, rules and forms found in that avenue.[20] This local coherence means that an equilibrium emerges not across the legal discipline as such – and importantly not even across adjudication as a function within the legal discipline – but within each of the avenues of adjudication.

The picture of adjudication as a bricolage made up of the different avenues is primarily a result of, as Raz noted, the haphazard development of the law and the legal institutions. Again, the lack of a masterplan for how to conduct environmental adjudication in England and Wales becomes important. Central to the development of environmental adjudication in England and Wales is that the system represents incremental responses to practical and legal problems emerging over time as environmental law has developed and matured as a legal discipline.[21] A central feature of our understanding of bricolage is the fact that that institutions of adjudication have emerged from structures of adjudication already in place. Consider, for example, the response adopted following the UK's accession to the Aarhus Convention, posing practical challenges for the existing adjudicatory structures for environmental law in the UK. The response by the UK government was to

[19] See eg OW Pedersen's review of E Scotford, *Environmental Principles and the Evolution of Environmental Law* (Oxford, Hart Publishing, 2017) in (2018) 30 *Journal of Environmental Law* 359 and more generally Balkin, 'Understanding Legal Understanding' 128.

[20] On local coherence see BB Levenbook, 'The Role of Coherence in Legal Reasoning' (1984) 3 *Law and Philosophy* 355.

[21] NE Simmonds, 'Bluntness and Bricolage' in H Gross and R Harrison (eds), *Jurisprudence: Cambridge Essays* (Oxford, Clarendon Press 1992) 1–28, 24.

rely steadfastly on existing adjudicatory structures of judicial review and statutory appeals, subsequently with some tweaks to the costs regime in the Civil Procedure Rules. In other words, when responding to the requirements of the Convention, the ultimate response was developed through reliance on structures already in place. In that process, invitations to make wholesale changes to the adjudicatory landscape, which was a distinct possibility, although not necessarily required by the Convention, were declined. The reasons for relying on existing avenues and structures and the merit of developing new institutions are largely irrelevant in this context. What matters from the perspective of the bricolage metaphor is that, as a matter of description, well-established means of adjudication were utilised as the base for complying with the Convention.

Similarly, as noted above, the picture of environmental adjudication as bricolage emerges because the law and legal structures lack commitment to a single overarching principle.[22] As demonstrated in the preceding chapters, each of the different avenues of adjudication contains its own standards, rules and principles, shaping the form and function of adjudication within the avenue. Central to the metaphor of bricolage is thus the argument that the bricolage emerges using a heterogeneous repertoire, which does not necessarily bear any relation to the larger project at hand.[23] In the context of environmental adjudication, this prevalence of building structures of adjudication through 'whatever is at hand' without an articulated commitment to an overarching principle is particularly striking. Many, although not all, of the avenues described in the previous chapters are avenues of adjudication developed over time applied to adjudication of environmental claims but without having been designed or structured specifically with environmental adjudication in mind. That is, the avenues are 'the contingent result of … the remains of previous constructions'.[24] This also explains why judicial review is prominent because judicial review has been (for very good reasons) the historical method of adjudication in the context of the administrative state.

Increasingly, however, the number of statutory reviews has increased dramatically hand in hand with environmental law becoming increasingly statutory in general and, more recently, we have encountered a move towards administrative adjudication by specialist administrative agencies or tribunals. These developments have taken place without much concerted commitment to general theories or principles of environmental adjudication. But as we have demonstrated in chapters five to seven, the application of existing avenues to the context of environmental adjudication imposes constraints and limitations on the adjudicatory process as a result of the legal culture of each avenue and by reference to the 'use for which it was originally intended'.[25] The avenues forming the bricolage of adjudication are,

[22] See eg Simmonds above who terms this lack of commitment 'bluntness', Simmonds, 'Bluntness and Bricolage'.

[23] C Levi-Strauss, *The Savage Mind* (Chicago, University of Chicago Press 1966) 17.

[24] ibid 17.

[25] ibid 19.

to use Levi-Strauss's term, 'pre-constrained', limiting the 'freedom [of each avenue] to manoeuvre'.[26] These constraining functions of the avenues and the metaphor of environmental adjudication as a bricolage necessarily have implications for how we understand what adjudication is.

III. Understanding Good Adjudication

There are two main implications following from approaching environmental adjudication as a bricolage, which primarily makes structural sense once we break down these into separate avenues. One relates to our understanding of environmental law and the adjudicative systems forming part of the law, and the other relates to how environmental lawyers and scholars further our knowledge and understanding of environmental adjudication. To begin with, our understanding of environmental law and adjudication as a legal field entails an argument that ideas and concepts of environmental adjudication make very little sense – or at least, do not take one very far – on a general and abstract level. Only when we approach environmental adjudication on the 'micro' level of each individual avenue can we begin to make some structural and conceptual sense of what it is that courts and other adjudicators do when hearing environmental claims. This in turn means that discussions about, for example, whether courts are suitable places for the resolution of environmental dispute; whether adjudicators are environmentally myopic; whether environmental claims deserve tailored forums of adjudication; and whether environmental concerns ought to receive particular attention from such decision-makers, must bear in mind the disparity and variety identified across the spectrum of environmental adjudication here. In short, assertions and assumptions about environmental adjudication ought to bear in mind that environmental adjudication in England and Wales reflects a bricolage, which itself encapsulates a wide range of avenues, each containing its own functions. Because the avenues shape the function and role of the adjudicator, any normative considerations about environmental adjudication ought to be placed in the contingent context of the individual avenue rather than at the general 'macro' level. Simply because the adjudication in each avenue is fundamentally different from adjudication in another avenue (though the variety naturally varies), this contingency of adjudication must be borne in mind when debating environmental adjudication.

In response to the many attempts to furnish strong legal foundations of environmental law, for example through appeal to environmental principles, Scotford has convincingly highlighted how these attempts are necessarily hampered by the strong pressure exerted by the contingency of environmental law.[27] The emphasis on contingency in our argument is slightly different insofar as, in the present

[26] ibid.
[27] eg Scotford, *Environmental Principles*.

context, the element of contingency is not made in response to those who seek to furnish a disciplinary foundation of environmental law on a ground that ultimately might not be able to bear it (for scholarly and legal reasons). Instead, our emphasis on contingency is made in order to highlight the need to draw out the multiple avenues and the variety present in environmental adjudication. On this point, the argument of contingency is akin to the claims made by Scotford, insofar as our argument seeks to drive home the need to appreciate context when we talk about environmental adjudication.

One consequence ensuing from the need to appreciate the contingency of adjudication across the different avenues consequently follows from the argument made in chapters five and six about the ways in which each avenue shapes and limits the reasoning and types of arguments that can be heard. In the decision by the FTT in *Warren v Natural England* the Tribunal takes great care to set out the confines of its jurisdiction and how this differs from claims heard in judicial review.[28] Judge McKenna consequently draws out how the Tribunal has no inherent jurisdiction but can only go where Parliament has afforded it statutory authority. Unlike in judicial review claims, however, this means that the Tribunal undertakes a de novo assessment rather than a review of the reasonableness of Natural England's decision to serve a stop notice. The Tribunal is, as a consequence, entitled to reach what Judge McKenna calls a 'fresh decision'.[29] For all intents and purposes, the Tribunal steps into the shoes of the regulatory agency and makes its own administrative decision. And yet, when this same question was put before the Upper Tribunal, whilst the tribunal agreed as to the scope of the power, it emphasised that the role is not the same.[30] Nor could it (the Upper Tribunal) carry out its own tasks in the same way as the FTT, who in turn could not step into the shoes of Natural England.[31] Each decision-maker could make a 'fresh' decision, but none can do so in exactly the same way, or on the same constitutional and functional underpinning, as its predecessor.

The statutory review approach is, as is well established, in sharp contrast to the approach taken in judicial review. Consider the Court of Appeal decision in *Downs* discussed in chapter four, where Sullivan LJ, delivering the Court's opinion, overturned the High Court's evaluation of the considerations, which formed part of the decision by made DEFRA.[32] Much like Judge McKenna in *Warren*, Sullivan LJ is keen to set out the confines of the court's jurisdiction when hearing judicial review claims. In judicial review claims, it is not, unlike in the claim in *Warren*, the adjudicator's job to reach a 'fresh' decision by substituting the administrative agency's decision with its own.

[28] *Warren v Natural England* [2018] UKFTT NV_2018_0006 (GRC), [11].
[29] ibid [9].
[30] *Natural England v Warren* [2019] UKUT 300 (AAC).
[31] ibid [189].
[32] *Secretary of State for Environment, Food and Rural Affairs v Downs* [2009] EWCA Civ 664, [2010] Env LR 7.

These points are important in the context for how we understand environmental adjudication because each of the decisions speak to what it is an adjudicator does when hearing a claim within a particular avenue. When Sullivan LJ rebukes Collins J in the High Court for having substituted DEFRA's decision for his own, he is effectively telling him that he has strayed off the path of what it means to hear a claim in judicial review. The decision of Collins J is, in other words, closer to the type of adjudication undertaken by Judge McKenna in the FTT. Unfortunately for Collins J, he happened to sit in the Administrative Court and not in the Tribunal. Once an adjudicator strays too far from the confines of a given avenue, the adjudicator's activities lose legitimacy because they do not conform to the practices and rules of that avenue. This in turn means that in order for a given activity of adjudication to constitute adjudication within the confines of a particular avenue, the adjudicator must 'play by the rules' of that avenue. In other words, the adjudicator must commit herself to the avenue in which she adjudicates. If the adjudicator veers too far off the confines of the avenue, her activity ceases to be adjudication and instead becomes something different.

This does not mean that there is no flexibility and there are outliers of decisions delivered from the confines of a particular avenue. Some decisions might therefore reasonably be seen as pushing the boundaries of the avenue from which it is delivered. One such example is the decision in *ClientEarth (No. 2)* where the Court intensively probed the underlying administrative decision made by the Secretary of State.[33] The level of scrutiny applied by the Court consequently led some commentators to question whether the decision signalled a change in judicial willingness to scrutinise administrative decisions.[34] As Bell points out, however, the decision in *ClientEarth (No. 2)* is, at present, best viewed as a product of the particular statutory context of the Air Quality Standards Regulations 2010[35] and the mandatory requirements found therein rather than a new benchmark for scrutiny in judicial review.[36] Having said that, the decision highlights the inherent contingency of each adjudicatory avenue and context of each case and thereby also the importance of context when it comes to environmental adjudication.

Flexibility and contingency within each avenue aside, the main point that adjudication entails a commitment by the adjudicator to operate within the confines of an avenue is important – the rules of each avenue, as these pertain to power, reasons and remedies, serve, as we have discussed in chapters five to seven, to give each avenue of adjudication its distinctiveness.[37] This distinctiveness is central because it provides a basis for excluding certain issues from consideration when

[33] *ClientEarth (No. 2) v Secretary of State for the Environment, Food and Rural Affairs* [2016] EWHC 2740 (Admin), [2017] Env LR 16.

[34] J Bell, '*ClientEarth (No 2)*: A Case of Three Legal Dimensions' (2017) 29 *Journal of Environmental Law* 2017.

[35] Air Quality Standards Regulations 2010, SI 2010/1001.

[36] Bell, '*ClientEarth (No 2)*: A Case of Three Legal Dimensions'.

[37] See in general, S Fish, *Professional Correctness* (Cambridge, MA, Harvard University Press 1995) 19–39.

hearing a claim. As noted above, in the absence of direct statutory authority to do so as in *Clientearth (No. 2)*, the avenue of judicial review effectively excludes a wide range of arguments from being put to the adjudicator and excludes the adjudicator from doing certain things. This means that claims launched within that avenue will need to play by the rules of that avenue to be entertained by the adjudicator. But it also means, as we have touched upon in chapter five, that environmental considerations are necessarily limited, highly variable and might not play as central a role as claimants might prefer. The reason for this is that were environmental concerns to be given a priori dominant preference (in the absence of statutory justification), each avenue of adjudication would lose its distinctiveness. That is, judicial review would cease to be judicial review as we commonly understand it were environmental interests to be given preference. That is not to say that specific avenues of environmental adjudication, affording special consideration to environmental interests, cannot be created as part of the bricolage of adjudication. Indeed, some jurisdictions seem to have gone down that road and created specific environmental tribunals with distinctive rules of procedure.[38] The point is instead that up until one such avenue has been created, and there might well be good reasons for creating one such, there are likely to be limits on the extent to which existing avenues of environmental adjudication are able to afford a priori special consideration to environmental interests. Doing so, would, as noted, undermine the distinctiveness and integrity of each adjudicatory avenue.

The pressure asserted by distinctiveness, which self-referentially serves to maintain the powers, reasons and rules of each avenue, necessarily also preserves the lack of conformity across the avenues of adjudication and ultimately the bricolage of environmental adjudication. Up to this point, we have focused primarily on describing this feature, but the metaphor of bricolage necessarily entails considerations as to whether this untidy structure is at all appropriate. Are there perhaps better ways of accommodating the challenges of environmental adjudication than in a system of bricolage, which seemingly lacks the ability to provide environmental concerns the central stage sought by claimants? The answer to this question is twofold. First, as indicated in chapter six, although environmental interests are not necessarily the primary consideration in many cases, there are examples in the case-law where adjudicators are able to afford special weight to environmental interests, either as a result of statutory requirements or through common law. In other words, the picture might not be as bad as first thought. To paraphrase Simmonds, crooked roads can still possess ingenuity.[39]

Second, within the bricolage of environmental adjudication in England and Wales we have seen, in recent years, a move towards more specialised forums of adjudication primarily in the avenue of statutory appeal. The creation of the Environment Chamber within the FTT's General Regulatory Chamber, as well

[38] eg G Gill, *Environmental Justice in India: The National Green Tribunal* (Abingdon, Routledge, 2016).

[39] Simmonds, 'Bluntness and Bricolage' 25. See also Levi-Strauss, *The Savage Mind* 22.

as the 'Planning Court' within the Administrative Court, signals a move towards the creation of distinctive structures of environmental adjudication. Importantly, however, these developments have taken place against a background and through use of the existing avenues of adjudication. The FTT primarily hears statutory appeals (although it has scope to hear some judicial review claims) and the Planning Court hears primarily judicial review claims or statutory challenges under section 288 of the Town and Country Planning Act 1990. As such, the novelty of these developments is somewhat limited. That does not mean that a more radical change is not possible and it might well be that one such will be pursued in the future. As it stands, however, the argument put forward here indicates that the bricolage of environmental adjudication and the lack of tidiness that inevitably goes with it is an enduring feature of environmental adjudication in England and Wales.

IV. Conclusions

The likelihood of the bricolage of environmental law adjudication enduring has implications for the perceived role of adjudicators in environmental law. If this bricolage is a central feature of environmental adjudication, it means that there are limits to the level of coherence we can expect individual adjudicators to deliver. When Carnwath LJ suggests that 'the courts can ensure that [environmental] policy is rational and coherent',[40] the real focus of this adjudicatory assistance is likely to be from within the confines of a given avenue of adjudication (eg judicial review or statutory appeal) rather than across the discipline of environmental law as such. This is because, as noted above, each adjudicator, as matter of professional practice, is committed to the constitutional roles and powers, historical baggage, legal culture and reasoning of each avenue of adjudication. Any failure of an adjudicator to commit to, and to operate within, a given avenue runs the risk of being censored by adjudicators higher up in the appellate hierarchy. As Lucy argues: 'Bricoleurs that look beyond the horizons of their practice are unlikely to remain bricoleurs for long.'[41] Consequently, scholars and advocates of environmental law who in their scholarship or briefs and submissions invite adjudicators to step outside of the confines of an avenue in an attempt to develop particular novel environmental law doctrines or arguments, face a significant challenge.

Moreover, the commitment of each adjudicator to fulfil their constitutional purpose, as expressed in a given avenue of adjudication, has a knock-on effect on the legal reasoning we encounter in environmental law. As claimants and litigators

[40] R Carnwath, 'Environmental Law in a Global Society' [2015] *Journal of Planning and Environmental Law* 269, 278.

[41] W Lucy, 'Private Law: Between Visionaries and Bricoleurs' in Cane and Gardner, *Relating to Responsibility* 207.

are forced to 'fit' their claims within the confines of the adjudicatory avenues, the legal reasoning encountered in environmental law necessarily becomes a patchwork – a patchwork reflecting the power structures, reasoning and remedies available in whichever avenue a claimant finds herself in. At this point, the argument that environmental adjudication resembles a bricolage spills over into the disciplinary characteristics of environmental law. This is because, if adjudication takes place across a bricolage of avenues, each with its individual power structures, rules of reasoning and remedies, and if adjudication is a central feature of the discipline (which it is), then one would expect this to have some impact on the overall discipline. The main consequence of this is that the understanding of environmental adjudication as a bricolage necessarily entails a need to accept, within the discipline of environmental law, the variety and patchwork that comes with the bricolage and the fact that this shapes legal reasoning in environmental law more generally.

This also means that our understandings of environmental adjudication and environmental law will need to reflect the likelihood that the unifying theme in environmental adjudication (to the extent that there is one across the different avenues) is not necessarily an adjudicatory desire to deliver coherence across the discipline of environmental law or to promote environmental protection. Instead, the unifying theme is the commitment by adjudicators to ensure an internally consistent process of adjudication. That is, instead of a commitment to a purpose external to the process of the adjudication, such as environmental protection or disciplinary coherence (by external we do not mean to suggest that environmental concerns are not relevant at all – chapter six clearly shows that there is scope for flexibility), the commitment is an internal one to legal consistency within an avenue of adjudication. Whilst this might come across as overly narrow, it is important to remember that the internal commitment to a given avenue secures important legal qualities, including consistency, integrity and ultimately the rule of law. Whilst these qualities are not specifically aimed at promoting environmental objectives or necessarily conducive to a high level of environmental protection, they nevertheless serve the discipline of environmental law well. This is because the internal commitment to the qualities of consistency, integrity and the rule of law are important stepping-stones to any mature system of law.

SELECTED BIBLIOGRAPHY

Adshead, J, 'Doing Justice to the Environment' (2013) 77 *Journal of Criminal Law*.

Ahmed, F, 'Standing and Civic Virtue' (2018) 134 *LQR* 239.

Arvind, TT and Stirton, L, 'The Curious Origins of Judicial Review' (2017) 133 *LQR* 91.

Balkin, JM, 'Understanding Legal Understanding: The Legal Subject and the Problem of Legal Coherence' (1993) 103 *Yale law Journal* 105.

Bell, J, 'Kent and Oakley: A Re-examination of the Common Law Duty to Give Reasons for Grants of Planning Permission and Beyond' (2017) 22 *Judicial Review* 105.

—— '*ClientEarth (No 2)*: A Case of Three Legal Dimensions' (2017) *Journal of Environmental Law* 343.

—— 'Reflections on Open Justice and the Status of the General Common Law Duty to Give Reasons' (2018) 77 *Cambridge Law Journal* 240.

Bell, S, et al, *Environmental Law*, 9th edn (Oxford, Oxford University Press, 2017).

Blundell, D, 'Of Evidence and Experts: Recent Developments in Fact-finding and Expert Evidence in Judicial Review' (2018) 23 *Judicial Review* 243.

Bjällås, U, 'Experiences of Sweden's Environment Court' (2010) 3 *Journal of Court Innovation* 177.

Brudner, A, 'Imprisonment and Strict Liability' (1990) 40 *University of Toronto Law Journal* 739.

Brudney, JJ and Ditslear, C, 'Canons of Construction and the Elusive Quest for Neutral Reasoning' (2005) 58 *Vanderbilt Law Review* 1.

Cardozo, B, *The Nature of the Judicial Process* (New Haven, CT, Yale University Press, 1921).

Carnwath, R, 'Environmental Enforcement: The Need for a Specialist Court' [1992] *Journal of Planning and Environmental Law* 799.

—— 'Environmental Law in a Global Society' [2015] *Journal of Planning and Environmental Law* 269.

Chapman, B, 'The Rational and the Reasonable: Social Choice Theory and Adjudication' (1994) 61 *University of Chicago Law Review* 41.

Chayes, A, 'The Role of the Judge in Public Law Litigation' (1976) 89 *Harvard Law Review* 1281.

Coyle, S and Morrow, K, *The Philosophical Foundations of Environmental Law* (Oxford, Hart, 2004).

Craig, P, 'English Administrative Law History: Perception and Reality' (2019) Oxford Legal Studies Research Paper No 48/2019, https://papers.ssrn.com/sol3/papers.cfm?abstract_id=3404029.

Culler, J, *Literary Theory: A Very Short Introduction* (Oxford, Oxford University Press, 2011).

Davies, ACL, *Accountability: A Public Law Analysis of Government by Contract* (Oxford, Oxford University Press, 2001).

Dewey, J, 'The Development of American Pragmatism' in LA Hickman and TM Alexander (eds), *The Essential Dewey*, vol 1 (Bloomington, Indiana University Press, 1998).

Dickinson, J, 'Interpretation and Coherence in Legal Reasoning, https://plato.stanford.edu/entries/legal-reas-interpret/ (29 May 2001, revised 10 February 2010 – accessed 28 January 2010).

Diver, CS, 'The Judge as Political Powerbroker: Superintending Structural Change in Public Institutions' (1979) 65 *Virginia Law Review* 43.

Dorf, MC, 'Legal Indeterminacy and Institutional Design' (2003) 78 *New York University Law Review* 875.

DuPont, C and P, Zakkow, *Trends in Environmental Sentencing in England and Wales* (London, DEFRA, 2003).

Dworkin, R, *Law's Empire* (London, Fontana Press, 1986).

Easterbrook, FH, 'Cyberspace and the Law of the Horse' (1996) *University of Chicago Legal Forum* 207.

Editor, 'Legal Aid for Environmental and Planning Litigation?' (2017) 24 *Irish Planning and Environmental Law Journal* 54.

Endicott, TAO, 'Questions of Law' (1998) 114 *LQR* 292.

Farber, DA, 'Adjudication of Things Past: Reflections on History as Evidence' (1998) 49 *Hastings Law Journal* 1009.
Faure, M, 'The Revolution in Environmental Criminal Law in Europe' (2017) 35 *Virginia Environmental Law Journal* 321.
Finnis, J, *Natural Law and Natural Rights* (Oxford, Oxford University Press, 1980).
Fish, S, 'Interpretation and the Pluralist Vision' (1981–82) 60 *Texas Law Review* 495.
—— *Professional Correctness* (Boston, MA, Harvard University Press, 1995).
Fisher, E, 'Unpacking the Toolbox: Or Why the Public/Private Divide Is Important in EC Environmental Law' (2001) FSU College of Law, Public Law Working Paper No 35, http://ssrn.com/abstract=283295 or http://dx.doi.org/10.2139/ssrn.283295.
—— *Risk Regulation and Constitutionalism* (Oxford, Hart, 2007).
Fisher, E, et al, ' The Legally Disruptive Nature of Climate Change' (2017) 80 *MLR* 173.
—— 'Rethinking Judicial Review of Expert Agencies' (2015) 93 *Texas Law Review* 1681.
Fiss, O, 'Objectivity and Interpretation' (1982) 34 *Stanford Law Review* 739.
Fletcher, WA, 'The Discretionary Constitution Institutional Remedies and Judicial Legitimacy' (1982) 91 *Yale Law Journal* 635.
Freeden, M, *The Political Theory of Political Thinking: The Anatomy of a Practice* (Oxford, Oxford University Press, 2013).
Fuller, L, 'The Forms and Limits of Adjudication' (1978) 92 *Harvard Law Review* 353.
Gardner, J, 'The Purity and Priority of Private Law' (1996) 46 *University of Toronto Law Journal* 459.
Graham, KW, Jr, '"There'll Always Be An England": The Instrumental Ideology of Evidence' (1987) 85 *Michigan Law Review* 1204.
Gill, G, *Environmental Justice in India: The National Green Tribunal* (Oxford, Routledge, 2016).
Gutting, G and Oksala, J, 'Michael Foucault', https://plato.stanford.edu/entries/foucault/ (first published 2003, amended 2018 – accessed 14 August 2019).
Halper, T, 'Logic in Judicial Reasoning' (1968) 44 *Indiana Law Journal* 33.
Hampton, P, *Reducing Administrative Burdens – Effective Inspection and Enforcement* (London, HM Treasury, 2005).
Hart, HLA, *The Concept of Law*, 2nd edn, with a postscript edited by P Bulloch and J Raz (Oxford, Clarendon Press, 1994).
—— 'Positivism and the Separation of Law and Morals' (1958) 71 *Harvard Law Review* 593.
Hawken, F, 'Failed Justice: The Impact of the Legal Aid, Sentencing and Punishment of Offenders Act 2012 on the Legal System of England and Wales' (2019) 24 *Coventry Law Journal* 129.
Honoré, A, 'Groups, Laws and Obedience' in *Making Law Bind* (Oxford, Oxford University Press, 1987).
Howarth, D, 'Environmental Law and Private Law' in J Viñuales and E Lees (eds), *The Oxford Handbook of Comparative Environmental Law* (Oxford, Oxford University Press, 2019).
—— *Law as Engineering: Thinking About What Lawyers Do* (Cheltenham, Edward Elgar, 2014).
Horwitz, MJ, 'The History of the Public/Private Distinction' (1982) 130 *University of Pennsylvania Law Review* 1423.
Lord Irvine of Lairg, 'Judges as Decision-Makers' [1996] *PL* 59.
Jackson, F, *From Metaphysics to Ethics: A Defence of Conceptual Analysis* (Oxford, Clarendon Press, 1998).
Jasanoff, S, 'The Practices of Objectivity in Regulatory Science' in C Camic, N Grocc and M Lamont (eds), *Social Knowledge in the Making* (Chicago, University of Chicago Press, 2011).
Kennedy, D, 'The Stakes of Law, or Hale and Foucault' (1991) 15 *Legal Studies Forum* 327.
Khushal Murkens, JE, 'Judicious Review: The Constitutional Practice of the UK Supreme Court' (2018) 77 *Cambridge Law Journal* 349.
Kidd, M, 'The Use of Strict Liability' (2002) 15 *South African Journal of Criminal Justice* 23.
Kress, K, 'Legal Indeterminacy' (1989) 77 *California Law Review* 283.
Komesar, N, *Imperfect Alternatives* (Chicago, University of Chicago Press, 1995).
Ky, P, 'Qualifications, 'Qualifications, Weight of Opinion, Peer Review and Methodology: A Framework for Understanding the Evaluation of Science in Merits Review' (2012) 24 *Journal of Environmental Law* 207.

Lazarus, R, 'Assimilating Environmental Protection into Legal Rules and the Problem with Environmental Crime' (1994) 27 *Loyola of Los Angeles Law Review* 867.

—— 'Meeting the Demands of Integration in the Evolution of Environmental Law: Reforming Environmental Criminal Law' (1995) 83 *Georgetown Law Journal* 2407.

Lees, E, *Interpreting Environmental Offences* (Oxford, Hart, 2015).

—— 'Allocation of Decision-Making Power under the Habitats Directive' (2016) 28 *Journal of Environmental Law* 191.

—— 'Environmental Law and Criminal Law' in E Lees and J Viñuales (eds), *Oxford Handbook of Comparative Environmental Law* (Oxford, Oxford University Press, 2019).

—— and Shepherd, E, 'Morphological Analysis of Legal Ideology: Locating Interpretive Divergence' (2018) 10 *Journal of Property, Planning and Environmental Law* 5.

Leiter, B and Etchemendy, MX, 'Naturalism in Legal Philosophy' in *Stanford Encyclopedia of Philosophy*, https://plato.stanford.edu/entries/lawphil-naturalism/ (15 July 2002, amended 27 March 2017 – accessed 17 July 2018).

Levenbook, BB, 'The Role of Coherence in Legal Reasoning' (1984) 3 *Law and Philosophy* 355.

Levi, EH, 'The Nature of Judicial Reasoning' (1965) 32 *University of Chicago Law Review* 395.

Levi-Strauss, C, *The Savage Mind* (Chicago, University of Chicago Press 1966).

Llewellyn, K, *The Bramble Bush* (New York, Oceana, 1930).

Loughlin, M, *Foundations of Public Law* (Oxford, Oxford University Press, 2010).

Lucy, W, 'Private Law: Between Visionaries and Bricoleurs' in P Cane and J Gardner (eds), *Relating to Responsibility: Essays in Honour of Tony Honore on his 80th Birthday* (Oxford, Hart, 2001).

Macrory R, and Woods, M, 'Modernising Environmental Justice: Regulation and the Role of an Environmental Tribunal' (Centre for Law and the Environment, UCL, 2003).

McCartney, F, 'Public Interest and Legal Aid' (2010) 37 *Scots Law Times* 201.

McEldowney, J and McEldowney, S, 'Science and Environmental Law: Collaboration across the Double Helix' (2011) 13 *Environmental Law Review* 169.

Moore, MS, 'The Semantics of Judging' (1981) 54 *Southern California Law Review* 151.

—— 'A Natural Law Theory of Interpretation' (1985) 58 *Southern California Law Review* 277.

Mullen, T, 'Protective Expenses Orders and Public Interest Litigation' (2015) 19 *Edinburgh Law Review* 36.

Ormondroyd, C, 'Access to Environmental Justice' [2011] *Journal of Planning and Environmental Law* 251.

Osiel, MJ, 'Ever Again: Legal Remembrance of Administrative Massacre' (1995) 144 *University of Pennsylvania Law Review* 463.

Pedersen, OW, 'Modest Pragmatic Lessons for a Diverse and Incoherent Environmental Law' (2013) 33 *OJLS* 103.

—— review of E Scotford, *Environmental Principles and the Evolution of Environmental* Law (Oxford, Hart, 2017) in (2018) 30 *Journal of Environmental Law* 359.

—— 'A Study of Administrative Environmental Decision-Making before the Courts' (2019) 31 *Journal of Environmental Law* 59.

Pontin, B, 'Integrated Pollution Control in Victorian Britain: Rethinking Progress within the History of Environmental Law' (2007) 19 *Journal of Environmental Law* 173.

Porter, S, 'Do the Rules of Private Nuisance Breach the Principles of Environmental Justice?' (2019) 21 *Environmental Law Review* 21.

Preston, B, 'Judicial Specialisation through Environment Court: A Case Study of the Land and Environmental Court of New South Wales' (2012) 29 *Pace Environmental Law Review* 602.

—— 'Characteristics of Successful Environmental Courts and Tribunals' (2014) *Journal of Environmental Law* 4.

Pring, G and Pring, C, *Environmental Courts and Tribunals: A Guide for Policy-Makers* (UN Environment Programme, 2016).

Putnam, H, *Pragmatism: An Open Question* (Hoboken, NJ, Blackwell 1999).

Rawlings, R, 'Modelling Judicial Review' (2008) 61 *Current Legal Problems* 95.

Raz, J, *Authority of Law: Essays on Law and Morality* (Oxford, Oxford University Press, 1979, online edn 2012).
—— 'The Relevance of Coherence' (1992) 72 *Boston University Law Review* 273.
Redish, MH and Marshall, LC, 'Adjudicatory Independence and the Values of Procedural Due Process' (1986) 95 *Yale Law Journal* 455.
Rigoni, A, 'Common-Law Judicial Reasoning and Analogy' (2014) 20 *Legal Theory* 133.
Robinson, D, 'Regulatory Evolution in Pollution Control' in T Jewell and J Steele (eds), *Law in Environmental Decision-Making* (Oxford, Clarendon Press, 1998).
Robinson, N, 'Ensuring Access to Justice through Environment Courts' (2012) 29 *Pace Environmental Law Review* 363.
Rodriguez-Blanco, V, 'Is Finnis Wrong? Understanding Normative Jurisprudence' (2007) 13 *Legal Theory* 257.
Rosen, A, 'Statutory Interpretation and the Many Virtues of Legislation' (2017) 37 *OJLS* 134.
Rubin, EL, 'The New Legal Process: The Synthesis of Discourse, and the Microanalysis of Institutions' (1996) 109 *Harvard Law Review* 1393.
—— *Beyond Camelot* (Oxford, Oxford University Press, 2005).
Sadeleer, N De, *Environmental Principles – From Political Slogans to Legal Rules* (Oxford, Oxford University Press, 2002).
Scotford, E, *Environmental Principles and the Evolution of Environmental* Law (Oxford, Hart, 2017).
Shapiro, DA, 'In Defense of Judicial Candor' (1987) 100 *Harvard Law Review* 731.
Simmonds, NE, 'Bluntness and Bricolage' in H Gross and R Harrison (eds), *Jurisprudence: Cambridge Essays* (Oxford, Clarendon Press, 1992).
Spann, GA, 'Expository Justice' (1983) 131 *University of Pennsylvania Law Review* 585.
Steele, J, 'Assessing the Past: Tort Law and Environmental Risk' in T Jewell and J Steele (eds), *Law in Environmental Decision-Making* (Oxford, Clarendon Press, 1998).
Stone, CD, 'Should Trees Have Standing? – Toward Legal Rights for Natural Objects' (1972) 45 *Southern California Law Review* 450.
Summers, RS, 'Pragmatic Instrumentalism in Twentieth Century American Legal Thought – A Synthesis and Critique of Our Dominant General Theory about Law and its Use' (1981) 66 *Cornell Law Review* 861.
Sunstein, CR, 'The Problem with Rules' (1995) 83 *California Law Review* 953.
—— 'Standing and the Privatization of Public Law' (1988) *Columbia Law Review* 1446.
Sypnowich, C, 'Law and Ideology' in *Stanford Encyclopedia of Philosophy*, https://plato.stanford.edu/entries/law-ideology/ (first published 2001, amended 2019 – accessed 14 August 2019).
Uncovska, E, 'The Impact of Legal Aid Cuts on the Right to a Fair Trial' (2019) 24 *Coventry Law Journal* 136.
Vaughan, S, 'The Contaminated Land Regime: Still Suitable for Use?' [2010] *Journal of Planning and Environmental Law* 142.
Vermeule, A, *Law's Abnegation* (Boston, MA, Harvard University Press, 2016).
Vogenauer, S, 'A Retreat from *Pepper v Hart*? A Reply to Lord Steyn' (2005) 25 *OJLS* 629.
Waits, K, 'Values, Intuitions, and Opinion Writing: The Judicial Process and State Court Jurisdiction' [1983] *University of Illinois Law Review* 917.
Warnock, C, 'Reconceptualising Specialist Environment Courts and Tribunals' (2017) 37 *Legal Studies* 391.
—— and Pedersen, OW, 'Environmental Adjudication: Mapping the Spectrum and Identifying the Fulcrum' (2017) *Public Law* 643.
Watson, M, 'Environmental Offences: The Reality of Environmental Crime' (2005) *Environmental Law Review* 190.
Woolf, H, 'Are the Judiciary Environmentally Myopic?' (1992) 4 *Journal of Environmental Law* 1.
Zane, JM, 'German Legal Philosophy' (1918) 16 *Michigan Law Review* 287.

INDEX

Note: Alphabetical arrangement is word-by-word, where a group of letters followed by a space is filed before the same group of letters followed by a letter, eg 'legal rules' will appear before 'legality'. In determining alphabetical arrangement, initial articles and prepositions are ignored.

www.ingramcontent.com/pod-product-compliance
Ingram Content Group UK Ltd.
Pitfield, Milton Keynes, MK11 3LW, UK
UKHW020803290926
15470UKWH00003B/922

9 781509 931460